GLAUCUS
AND OTHER PLAYS

AMERICA'S LOST PLAYS
VOLUME III

A series in twenty volumes of hitherto unpublished plays collected with the aid of the Rockefeller Foundation, under the auspices of the Dramatists' Guild of the Authors' League of America, edited with historical and bibliographical notes.

BARRETT H. CLARK
GENERAL EDITOR

Advisory Board

ROBERT HAMILTON BALL, QUEENS COLLEGE
HOYT H. HUDSON, PRINCETON UNIVERSITY
GLENN HUGHES, UNIVERSITY OF WASHINGTON
GARRETT H. LEVERTON, FORMERLY OF NORTHWESTERN UNIVERSITY
E. C. MABIE, UNIVERSITY OF IOWA
ALLARDYCE NICOLL, YALE UNIVERSITY
ARTHUR HOBSON QUINN, UNIVERSITY OF PENNSYLVANIA
NAPIER WILT, UNIVERSITY OF CHICAGO

GLAUCUS

& *Other Plays*

BY GEORGE HENRY BOKER

EDITED, WITH INTRODUCTION AND NOTES
BY SCULLEY BRADLEY

WILDSIDE PRESS

CONTENTS

Introduction   vii

The World a Mask   1

The Bankrupt   57

Glaucus   119

INTRODUCTION

IN PRESENTING these three plays of George Henry Boker, it must be said at once that they do not represent his best literary work, and that they fail to reflect adequately his importance to the American theater. Their appearance here is justified by the fact that they are good examples of types of play that once flourished on our stage, and thus take on a peculiar value for students and lovers of the theater. They also constitute all that remained unpublished of the work of an important dramatist in the history of our national literature. George Henry Boker is the author of a great poetic tragedy, *Francesca da Rimini,* which alone should be enough to preserve his memory to posterity. It is difficult to think of another romantic tragedy written in English in the nineteenth century, which combined so well as *Francesca da Rimini* the power of poetry and the quality which keeps a dramatic work alive upon the stage for many years to delight and move successive generations of playgoers. Written in 1853, it was performed by E. L. Davenport during a short run in New York and Philadelphia in 1855; in 1882, at the height of his career, Lawrence Barrett discovered the play and made it one of his principal vehicles during the remaining nine years of his life. Ten years later, during the season of 1901-1902, Mr. Otis Skinner, Barrett's first Paolo, revived the play for the road and played the part of Lanciotto in the principal cities of the country, achieving a triumph which many of his admirers regard as the artistic pinnacle of his career.

Yet this play is by no means the sum of its author's artistic achievement. *Calaynos* and *Leonor de Guzman* are almost on the same high level of achievement, and in more fortunate circumstances or in different times they might well have won lasting success, instead of falling, after a brief recognition, victims to the unhappy circumstances which prevailed in the theater of the day. Altogether Boker wrote eleven plays, of which seven were on the stage and eight were published, although not all of his acted plays found publication. The three plays in this volume will bring to light all that remained unpublished. *Francesca da Rimini, Leonor de Guzman* and *Calaynos* have been mentioned as the masterpieces of Boker, but besides these, one should suppose that five others, *Anne Boleyn, The Betrothal, Königsmark, Nydia,* and *Glaucus* might hold a permanent place among the best dramatic literature of their times. One of these, *Glaucus,* is here published for the first time.

Boker had the natural gifts of the born dramatist, but he was a poet as well. The seven published volumes of his poetry, together with his fugitive poems published in magazines, constitute a major contribution to our literature. Neglected at the time of his death in 1890, and for many years afterward, his poetry has won critical recognition in recent times, and begins to take a well deserved position in the anthologies among the memorable works of his countrymen.

The explanation of the neglect of so much of Boker's work during his lifetime would involve a biographical study inappropriate to this place. It has been said that, as a gentleman who inherited great wealth in Philadelphia, he was too prosperous to be picturesque, but this hardly explains his relationship to a community which had remained equally oblivious to the variegated picturesqueness of Edgar Poe and Walt Whitman. As in the case of these others, both the time and the place were unfavorable to the work that Boker had to do. He was a belated romantic in a world attuned to the new realism; and failing to achieve the recognition that his nature craved—a recognition which Whitman, at least, knew how to do without—he turned his active energies more and more to public life, to the organization of Northern sentiment in the Civil War, and later, to foreign diplomacy.

Of the three plays here published, two were presented on the stage: *The World a Mask* in 1851, and *The Bankrupt* in 1855. That they both had short runs is not a significant fact in those days when actors and managers would rather revive an old or foreign play than present a recent native work and pay royalty to its author. The support of a native dramatist was assured only in case his work proved an extraordinary popular success; and in that event, even, the actor or manager was usually not interested in continuing it on the stage unless he could persuade its author to sell it outright to him for a sum ridiculously less than the profit that the play would bring him. The familiar story of the relationships of Forrest with the authors Robert Montgomery Bird and John Augustus Stone is indicative of the situation which prevailed. In the case of Boker's two comedies, however, there was no such overwhelming popular approval, and the plays were retired from the stage after the average short runs to which even good American plays in that day were limited. The fact is, however, that any native play of the period which succeeded in reaching the stage at all, against such overwhelming handicaps as were inherent in the business organization of the theater, must of necessity be of interest in the history of the American stage. Boker's plays are no exception in this respect.

Glaucus, the last play in the present volume, presents a somewhat different problem. Unlike the earlier comedies, it is in blank verse, and ranks, indeed, among its author's best literary productions. It is a work of the poet's last period of artistic maturity, written in 1885, at Lawrence Barrett's suggestion. It was written directly for the stage and might perhaps have stood near to *Francesca da Dimini* in the actor's repertoire of popular plays, but for a personal disagreement between the writer and the actor which caused the latter to refuse the work.

It may be of value to give some account of the history and the manuscripts of each play, and to explain the relationships between the text here presented and the notes which appear at the end of this volume. The fact that there are several manuscripts of each play has presented an editorial problem. Variant readings among the manuscripts are of three sorts: corruptions and errors of transcription; differences between the "literary" and the "acting" form of a play; and actual changes in the author's intention. The texts here reproduced represent what appears to be Boker's latest judgment concerning each passage for reading as a work of literature. Variants, and cuts for stage presentation are indicated in the notes at the end of the volume. A short account of each play is given below.

THE WORLD A MASK

The World a Mask[1] represents an experimental stage in the development of its author. He had already written, within two years, three plays in blank verse. *Calaynos* and *Anne Boleyn,* both tragedies, had satisfied his artistic conscience; and his romantic comedy, *The Betrothal,* was successfully on the stage of the Walnut Street Theatre in Philadelphia in September 1850, at the very time when its author was beginning his work on *The World a Mask.* The latter play was composed with an eye to a popular taste of the day. This called for prose comedy, with a melodramatic complexion, preferably concerned with English high life. It was a bad taste to begin with, and in the second place, it required a different talent from that of Boker to succeed with this artificial type of play.

As a result, this dramatist, who was later to rise to the accomplishment of such fine plays as *Leonor de Guzman* and *Francesca da Rimini,* produced in this case a play that was just about average for its time and sort. That is another way of saying that it was rather bad—and no one knew it better than the author. He finished the play in December 1850. In January 1851, when he wrote to his friend Bayard Taylor that it was about to be produced, he recounted with amazement the admiration of the audience of actors—prob-

[1] The manuscripts are in the Princeton University Library.

ably the stock company at the Walnut Street Theatre—to whom he had read it. To Taylor, Boker summed up his own reaction: "It is a damn bad play and all the praise in the world can make it no better."

Nevertheless the piece was put in rehearsal at the Walnut Street Theatre on April 15, 1851, and opened on April 21 for a run of eight successive performances. The cast was composed of regular members of the company. Charles Couldock, famous "heavy," played the villain, Galldove, and Mme. Ponisi the unfortunate Teresa, the sham countess.

Apparently, judging from the praise of the press, the comedy was successful; but its author remained unconvinced by these encomiums. On the day after the opening he wrote Bayard Taylor, "Never was a comedy worse played to a better-natured audience . . . the best effects were marred, and the whole edge taken off the wit (such as it is). . . . Why, notwithstanding all this, the curtain fell amid cheers and calls, instead of flying benches, catcalls, and yells of derision, the devil, who must have had a proper care of the whole thing, only knows. The piece was completely successful, much to my astonishment."

This play has had four titles. On October 15, 1850, Boker wrote Bayard Taylor, "I am hard at work on 'The Sycophant,' a detestable wretch; but I hope to bring him to justice somewhere in the fifth act." The earliest surviving manuscript, in Boker's hand, is entitled *All the World a Mask*. This, which affords the best version for reading, has been made the basis of the present text. It is referred to in the notes as MS I. A second manuscript, referred to as MS II, is apparently the version used in the performance of the play. It is in longhand, not Boker's, and may be the work of a theater copyist. The acts are bound separately and Act I bears a printed title-page with the title, *The World a Mask*, which has been retained here as the best title for the play. In this copy there are some corruptions, and a good many "cuts" to hasten performance. The stage directions have been greatly amplified and scene plots have been added. The original ending has been cut and several new speeches added to form a new ending, with the apparent intention of heightening the comic nature of the concluding situation. From a literary point of view the second ending was distinctly not an improvement. The latest manuscript, here referred to as MS III, is a typed copy dated 1886, the year when the dramatist, probably in contemplation of a complete edition of his works, had typed copies of several of his plays prepared. This version is entitled *Under a Mask*. The authority of MS III is in serious doubt. There are no marks on it to indicate either supervision or revision by the author and it abounds in errors which he would not have made. The typist, apparently

INTRODUCTION

consulting both previous manuscripts, has followed the one or the other with apparent indiscrimination and frequent confusion.

For the present text the three manuscripts have been critically collated with a view to presenting the play in its most readable form. With this end in view it was found desirable to retain Boker's original version, MS I, in almost every case, indicating all variant readings in the notes, to which the superimposed numbers in the text refer. All "cuts" and additions in MS II have been thus indicated. A very few of the additions of MS II have been retained in the printed text, with proper annotation, when they seemed to improve or clarify the reading. The stage directions of MS II have been reproduced in the text, since the original version was deficient in this respect; but scene plans and the occasional director's notes and comments have been ignored. The names, which were frequently abbreviated in all the manuscripts, have been given in full. The very few variants in MS III which might prove critically interesting, have been included in the notes.

THE BANKRUPT

Boker wrote his greatest tragedy and his least successful comedy in the same year, 1853. Having finished *Francesca da Rimini* in March, he made an excursion into a field new to him, the portrayal of melodramatic materials from the contemporary scene. *The Bankrupt*[2] was not a bad example of the type of play that it represents; but the type itself was bad, and Boker was dissatisfied with the result of his effort. Although he permitted the play to reach the stage in 1855, he withheld his name as author. No mention of it has been found in his correspondence. He did not include it in his collected works in 1856.

To the reader of the present, however, it serves as a good example of a sort of melodrama which enjoyed a long vogue upon the stage—although that interesting consideration does not alter the fact that like most surviving plays of this variety, it is deficient in reality of character, artificial in dialogue and extravagant in situation. Two other facts, connected with the plot of this play, are of great interest for the historian. First, it is a very early example of the use of modern financial operations as material for dramatic situation; and in its combination of the domestic drama with the financial crisis it looked forward to plot material which was to find its popular use much later, in the work of Bronson Howard and subsequent authors. Also *The Bankrupt* represents an early, if indeed not the first instance of the employment on the stage of the wily and omniscient detective pitted against the force of a master criminal mind. Poe had already popularized this situation in prose fiction,

[2] The manuscripts are in the Princeton University Library.

and it is most interesting to observe that, in the last scene, Pike, the detective, informs Shelvill, the crook, that he has been trapped at last by a writing in cipher that has been interpreted by a poet whom he employed, a Mr. Poe.

The Bankrupt was advertised for performance in 1855, as a part of the repertory of Julia Dean (Mrs. Hayne) when that actress fulfilled an engagement from November 12 to December 12 at the Broadway Theatre, New York. It was first performed on December 3, and ran for four successive performances, until December 6. The newspaper criticism was lukewarm, and there is no record to indicate that the play was ever subsequently revived.

In 1886, when Boker apparently considered a complete edition of his plays, which never materialized, he prepared a new version of this play, of which the typescript survives, entitled *A Commercial Crisis*. It was possibly at this time that extensive cuts were made in the original speeches, resulting in a decided improvement. These changes may, however, have been made much earlier with a view to the stage performance in 1855. At any rate, long passages are stricken out in the original manuscript and not reproduced in the typescript of 1886. The present text represents the later version, but all variant readings have been indicated in the notes. For this purpose the original longhand manuscript of 1853 is referred to as MS I; the typescript of 1886, as MS II.

GLAUCUS

It has already been stated that *Glaucus* is the most satisfactory of the three plays in the present volume, both for its literary quality and its adaptability for performance on the stage. It was, in fact, written directly for the stage, in 1885, at the request of Lawrence Barrett, who was at that time appearing with great success in a revival of Boker's *Francesca da Rimini*. I have, in another connection, recorded in some detail the curious circumstances which prevented the play from reaching the stage.[3] The facts, briefly, are these: Barrett had asked Boker to write "a play in which he could introduce a number of gorgeous spectacular effects . . . something that would give the ingenuity of the stage carpenter, the scene painter and the costumer a chance." Using the story of Bulwer-Lytton's *Last Days of Pompeii*, Boker first supplied the actor with the blank verse play, *Nydia*.[4] Barrett declined this play, probably on the grounds that the principal character was Nydia, the blind slave. This assumption is justified by the fact that Boker at once began work on another and independent treatment of the same story, diminishing the

---

[3] *George Henry Boker, Poet and Patriot*, The University of Pennsylvania Press, Philadelphia and London, 1927; pp. 333-40.

[4] Edited by Sculley Bradley, University of Pennsylvania Press, Philadelphia and London, 1929.

part of Nydia and emphasizing that of Glaucus. This play, also in blank verse, was completed on January 9, 1886, and tentatively accepted by the actor. Before final arrangements were made, however, a misunderstanding arose between the actor and the author. It seemed to Boker that Barrett, knowing that the author was exceedingly well-to-do, was attempting to secure royalty terms for the successful *Francesca da Rimini* which would have been ruinous for any author who was forced to earn his living by his pen. On this point Boker, who had been a leader in the agitation to secure better protection for American authorship, was not to be dissuaded. The popularity of *Francesca da Rimini* was so great that the actor was compelled to compromise with Boker in respect to the earlier play. However, he nursed for some time a strong sense of injury which caused him to abandon the plans for the production of *Glaucus*.

There are two manuscripts of *Glaucus*, both typewritten.[5] It seems likely that an earlier manuscript in longhand may have existed, but it has not been found. MS I is the earlier of the two surviving manuscripts. It bears the typed notation on the first page, "Begun Oct. 18, 1885 and finished January 9, 1886 —83 days." It seems that the poet may have discussed this manuscript with the actor, for it bears extensive suggestions for "cuts," which, as a general thing do not heighten the literary quality, and serve only to shorten the acting duration of the play. A second manuscript is undated, but is consistent in form with several manuscripts of the poet's other plays which were prepared in 1886 for a complete edition which did not materialize. This has been designated as MS II in the notes for the present edition. Most of the "cuts" suggested in MS I were also indicated in MS II, although the actual text was unaltered. For this reason it seems probable that the longer, and uncut form of the play is the version which the poet preferred and the one which he probably would have printed. In the present edition care has been exercised to indicate in the notes all the deletions which were suggested for the purpose of acting.

There is a curious addendum to MS II, consisting of new material to follow note 21 on p. 164 of the present edition. It consists of a shorter version of Act II from that point and another Act III, also abbreviated, but not different in the narrative. Possibly it was an additional suggestion for curtailing the duration of the play on the stage. It is not reproduced in this edition.

It is a pleasure to acknowledge my indebtedness and to offer my thanks for the assistance of others in the publication of this volume. My colleague, Professor Arthur Hobson Quinn, the first American historian to direct at-

[5] Princeton University Library.

tention to the poetry and plays of Boker, has assisted me in ways too numerous to specify. I am grateful to Mr. Barrett H. Clark for the devotion to our native drama which has materialized in the series of publications of which this volume is a part. To the Princeton University Library I am deeply indebted for their courtesy in according me the freest possible access to these manuscripts, all of which are in their collection.

SCULLEY BRADLEY
Professor of English, University of Pennsylvania

THE WORLD A MASK

A COMEDY

DRAMATIS PERSONAE[1]

SIR HUGH BLUMER

GALLDOVE } *His Nephews*
RYLTON

FERNWOOD

GARNISH

LORD REW

CAPTAIN FLEET, *An Adventurer*

RABY, *A Clergyman*

MATHEW, *Servant to Sir Hugh*

TERESA CESPO, *Passing as Countess di Cespo*

LUCY WILLBURG, *Betrothed to Rylton*

LADY WILLBURG, *Her Mother*

MISS GARNISH, *Sister to Garnish*

BETSY, *Sir Hugh's Chambermaid*

GUESTS, OFFICERS, SERVANTS, ETC.

SCENE, LONDON. TIME 1851

ACT I.

SCENE: *A reception room in Lady Willburg's house. Garnish and Miss Garnish discovered. Lord Rew enters and then retreats.*

MISS G. Lord Rew, Lord Rew, for pity sake, come back! You would not leave me alone with my brother? [*Lord Rew returns*]²

GAR. What a prudent young innocent! Come back, Rew; she's afraid of the scandal.—Her honor hangs by such a thread.

LORD R. [*Returning*] Garnish is such an uncertain, hard-mouthed brute. Could not hold him for a minute.

MISS G. He promised to behave himself, if I would take him out.

GAR. That's a fib, Hetty. I had to give you a hundred pounds before you got into the carriage.³

LORD R. See that! He's off. Don't tell me his points, Miss Garnish. I've known him from a foal. He'd run away with a prizefighter. It's a hollow thing—indeed it is. [*L.2.E. going*]⁴

MISS G. My lord, 'tis scarcely fair to make game of my brother's infirmities. The poor fellow!—I have some feeling, sir. [*Weeps*]

LORD R. There! woman's old trick! [*Aside*] Come ashore, come ashore, Miss Garnish! Only leave the water, and I'll stand here, till my legs let down. I'm not in the best sorts today; little off my feed. The more I coax, the worse she goes. [*Aside*] Now, my dear Miss Garnish—

GAR. What is Hetty crying about? Don't get excited, Rew. She always crys for what she wants: She'd grin for it⁵ as easily—if she had better teeth.

MISS G. Grin! You brute! [*Rising and going down C.*]

GAR. See that. She can blow as well as rain.

MISS G. Will you leave Garnish alone, my lord?

LORD R. Certainly. Lady Willburg shown yet?

MISS G. Not yet.

LORD R. Rylton and Lucy are off at last. All made public—too bad.

GAR. Isn't it dreadful, Hetty? So young too! Poor Lucy!⁶

LORD R. What's the matter? Marriage is as common as flats at Epsom.

GAR. Why, you spoke as if she were to be hung, drawn and quartered.

LORD R. Pshaw! too bad to match her with that spooney, Rylton.⁷

GAR. Oh! that's all. I thought—

Miss G. Garnish! You grow worse as you grow older.[8] You have driven all my friends from me—you have driven me into three nervous fevers, and you'll drive me into my grave at last. [*Aside to Garnish*]

Gar. Will I? Deduct the cost of a stylish funeral then, and see how rich I'd be, Rew. My! Hetty, what a lying tomb stone I'd put over you! As full of virtues as a quack's label. Just think of the grief you'd give the newspapers! "Miss Garnish departed this life full of years and honors—"

Lord R. Poh! poh! Garnish, you haven't the heart of a plough-horse.

Gar. When you were playing piquet with me—

Lord R. [*Aside to him*] Not a word about the cards.

Gar. I wasn't going to tell what you won. Lord Rew said that you were the only heavy drag on my property; and if heaven would be merciful enough to take you away, I ought not to make an Irish wake of your funeral,[9] or—[10]

Lord R. Garnish, my hair turns with horror.

Gar. What a credit to your barber! That wig—

Lord R. Can't stand this spurring, Miss Garnish. The fellow's worse than Tiffany at the last quarter. [*Enter Lady Willburg, L.2.E.*]

Lady W. Excuse me for detaining you. What has disturbed Miss Garnish and Lord Rew? [*Aside*]

Lord R. Hem! Hem! [*Going down L. of her*] Hem! Hem! Hope we find your ladyship in tip-top condition.

Lady W. I have almost a superfluity of health and vivacity.

Gar. Does your ladyship never feel a little flighty of mornings? You know 'tis in your family. Your mother died in a—

Miss G. [*Aside to Garnish*] For Heaven's sake, Garnish!

Gar. You told me so yourself. Where's the harm? If Lady Willburg did rob her poor mother of her wits, I am sure no one would accuse her of having kept them.[11]

Lady W. You were observing, Lord Rew?

Lord R. Glad to hear the affair between Miss Lucy and Mr. Rylton is to come off so soon. Rylton is a nice catch—

Lady W. Nice catch!

Lord R. Catch weight, I mean. Light hand—a perfect feather.

Gar. You told Hetty he was spooney! Didn't he, Hetty? What difference can his weight make to Lady Willburg? Is he to jockey her in a hurdle race?

Lady W. [*Turning a little up stage*] If you will desert us, Mr. Garnish?—

Gar. I was not going.

Miss G. Yes, yes! You know you have an engagement at Tattersalls.

Gar. Have I? Oh, well, I suppose I had better go and buy another horse. [*Crosses to L.C. between Rew and Miss Garnish*] I don't see the sense of it, Hetty. You send me there one day to buy a horse, and the next day to sell him. But I'll go.—Hetty, shall I carry your bundle of rouge home for you? [*Loud and pointedly*]

Lord R. Hurry, Garnish; Mulberry is under the hammer by this time. Nicest beast you ever pulled a rein over.

Gar. A horse of yours, I suppose. Do you understand this, old fellow? [*Motions as if dealing cards*] I'll be there. What a row Hetty would make if she knew! [*Exit L.2.E.*]

Lord R. [*Aside*] Bolted at last. [*Turns up stage a little*]

Miss G. [*Aside*] Oh, bless me! [*Takes stage a little to R.*]

Lady W. [*Aside*] What a relief! [*Going down stage 2 or 3 paces L.H. to give Rew the opportunity of going down center. L.2.E. Enter Servant, and gives a card to Lady Willburg*]

Lady W. [*Reads*] Mr. Galldove! Are you acquainted?

Lord R. Sired by old Galldove—that side of the stock was always tricky; dam, own sister to Sir Hugh Blumer—that's better blood. Just returned from a canter over Italy.

Miss G. A vastly agreeable man; but no match—none whatever.[12]

Lady W. Mr. Rylton's cousin. I am at home. [*Exit Servant L.2.E.*]

Miss G. He left England in a hurry, some years ago, and with a terrible character—perfectly shocking. A delightful man, nevertheless. [*Enter Galldove. L.2.E.*]

Gal. Lady Willburg! Just as I left her, Heaven knows how many years ago.

Lady W. Indeed, sir? [*Aside*] He talks of me as if I were an Egyptian mummy in a remarkable state of preservation!

Gal. Ah! But your ladyship must remember that your absence has measured my time. What a long year would that be on which the sun never shone!

Lord R. [*Aside to Miss Garnish*] Bless his impudence. The old lady bolts it all too!

Miss G. [*Aside to him*] Did you ever hear such gross stuff? Why, my poor friend, Lady Willburg, has gone all to pieces in the last few years.

Gal. Miss Garnish, too. Still torturing the poor men![13]

Lady W. [*Aside*] With her odious attentions.

Gal. As cruel a belle as ever, no doubt! When will you bless somebody with that bewitching little hand?

Lady W. [*Aside*] When somebody will indulge her with an opportunity.

Lord R. [*Aside*] He talks like a parrot. It's pretty poll to everybody.

GAL. You were a standing toast with our English Club, in Italy. "Miss Garnish!" with all the honors.

MISS G. You are too kind, Mr. Galldove.

GAL. [*Aside*] Am I?

LORD R. Phew! This fellow can distance the devil at his own race.

GAL. I have found all my friends at once. I am delighted to see your lordship. [*To Rew*] By the by, can you tell me which horse will win the St. Leger? You know they call you an oracle in such matters. I must bet a little; though I might stake my whole estate on your judgment, without fear of loss. Ah! [*Aside*] there is more truth there than I meant. Now, come, come, do let me behind the curtain—just a peep—a hint. Lord Southpate told me of your remarkable prophecy about the Doncaster.

LORD R. [*Aside*] The devil he did! The fellow won all I lost.

MISS G. [*Aside to Lady Willburg*] Poor Rew! that race nearly sent him to the Continent.

LORD R. Well, well; if my book had only changed with my judgment.

MISS G. [*Aside to Lady Willburg*] Just as the horses were coming in.

GAL. What then, my lord?

LORD R. That puppy, Southpate, would have had less to say about it—by a damned sight! Excuse me, ladies.

GAL. Ah! these little slips will happen, even with prophets.

LORD R. Judgment is a good horse to back; but, on the whole, I don't know but that the winner is better.

GAL. A very sapient idea, my lord; and very clearly expressed.

LORD R. [*Aside*] A handy fellow, on my soul! I'll put him on the visitor's list at the "Jockey."[14] [*Re-enter Garnish*]

LADY W. [*Aside*] That horror again!

MISS G. [*Aside*] My incubus!

LORD R. Girth's broke.

GAR. No sale at Tattersall's today. Did you think this was the first of April? Who's that, Hetty?

MISS G. Mr. Galldove.

GAR. What, old Thingumabob's nephew? Are you the man that ruined yourself: Why, you don't look seedy. What do you live on now?

GAL. Upon what will never support you—my wits. Faith, you deserved it, Garnish—upon my life you did! Ha! Ha! excuse my freedom. [*Laughing*] Ever facetious, I see. They told all your jokes in Italy.

GAR. Did they? People call me a fool here, because I am too honest for their wisdom. I think of printing "fool" on my forehead some day—

GAL. As a warning to honesty?

Gar. Yes.

Gal. That were superfluous. Nature has been so provident towards you.

Gar. Why, yes; she's not ashamed of her folly, but she takes care to hide her villainy snugly enough; Hey, Mr. Galldove, you know—don't you? [*Exit to L.H. meaningly*]

Gal. [*Aside to Lord Rew*] That's "awful Garnish," is it? His nickname must have fallen from Heaven.

Lady W. Can you inform us who the Countess di Cespo is?

Gal. Indeed I cannot. Probably she is from the north of Italy; I resided in the south. Did she bring no letters? [*Crosses to center*]

Miss G. To everybody.

Lady W. The most unexceptionable letters from Lord Merry and Sir John Fouth. But Lord Merry has undertaken a long peregrination into Persia, and Sir John was unfortunately destroyed, by a casualty, the day after his letters were addressed.

Gal. [*Aside*] The day before, if I remember rightly.

Lady W. We are becoming slightly suspicious of foreigners in society.

Gal. Very justly, very justly, madam. Prince Français sent over his valet, letters and all, as Count Somebody, just for the joke's sake. You know Français hates everything English, from a line of battle ship to a bottle of Harvey's sauce. He takes the *Times* to burn it unread; eats beef, against his taste, simply[15] because it reminds him of a slaughtered bull; buys a picture of the Queen to practise at with pistols; and has actually gone so far as to translate Shakespeare[16] into his abominable language, for the purpose of depreciating a fame as immortal as the stars! The valet was the crowning victory, however. The sham count took; and carried back to his princely master a huge bundle of love-letters from half the fairer side of the Court.

Gar. And some from the uglier side. Hetty, don't you remember the moustache you wrote a sonnet to?

Miss G. Good Heaven, Garnish!

Gal. I should not wonder if this Countess di Cesto—

Miss G. Cespo, Cespo, Mr. Galldove.

Gal. Ah! Cespo. I should not wonder, if she were some adventuress.

Lady W. The countess is certainly a lady.

Lord R. Thoroughbred.

Miss G. A belle, sir.

Gal. Have you abdicated the kingdom of hearts to a stranger?

Miss G. Ah! Mr. Galldove.

Lord R. She walked round the course. No entries against her.

Gal. [*Aside*] All goes fair.

LORD R. She dances like Franconi's gelding.

MISS G. Sings so charmingly!

LADY W. Performs everything which she undertakes so admirably!

GAL. Indeed?

GAR. I don't like her singing and dancing, Hetty. She sings as if her heart were sticking in her throat, and dances as if it were in her shoe, and getting trodden upon. My! what a sorrowful way of being gay she has!

GAL. [*Aside*] The fool sees beyond them all. But, Mr. Garnish—

LORD R. [*Aside to Galldove*] For Heaven's sake don't rouse him. You cannot know his temper.—Headstrong as a ram. [*Enter Servant and gives card to Lady Willburg*]

LADY W. The Countess herself! At home, assuredly. [*Exit Servant, L.2.E.*]

GAR. Talk of the dev—

MISS G. [*Going to window*] Garnish, Garnish! is that horse running away?

GAR. [*Following her*] Horses don't run away with a brewer's dray and six barrels behind them.

MISS G. Don't they?

GAR. No, you goose! [*Enter Teresa Cespo, L.2E.*]

LADY W. I am delighted with your visit, madam.

TER. [*Aside*] He's here! Had I but known it! Why will he not look at me? It gives me much pleasure—[*Aside*] Oh, this vile masquerade—to return your ladyship's visit this early. I—[*Aside*] How can he feign so? Miss Garnish, Lord Rew, good morning!

LADY W. Allow me, countess, to present Mr. Galldove.

TER. [*Sighing*] Ah!

GAL. [*Aside to Teresa*] Teresa!

LADY W. You sigh?

TER. I was thinking of home. I have heard of Mr. Galldove in Italy.

GAL. You flatter me.

TER. Sir, you will flatter me more by valuing my esteem.

GAR. [*Aside to Galldove*] Hey! Mr. Galldove, that was a pretty dash! I'd give my ears for half so much.

GAL. [*Aside to Garrish*] What, no more, sir? You underrate her smiles. Ears are no ornaments to certain heads. I have seen a creature that would part with his, and thank the taker.

GAR. Oh, what, an ass?

GAL. How apt you are at guessing! [*Enter Rylton and Fernwood, L.2E.*]

RYL. All hail to Fernwood! safely back again from his long travels. Gentlemen, tremble before your master—ladies, salute your idol! [*All bow to*

Fernwood] I pulled our stock and stone in here, by main force, like a good pagan. Look what a stormy brow he wears! Something sits heavily on his mind today. Therefore hope nothing from his golden mouth; if he should only roll his sacred eyes, be happy, and adore.[17]

FERN. Pshaw! Rylton, Rylton, what a light thing you are!

RYL. To weight against your leaden majesty. The Countess and my cousin! What a fool I am!

FERN. I always said so.

RYL. What a nose for fools! But that's no wonder with your practice.

FERN. Why?

RYL. You have one under it from morn till night.[18] Pardon me, Countess, but we all love Mr. Fernwood so much that we are proud to parade our feelings.

TER. A strange parade for love.

RYL. This dress is motly; but the heart beneath takes no taint from the coat.[19] Fernwood, allow me to introduce you to my cousin, Mr. Galldove— He has—

FERN. [*Starting*] Who?

GAL. How have I offended the idol? Good Magog—

FERN. Sir, this banter, though harmless from a friend, is insult from a— from a stranger. [*Aside to Rylton*] What is his name?

RYL. Thomas Galldove, Esquire, late from Italy.

FERN. From Italy! What part?

RYL. Taranto.

FERN. So! your cousin?

RYL. Heavens! Fernwood, what's the matter now?

FERN. Nothing, nothing.

RYL. A very remarkable nothing. Let me feel your pulse.

FERN. Pshaw! a mistake. Excuse my rudeness, Mr. Galldove, [*crosses to him*] I made a painful error[20] in your name.

GAL. Nay, sir, I am glad my poor name could awaken such interest in you. An acquaintance so strangely begun, should have no common issue. You shall not purchase my forgiveness, however, by anything less than your friendship. [*Fernwood turns away; Galldove regarding him amazedly*]

FERN. Lady Willburg, who—who is that lady near the table?

GAR. Why, Mr. Fernwood, what have you been drinking?

LADY W. Allow me to present you. [*Going slightly up to Fernwood*]

FERN. Yes, at once—at once.

Ryl. Farewell, Fernwood, I am going to find a comfortable asylum for you.

Fern. Madam, I wait for you.

Ryl. Is the man sane? No word for me? Why, Fernwood!

Fern. Well, well, madam!

Ryl. Why, Fernwood, Fernwood!

Fern. Well, sir!

Ryl. A fair day to you, and a clearer brain. [*Exit, L.2E., bowing to others*]

Fern. [*Takes stage a little L.H.*] Now, Lady Willburg. [*Crosses with Lady Willburg to Teresa*]

Lady W. [*Introducing them*] My friend, Mr. Fernwood, Countess di Cespo.

Fern. Good Heaven, as I feared!

Lady W. Mr. Fernwood!

Gar. Drunk! that's clear.

Miss G. Strange conduct for a gentleman, Mr. Galldove.

Gal. For a gentleman! What—who—whence came that man?

Miss G. You equal him in passion.

Gal. I, what, I! Oh, no. [*Laughing*] But to a lady—See how they stare at each other. Dumb as death!

Miss G. As pale, too.

Gal. 'S blood![21] shall I trip at the first step? She speaks. [*Aside*]

Ter. Your friend seems moved, my lady. Pray, sir, have you known me before?

Gal. [*Aside*] So! well done, Terry—better than I hoped for.

Fern. [*Crossing to Teresa*] No, not before; or, if I have known you, not thus. [*Crosses to R.C.*]

Gal. [*Aside*] Dared I but speak. Oh, furies! should she forget herself.

Fern. Chance likenesses are strange. I knew a maid, a simple country girl, who much resembled you.

Ter. A sorry compliment.

Gal. [*Aside*] Brava. Well played!

Fern. Thus was it. Far away, in Italy—

Ter. In Italy? My country.

Gal. [*Aside*] She's gone! Green, half-ripe fool, would you had rotted in the bud! I must—[22] In what part, sir? [*Crosses to L.C.*]

Fern. Come not too near me! By yon blessed light,
Your life is trembling in the scales of fate!

Gal. This is outrageous!

THE WORLD A MASK

FERN. Pardon me again:
    You broke upon my story.
    Thus was it, lady.—Upon a narrow arm
    Of that wide sea, whose mournful waters sigh
    Around the fading things, with which old Rome
    Strewed, in her lavish grandeur, Italy—
    A maiden lived. Her father, mother, brother
    Dwelt in the cot, but she was star of all.
    Their cot was built between two stately columns,
    Whose fluted shafts the senatorial purple
    Had brushed in former days; and over it
    Hung a vast sculptured frieze, threatening the roof
    With sudden rain.

TER.   [*Aside*] My home, my home!

GAL.   [*Aside to her*] Teresa!

FERN. The maiden's father died; her mother drooped,
    And followed her old mate; her brother drowned
    Far from his home, upon some stormy coast:
    So she was left alone; with nothing but
    The time-notched pillars and the dusty frieze,
    With a stray flower or two, for friends. But hark!
    Draw nearer, Galldove—listen, lady, listen;
    For this lone maid was wonderous, like yourself
    In more than feature.—An infernal villain—
    With all the vices of the neighboring town
    Crammed in a heart that harmonized with guilt,
    And fed upon it as a natural food—
    Stole to her side!—Fair promises, fair words;
    And so she fell!

TER.   'Tis false!

GAL.   [*Aside*] Fool, fool!

FERN. Ha! what do you know?

TER. Oh, nothing; but that the tale seemed false.

GAL. [*Aside*] Good, good! Give me a woman for deceit.

FERN. Too true. When next I met her what did I behold?—Can you tell, Mr. Galldove?

GAL. 'S death, not I! I have no knack at getting up romances.

FERN. Indeed! You have a most fictitious look.
    Then I will tell you Galldove: I beheld
    That once pure nature sunk beneath the wretch

With whom she wandered. Ay, that pliant girl
Was a mere tool—a thing to use and spurn—
In the foul fingers of her wronger. She,
Without the courage to commit a crime—
Without the merit that may be in guilt—
Became an humble instrument, and worked
The loathsome purposes she dared not plan—
Away, Teresa Cespo!

TER. Hear me—oh! [*She faints and is supported by Galldove*]
FERN. The game is up! Look, Galldove, to yourself! [*Exit L.2E.*]
GAR. Come back!—Tell us another story, Fernwood,—do!

TABLEAU

ACT II.

SCENE 1: *A boudoir in Teresa Cespo's lodgings. Teresa and Galldove discovered seated.*[23]

GAL. You wrote the note?
TER. Yes.
GAL. No answer yet?
TER. None. He may reply in person.
GAL. True. 'Tis plain this madman takes a powerful interest in you,[24] and should you have a chance of pleading face to face, 'tis all the world to nothing that you win.[25] This we must have by some means—his promise, his binding promise not to betray us.
TER. But how?
GAL. Pish!—let me see. Flirt—make love to him; or meet his love with comfort; or damn it! do something!
TER. Galldove!
GAL. Oh! not in earnest. Men are so weak, so vain. A little female flattery turned Anthony to cutting Roman throats. You know the story. That brown Egyptian thing was a mere tulip to my queenly rose. [*They rise and advance*]
TER. Love is too holy a thing for such false uses.
GAL. Out on your drowsy sentiment! Talk sense, plain sense—the wholesome mother of strong deeds. Bah! you would dream, and dream, letting this fair world slide through your listless hands, for want of power to close them.[26]
TER. Nay; be not angry. What am I to do if he refuse?

GAL. I'll care for him then.
TER. You would not harm him?
GAL. Did I say I would?
TER. He looked so kindly on me, while his words scorched to my very heart; within his eyes there dwelt a dove-like pity that disarmed his cruelest rage.[27]
GAL. Dreaming again![28] Who is this Fernwood? Why, he drew your wretched hut as if the air were canvas, and his tongue a painter's pencil.
TER. Heaven knows! Now I remember, once there was
A peasant lad who used to come by stealth,
And lean his pale cheeks 'gainst the orange blossoms,
Which hedged my father's house, for hours together:
And I have often watched the deep, full gleam
Of his dark eyes, that wandered after me—
Two brighter stars amid the glimmering flowers—
Resting on nothing but my humble self,
While all the glorious land of Italy
Was spread before them.
The neighbors said he loved me too:
But he was shy, and never spoke to me—
It may be he. Ah! that was long ago:
I was a child, and he scarce more. 'Tis he,
Perhaps;—Yet Fernwood is an English name;
I have forgotten the boy's. He seemed to pity me.
GAL. Pity!
TER. I have great need of it.
GAL. Perchance he loves you. If he does—
TER. Would you not be jealous?
GAL. I—how—I!
TER. I should be in your place. I have a heart—
GAL. Praise be Heaven, then, I have none, if that directs your tongue.[29]
TER. You wrong yourself![29]
GAL. You have my heart—There, don't wrangle, Terry dear. You have it. Fernwood, Fernwood? Who the devil can Fernwood be? Have you seen Rylton?
TER. Once or twice.
GAL. A handsome fellow—a brave handsome fellow, as honest as the sun. Do you not think so?
TER. Passable.

Gal. Nay, very handsome. But curse, curse his honesty! He thrives upon it, while I wither—[30]

Ter. What means all this? Why these vague questions? Why did you bind me to be ruled by you, then tricked me out as a countess—me, poor me;—and worst of all made us in public, strangers? I will not bear it longer, without a reason.

Gal. Will not, hey? Go out and starve then.

Ter. I would rather starve with you than flourish thus. Whence comes the money to support my irksome grandeur?

Gal. Starve with me! I have no appetite for starving. As for how we live—we live upon my brains. That's a rare diet, but far more solid than the heart you talk about.[31]

Ter. But why do I play countess, while you seem sunk almost to the dregs of penury?

Gal. These matters will explain themselves one day. Now, dear Teresa, do not vex yourself about my plans; but, as you love me, only further them.

Ter. What are your plans? I will be answered!

Gal. So willful! well, well; but should you hint them, love, I do not know what ill might not befall you.

Ter. Misfortune breeds misfortunes, sorrow, sorrows. Care has a most familiar look to me; I have known him from my cradle.—Oh, fie! I vex you. I have done.

Gal. Rylton and I are cousins—I, the elder—both bound by equal ties of blood to Sir Hugh Blumer. I am the natural, Rylton the real heir to our uncle's wealth. By some foul parchment or other,[31] Sir Hugh has the power—but, mark me, not the right, if he were just—to name his heir. So he and Rylton 'twixt them—curse them both!—withhold my just inheritance, roll in my gold, and leave me here to beg. I would reclaim my right. Now do you understand all that?

Ter. Most clearly. You would not right yourself by wronging Rylton?

Gal. Wrong him! How can I? He wrongs me—flourishes upon his wrongs to me—without so much as "By your leave" or "Thank you." [*Crosses to R.H.*]

Ter. But how am I concerned?

Gal. Patience sees everything. 'S death! do you doubt my honor?

Ter. Forgive my questions. I would not cross you. Doubtless you are right. We will toil together in this good cause; if my poor hands have any power for you—ay, and you say they have—Oh, happy thought! You will grow rich; and then—

Gal. [*Over towards R.H.*] Hist, Terry, hist! [*Enter a servant, L.C.*]

SER. Mr. Fernwood. [*Enter Fernwood*]

FERN. Good day, my lady! I am here; following the man who bore your note. Ha! Mr. Galldove? By the by, I owe you an apology for my strange conduct at Lady Willburg's. My brain is no better than my neighbor's; it will wander sometimes.

GAL. Sometimes it wanders on forbidden grounds; a trespass by law.

FERN. What did I say? These fits are like dreams; I forget them as soon as they are over. I have explained my vagary to our friends.[32]

GAL. [*Aside to Teresa*] Be on your guard, Teresa: trust dies in ditches.

FERN. You seem to ripen your acquaintance soon. Whispering!

GAL. My introduction dates with yours, and you are strangely forward. Some men we trust at once, others never. Sir, I would know you better.

FERN. As I would you.—Much better. Would you not trust him, Countess?

TER. With all my heart.

FERN. I thought so.

GAL. [*Crossing to center*] Excuse me, Countess. Mr. Fernwood, I have the happiness of leaving you—[*Fernwood looks surprised*] in the best company. [*Exit L.C.*]

FERN. Teresa Cespo—

TER. You forget my title.

FERN. Would to Heaven, you might forget it!

TER. Your thoughts wander again.

FERN. Ay, now they wander to a happy maiden who sang from Tasso, while her little herd nibbled the grass before her—to a holy maiden who, when the drowsy chimes came humming through the distance to her ears, sank down upon her knees beneath pure Heaven, with no more guile than her white yearling lambs. But the dream breaks; and I behold before me a woman deeply read in crime, and guileful as the Tempter. Do you know her?—A maid who left her flock and evening prayers, to herd with frauds and worship wickedness?

TER. You wrong me basely! Mercy! Who are you that draw these tears from me? [*Weeps*]

FERN. A friend—that sacred name stands next to His who is the friend of all. One who over Italy tracked you in vain, to find you here the plaything of a sensualist; sharing the honors of his meats and wines, and no more cared for.

TER. False, from first to last!

FERN. What, dare you—

TER. Sir, I dare say anything in defense of my slandered purity.

FERN. You do not mean—

TER. That in all save loving—and who that has a heart will blame me there?—I am as stainless as the Heaven which hears my solemn declaration. [*Sinks on her knees*]

FERN. Leap to my heart, and let it welcome you! No, no; the time is not ripe yet. [*Aside*]

TER. [*Rising*] Sir, are you mad? What do these passions mean? You are presuming on a nature weakened with many griefs.

FERN. To try innocence is to set a crown upon its brow.[33] Answer me, and answer truly; or I will blazon Galldove's tricks, until the world turn on him as one man. Deceit is useless; all your history is open to me.

TER. Then all our history will prove but this—that there are no such things as tricks in Mr. Galldove.

FERN. How came you in his hands?

TER. I—

FERN. Does that blush mean you love him?

TER. You know.

FERN. Oh! bitter fate! [*Aside*] Do you not see the danger you incur? Do—

TER. What danger?

FERN. His loathsome love.

TER. Would I could hate you! what is there in you that makes me bear those insults with tame patience? But I can smile at all you say of him, and of his love to me; for him and it I know.

FERN. And him and it I know! Foul-handed ruffian, working with a thing which angels name with reverence! Has the human heart fallen to such gross abuses?

TER. Base, base thought! Indeed you do not understand him. I would have you friends, and yet, I know not why; but I would have it so.[34]

FERN. What signs of his affection does he show?

TER. I am not practised in the ways of love. His brain is full, he has not time for me. You tax me sadly, sir. Must it be proven? Would it not puzzle you to tell me why you hate him?

FERN. [*Aside*] Love feeds on nothing, and is feasted.—Teresa, I love you.

TER. I knew you did. How else could I have trusted you? Promise me something.

FERN. Anything.

TER. Not to betray us.

FERN. Us! Galldove, you mean. Unless you wish it, never. You live apart?

TER. Oh, joy! he is safe; and I have saved him!

FERN. Do you live apart?

TER. Ah, yes; he is a mile away. I seldom see him.

FERN. Keep him there. His safety rests upon your honor. [*Aside*] Can this strange tale be true? It is! or sin has stamped a lie upon the whitest piece of purity man ever gazed on. [*Enter Galldove and Rylton*]

RYL. Here is the lunatic. An almanac! How stands the moon? We must address him by the calendar. Have you a dry, hot harvest madness now, or a dull watery fit? How goes it?

FERN. Thanks to this lady, sane once more. How, Mr. Galldove, back again? Two visits in one hour!

GAL. Rylton persuaded me to come.

RYL. No; you persuaded me.

GAL. Well, 'twas in some such way. Gods! if that man were dead! [*Aside*]

FERN. [*Crosses to Galldove*] Doubtless, doubtless. [*Aside to Galldove*] Galldove, you blunder sadly.

GAL. [*Taking Fernwood aside*] 'Ods mercy! who are you that tutor me?

FERN. One who knows your ways, my little man. Respect yon lady, or a new cell in Newgate shall be tenanted. Nay, do not frown. Go on, work all your aims: your way is clear, though somewhat crooked. Remember, no liberties with her. Do you hear, sir?

GAL. Yes, yes; but would not. 'Sdeath! sir—

FERN. Come, no fine rages. Why did you bring Teresa here?

GAL. She stuck to me; I could not get her off. 'Twas not my fault. Heaven knows I would be rid of her, if that may please you.

FERN. We shall meet again, fool, coward, liar! [*Exit C.D.*]

GAL. [*Aside*] Oh, damn you, beast! May every word come back to you a several poison!—Cousin, will you be kind enough to tell me who Mr. Fernwood is?

RYL. A man who has seen and learned everything between the poles. One who has driven the Esquimaux's dogs, mounted the Arab's mares, passed untasted through the Cannibals, drank water at Niagara, and tea at Pekin. One who has sailed through the mouth of the Niger, paddled in the head waters of the Nile. One who has thrown a Patagonian, lighted his chibouque with the Koran, eaten pork with a Rabbi, and pulled the great Tartar by the beard. A man of no particular age, and no particular country. He was born on the water with Noah, and will probably hobble at the Millennium. In short, a gentleman: who could say more?[35]

GAL. I do not think so.

RYL. What? the man who traduces him, strikes me a blow.

TER. You certainly will not deny Mr. Fernwood's gentility?

GAL. Oh no; I spoke at random. I would not offend you, cousin, think as I may. 'Tis true I do not like him as—

RYL. By that admission you deny yourself all claim to my respect.

TER. You cavil at a broken phase.

GAL. Indeed he does.[36] I meant to say, that I do not like him as well as you, perhaps; but, yet I like him vastly—vastly. You are too headlong for me, cousin. I'll call for you shortly. You know I dine with you! for I, alas, have no table of my own. Will I intrude?

RYL. What, intrude on my beef and port! No, no; you are welcome.

GAL. Thank you, thank you cousin. I have not dined since I left Italy—ah! ah! [*Sighs and exit*]

RYL. So wretched, and I know nothing of it! This must be looked to. Sir Hugh has some old prejudices against poor Tom, but he will surely help him at his need; and if he will not, let Galldove share my purse. Bless me, Countess, I am soliloquizing openly.

TER. And nobly. [*Aside*] Can Galldove wish the ruin of this man?[37]

RYL. Has such a trifle pleased you?

TER. 'Tis more than pleasure: It uplifts my soul to recognize such greatness.

RYL. Dear lady—

TER. But he—Mr. Galldove, I mean—deserves this at your hands. He speaks so well of you: praises your candor, your integrity, your very person; and in his commendation I join most heartily.[38]

RYL. You dress my beggarly deeds in so royal a guise, as to make them seem almost ridiculous. He is my cousin;[39] and some family pride is therefore blent with my desire to aid him.[40]

TER. If the just homage, which I pay your generosity is displeasing, I will lock it in my heart for other ears than yours.

RYL. [*Aside*] Her heart! What the deuce does the woman mean? Galldove is almost a stranger to her. Can all this be for me? Marry, Mr. Rylton, what a ladykiller you are becoming! Poh! nonsense! perhaps I have done some wonder without knowing it.—Lady, if there were more to encourage goodness, as you do, sin would be a scarcer commodity in this peddling world. Let us be friends.

TER. Most cheerfully. Would I had more such! [*Offers her hand, which he kisses respectfully. At this moment, enter Galldove, Sir Hugh Blumer, Lady Willburg, Lucy Willburg, Miss Garnish, Lord Rew and Garnish*]

GAL. [*Starting and almost treading on the feet of Lord Rew*] Ha! we have spoilt our welcome.

SIR H. How?

Lucy. What did you say, sir?
Gar. What did you jump at? Have you fits, as you say Fernwood has?⁴¹
Lady W. Preposterous! Mr. Galldove, I have a nervous system.
Lord R. What's loose? Have you cast a shoe? You nearly shied over me. [*Turns up R.C.*]
Gal. You surprise me. I was not aware that I did anything in particular—Ah! [*Sighs*]
Lady W. Explain yourself, Mr. Galldove.
Gal. I cry you mercy! What a to-do about nothing! [*Aside to Lucy*] Did you not see!
Ter. Welcome, ladies and gentlemen! You make a flattering show in honor of my poor house.
Gar. Yes; we always go in flocks, on the birds-of-a-feather principle.
Miss G. [*Aside to him*] Do hold your tongue, Garnish.
Gar. [*Aside to her*] Do go to the devil, Hetty! when I hear something better than my own conversation, I will stop. [*They seat themselves, all talk together, at the back of the scene*]
Sir H. [*Advancing*] Galldove, a word with you.
Gal. [*Advancing*] Am I not your nephew, Uncle?
Sir H. My sister was your mother—much to her discredit, I think. [*Aside*]
Gal. You will not forget my mother, when you speak to her own son?
Sir H. 'Ods love! I do though: you are so unlike her.
Gal. Am I? I would give the world to resemble her, Uncle.
Sir H. [*Aside*] The fellow has some feeling after all—why?
Gal. It might insure me some share of your affection.
Sir H. Or of my property.
Gal. By Heaven, 'tis ungenerous to make my poverty my reproach!
Sir H. The vices that begot your want are so many just reproaches.
Gal. Misfortunes, not vices, ruined me. I could have explained all this. Now, by all my sufferings, I never will, even to regain the only thing I prize—your cruelly prejudiced heart.
Sir H. [*Aside*] His passion seems honest. But Galldove—
Gal. I wish none of your charity, to disgrace my mother's memory. I cannot speak without your suspicion, therefore let all intercourse between us cease.
Sir H. Do you hope by headstrong passion—
Gal. Sir, I spoke without design. I hope nothing, I ask nothing. All I desire is to be allowed to suffer, without being forced to bear the unnatural sneers of my only relative.⁴²

Sɪʀ H. Nay, nephew, nephew.

Gᴀʟ. You forget, sir; I am a villain—a poor villain. Is it the villainy or the poverty which you loathe so much?

Sɪʀ H. Indeed, I had no wish to hurt your feelings. You know we have never agreed since you ruined poor Mary, my farmer's child.

Gᴀʟ. Another slander!

Sɪʀ H. But she charged you.

Gᴀʟ. Her seducer forced her to do that. I am always a victim for the crimes of my friends—Heaven help me! There is a certain gentleman who might tell you more—if he would.

Sɪʀ H. Do you mean Rylton?

Gᴀʟ. Oh, no; I am always blurting out something. I wish I were a fine, glossy gentleman, with a surface that reflects the world around so beautifully, and hides all that is within:—in faith, I do. Well, well, let us bury the past. Poor Mary! You remember how she used to skip along the hawthorn hedge, as white as the buds about her—ay, and as pure—as if nature's hand had just dropped among the flowers. Poor Mary—ah, poor Mary! She drowned herself, did she not? I wonder how her betrayer sleeps o' nights.

Sɪʀ H. [*Aside*] He must be innocent.—Look you, nephew, I have wronged you in one thing; perhaps in all. Here is my hand.

Gᴀʟ. [*Taking his hand timidly*] You are the only friend I have—on earth. [*Weeps*]

Sɪʀ H. Poor fellow! Bah! bah! we are both fit for a nursery. Come, let me settle an income on you. You will not refuse five hundred or so a year? That's but a trifle, nothing to make you feel obliged.

Gᴀʟ. No, sir; I'd rather beg! You will say tomorrow, that I ensnared you in your own goodness.

Sɪʀ H. If I do, hang me!

Gᴀʟ. Pray excuse me, dear Uncle. Your love contents me. I can work along: I am used to living on nothing. [*Aside*] Five hundred—Curse his impudence! Does he take me for a wornout lackey?

Sɪʀ H. Gods, sir! would you disgrace your family? Take the thousand pounds, or I will—damn it! I don't know what I'll do!

Gᴀʟ. [*Aside*] The old wretch is improving. A hundred would suffice my little wants; even that—

Sɪʀ H. Zounds! You dictate what use I shall make of my money! If you will not accept the fifteen hundred pounds, I shall swear you are too proud to love me.

GAL. [*Aside*] Hum! fifteen hundred pounds—that may do.—You shall never say it, dear Uncle, though I must humble my pride to receive your bounty. Gratitude—

SIR H. Damn gratitude! Your cheques will be honored at my bankers. Pluck up, nephew, pluck up! Life shall smile for you again. [*Going*] Excuse me ladies. [*Aside*] Could he have meant Rylton? Poor Mary, indeed!

RYL. [*Going up*] Uncle, Uncle—

SIR H. [*Regarding him fiercely*] Sir! [*Exit C.L.*]

RYL. Hillo! has your dog bitten you? [*Advances*]

GAL. [*Aside*] Thus do I twirl humanity around this little finger.

RYL. What were you and my uncle talking about?

GAL. He is my uncle too. Both you and he seem to forget it.

RYL. Well then, precisian, what were you and *our* uncle talking about?[43]

GAL. About the price of straws in Florence.

RYL. Straws in Florence!

GAL. Straw goods, forsooth. 'Tis evident you never soiled your dainty hands in trade. I was obliged to speculate with such trumpery, for a few ducats, to feed my vulgar mouth. 'Sdeath! you are always throwing my rags in my face!

RYL. Forgive me, cousin. Will Sir Hugh do nothing for you?

GAL. He offered me a beggarly hundred or two.

RYL. The squalid old brute! I'll swing him for this.

GAL. If you say a word, I'll never pardon you. Gods, sir! I have some pride left among my tatters. He measured his bounty by his affection—nothing for nothing.

RYL. He shall increase in both.[44] The mean old starver! I would not have thought this, for twice his fortune.

GAL. Anything dragged from him would spoil in using. Promise to say nothing. Think of my self-esteem.[45]

RYL. Right, man, I respect you. But allow me to help you along a little, and to speak well of you to Sir Hugh: there's no harm in that. [*Gives a pocket-book*] Now, now don't be angry. You can pay me when you please, and borrow what you like in the meantime. Why Tom, Tom, you are my cousin. You and our uncle make up for brother and father to me.[46] There, don't be sullen.

GAL. God bless you, Rylton!

RYL. Tears in your eyes! Pshaw, I'll disgrace myself before the women presently. By the by, you are not acquainted with my little enchantress, Lucy!

LUCY. [*Advancing. R.C.*] Mr. Rylton.

RYL. What?

Lucy. Mr. Rylton.

Ryl. Bitten by my uncle's dog! Have you no warmer term?

Lucy. Yes, for warmer times.

Gal. [*Aside*] Charming! What a pair of doves!

Ryl. Oh, bless me! little Lucy in her first pet. Here Galldove, you must soften her; my wit runs out. [*Aside to him*] You like to keep me wooing, do you?—My cousin, Mr. Galldove, Miss Lucy Willburg. [*Introducing them. Aside to her*] There, I was forced to *Miss* you for etiquette's sake.

Lucy. [*Aside to him*] You may miss me much more, if you carry your etiquette towards others much farther.—I have had this pleasure before.

Ryl. I double it then. [*Aside to her*] What are you driving at?

Lucy. [*Aside to him*] You forget your etiquette, sir. Introduce me to a gentleman, and then engross my conversation!

Gal. How pleasant are the secret ways of love!
    What wonders in a whisper! What great joys,
    Unknown to poorer souls, can lovers make
    Out of a snowdrop melting as it falls;
    Or any show that slips the common eye
    For want of love's sharp vision!
    What pretty lines! and, oh, how very true!
    What think you Miss Lucy?

Ryl. [*Aside to Lucy*] We'll end our battle yet, fair Amazon. [*Exit C.L.*]

Lucy. Mr. Galldove.

Gal. [*Advancing to Lucy*] Miss Willburg.

Lucy. You started, and cried "Ha!" as you came in.

Gal. I?

Lucy. Yes.

Gal. I stumbled upon something.

Lucy. What do you think it was?

Gal. I scarcely know. Something of the Countess'—perhaps her fan.

Lucy. Or, what is nearer to her—her hand.

Gal. So! My cousin has more care for that.

Lucy. Fie! sir, you make me merry.

Gal. Is it not pardonable to wring a laugh out of this wicked world? Ah! [*Sighs*]

Lucy. Will you be frank?

Gal. I will be anything for you.

Lucy. What did you start at, and why?

Gal. I dare not say.

Lucy. You promised me.[47]

GAL. 'Tis scarcely fair to force my thoughts from me. Did you not see?

LUCY. Yes, but 'tis your conduct I wish explained. Mr. Rylton's is above the need of it.

GAL. [*Aside*] What a sweet little lie!—Well, then—if you compel me to speak—when I saw Rylton kiss the Countess' hand, I thought 'twas not the manner of our time, and started,—fearing the Italian's beauty had conjured up some buried ancestor of mine.

LUCY. Not the manner of our time! I have seen such gallantry, in my young days, often—quite often.

GAL. I am glad you are satisfied.

LUCY. Perhaps it is the custom of her country.

GAL. I am almost a native of Italy, you know. Women are more chary of their favors there than here,—that is in public. Of course, my cousin was doing nothing which all the world might not have seen—with his permission.

LUCY. Of course not. [*Aside*] Oh, me!

GAL. Did you sigh?

LUCY. Oh, no! I have a slight neuralgic pain. 'Tis over now.

GAL. I see no harm, myself, in a gentleman's taking a lady's hand thus, [*Takes her hand*] and pressing it to his lips, thus—[*Offers to kiss her hand, which she withdraws violently*]

LUCY. Ha! ha! [*Laughingly*] Nor I.

GAL. Especially, if she permits it.

LUCY. True, true. I am not well. Excuse me—I shall be—I mean my mother will be pleased to see you—Indeed I am not exactly well.

GAL. A little more neuralgia, perhaps—in your left side?

LUCY. We fatigue the Countess by our stay.

GAL. We all remain too long. I have called here twice this very morning, to see my cousin.

LUCY. And found him both times, doubtless.

GAL. Yes, oh yes.

LUCY. [*Aside*] My heart, my heart! I'll take your arm across the room. Come Mother. [*At door*]

LADY W. [*Aside to her*] Lady Willburg, Miss Lucy. Never address me in that vulgar manner.—

LUCY. [*Aside*] Not one kind word for me in all the world! [*Lady Willburg and Lucy bow and exit, C.*]

MISS G. Come, Garnish, you grow tedious.

LORD R. [*Rising*] Heavy as dead weight on the last quarter.

GAR. [*Starting up*] Why, I've been sound asleep.

TER. A doubtful compliment.

GAL. [*Going down R.*] Lulled by the music of her voice,
   The grisly horror sank to rest!
GAR. Poverty and poetry! Are all poets beggars?
GAL. Worse, worse; they are all thieves.
GAR. Really!
GAL. Only of ideas. Nothing which you possess is in any danger.
GAR. You'll be hung for something worse than larceny then.[48] Come along, Hetty, Mr. Galldove, I'll give you half a crown, if you'll write something lively about the courtship of old Rew and Hetty. It has been going on these twenty years, and nobody has been fool enough to say a word about it yet. You can, without losing your character.
MISS G. Oh, if I were weeping over your body!
LORD R. Well, if Garnish can't strike a merry gait, cut my best snaffle. [*Exit all but Teresa and Galldove*]
GAL. [*L.*] Brava, brava, Teresa! Now you see the wisdom of your playing, Countess.
TER. [*R.*] I was happier a peasant.
GAL. Bah! you are a belle, a belle, a very despot. Your belleship has given me a start in the world, which I could never have gotten without you. Look, now; had you appeared in London as plain Teresa Cespo, you would have been worse than nothing to me.
TER. Am I a mere tool?
GAL. We are all mere tools; the greater use the less. But now you hold my fortune in your hands.
TER. You jest, to please me.
GAL. No; a word from you has lifted me to the pinnacle of fashion. Lord Haughty bows now, Lord Squalid has some pounds to lend, Duke Crafty courts me, all the world comes whimpering at my heels. What are rank, riches, talent, power, to fashion—to imperial fashion?
TER. A flimsy thing.
GAL. A solid power, in skilful hands. Here, in your house, I mingle with the world—here meet my uncle, and obtain a pension—
TER. A pension! Oh, happy fortune!
GAL. Nay, nay, 'tis not enough to marry on. A little longer, and this scanty sum shall swell, and swell, and swell—
TER. But Rylton—Are you just?
GAL. Oh, yes; he tries to buy me off. 'Sdeath! do you love him more than me? What of Fernwood?
TER. He promised all.
GAL. Victoria! He promised willingly?

TER. Without twice thinking.
GAL. Glorious! he loves you!
TER. He said as much.
GAL. Beautiful, most beautiful! What a butcher of men's hearts you are becoming! Keep him in hope—play him, Teresa. He is our only fear.
TER. How you abuse us! "Keep him in hope—play him!" He only loves me as a friend. Would I permit more?
GAL. More, or Eve's blood runs out in you. [*Aside*]
Well, well, keep your friend warm then.
He may be managed yet. Go dress yourself.
Ho! for the Court, the Park, the Opera—
The Ball, at which admiring morning winks
With playful wonder! All the world's astir.
Fashion is murmuring for its absent queen
To mount her throne, and make its state complete.
Away, away! the world is lost or won
While half its fools are sleeping! Up, awake!
Actors, not dreamers, toss this globe about!
[*Exeunt severally. Galldove R.1E. Teresa L.1E.*]

ACT III.

SCENE: *A Gaming House. Garnish and Lord Rew discovered L.H. playing at cards; others gaming at different table.*

GAR. Here, 'tis your deal. That's two thousand pounds this week. But you lost them to somebody: that's a satisfaction. You can't get ahead of me, old boy.
LORD R. Can't I? Made a turn on the St. Leger—trebled the stakes.
GAR. I am glad of that. Take good care of my money. Don't go about wasting it on horse-races and gaming tables. Did you hear the news about Fernwood?
LORD R. Mad?—got the staggers?
GAR. Worse.
LORD R. Hey!
GAR. In love.
LORD R. Poor fellow! All ended in that. With whom?
GAR. The Countess. She—
LORD R. Be hanged. Pull up, mind the game. [*They play. Enter Galldove and Rylton L.2E.*]

RYL. The silence of this place fills me with horror. A room full of men, and not one word among them all! This is terrible. Why did you bring me here?

GAL. To show you life on the darker side. Vice is like the smallpox; you must take it once, before you lose your dread of it.

RYL. Mere sophistry.

GAL. Pure common sense.

RYL. You have a loose way of touching on morality. Look around you here. See these hard faces that hang above the tables—these practical atheists who trust to chance alone. Can you not see the visible mask of hell crushing the god-like features underneath to its own horrid mould? What fearful gasps for the polluted air—what greedy clutching for the guilty gold that beggars him who gives it—what burning eyes on the devil's shining bait—what listening ears aching for sounds whose dismal sorcery makes the wild night to thicken, and the pitchy dark, grow dun as hell—what sighs come bubbling from the troubled heart—what raging oaths—what awful, awful groans! [*Crosses to R.H.*]

GAL. Save us! How you thunder at the merry world.

RYL. Galldove, here is a little picture of what your merry world would be, if chance indeed were God.

GAL. Your nurse must have been a shouting Methodist![49] Give up your gloomy thoughts. I have a secret for you—I play.

RYL. You!

GAL. Yes; gaming has been the one curse of my unfortunate life. But your generous trust has so touched my heart, that I have brought you here to see the full depth of my infamy, as well as the glory of my reformation. Tonight I play for the last time.

RYL. Why play tonight? I have no wish to see your vice.

GAL. That is my resolution. [*Aside*] Where can Fleet be?—Promise to keep my secret.

RYL. Ah, that you have such secrets to keep! Sir Hugh would never pardon you. Galldove, this scene has drained my spirits. I know not how it is; but when I am with you, a gloom seems to gather around me, and the hand of fate seems poised above my head.

GAL. The shadow of my ill-starred life falls upon you.

RYL. Well, well, if a few pounds can purchase your release, play on.

GAL. Remember your promise.

RYL. Remember yours as well. [*Enter Captain Fleet. No. 3 Down L.H. Galldove and Fleet talk apart*]

GAL. Where the devil have you been loitering?

Fleet. You told me to leave the note at old Blumer's house: that kept me. Don't growl at five minutes.

Gal. If you do it well, all that you seem to win is yours. Can you leave London tonight?

Fleet. My horse is at the door.

Gal. Well thought. Do not begin until I give the sign.

Fleet. Sharp's the word.[50] [*Galldove and Fleet cross to Rylton No. 3*]

Gal. Mr. Rylton, Captain Fleet. The Captain has seen some service— [*Aside*] in the French gallies.

Ryl. I am happy to know you, sir.

Fleet. Yours truly, as the letters say.

Gal. [*Aside to him*] Hold your cursed vulgar tongue! Perhaps you have heard of Captain Fleet's last exploit? Now don't be modest, Captain. He led Heaven knows how many prisoners, chained together like dogs, straight through the enemy's country, and put them all aboard, despite their best exertions to escape. [*Aside to Fleet*] You led the chain-gang, did you not?

Fleet. Oh, damn it, Galldove!—

Ryl. A brave exploit.

Gall. Important prisoners too, they were—Pensioners on Government.

Ryl. You deserve much of your country.

Gal. His country would probably have a care of him, if it could only get hold of the facts.

Fleet. Pshaw! A mere trifle, Mr. Rylton. The fleet could not put to sea without them.

Gal. I know not which to admire more, his worth or his modesty.

Fleet. Are you for a game tonight, Mr. Rylton?

Ryl. I never played a card.

Fleet. Indeed? How I should like to teach you! What you say, Mr. Galldove?

Gal. Agreed; but 'tis my last night. What shall the game be? Vingt-et-un?

Fleet. Certainly; here is a table. [*They seat themselves and play*]

Ryl. I'll get a breath of air; this room is stifling. [*Opens a large window. R.2E.*]

Gal. Rylton, Rylton, come and look over me: you have a lucky face.

Ryl. Very well, if you wish it. [*Looks on while Galldove and Fleet play*]

Gal. Will you take a card?

Fleet. Yes.

Gal. Another?

Fleet. Yes. I stand.

GAL. So do I. Nineteen.

FLEET. Twenty. I believe we play for the money?

GAL. Yes, yes. [*Takes Rylton apart. R.C.*] Have you anything about you?

RYL. You came ill provided for your last night.

GAL. The first hand swept my pocket. What you gave me this morning has gone to my creditors. Lord, man! I'll pay you directly. Fortune has a coquettish way of frowning at first on her favorites.

RYL. Here is my purse. [*Gives purse*] Lose all; but remember your pledge tomorrow.

GAL. Never fear.

FLEET. Will you talk till morning?

GAL. [*Violently*] What if I do?

RYL. [*Crosses to table R. and returns C.*] Go on with your game. [*They play*] A pack of cards is like a sorcerer's book, open it anywhere, and on the instant up spring a thousand fiendish passions to tear the rash intruder.

GAL. [*Looking at watch*] 'Tis just the hour. [*Aside*] Now, Captain, sharp's the word. I'll take a card—Content. Twenty-one.

FLEET. [*Cheating openly*] A natural.

GAL. Blast your luck!

RYL. [*Aside to Galldove*] Galldove, did you not see?

GAL. What, Cousin? [*They play again. Fleet bunglingly draws a card from his sleeve*]

FLEET. Twenty-one.

GAL. What luck, what luck!

RYL. [*Aside to him*] Why, Galldove, are you blind?

GAL. How, Rylton, how?

FLEET. [*Drawing a card from sleeve*] Another natural.

RYL. [*Crossing in front of the table and seizing Fleet's arm*] Swindler, I've caught you! Witness gentlemen—bear witness all—you too, Galldove—this fellow is a common cheat! [*Shakes cards from Fleet's sleeve, as others rise and group around them*]

GAL. You must be mistaken.

RYL. No; here is the proof upon the floor.

FLEET. Do you mean to charge a gentleman—

RYL. No; I mean to charge a rogue with his own practices.

FLEET. I will have satisfaction for this insult!

RYL. [*Taking stage to R.H.*] Satisfaction! I would not disgrace a cur with the same whip which you deserve. [*Enter Sir Hugh Blumer*]

GAL. [*Aside*] Ha! Sir Hugh! [*Aside to Fleet*] Strike him, Fleet, strike him.

FLEET. [*Crosses to Rylton, L.C.*] Take that! [*Strikes Rylton, who rushes at him. The others interpose*]

SIR H. [*R.C. A little up*] What, Rylton brawling in a gaming house!

RYL. Stand back! He is my enemy who touches me! Off, Galldove! I cannot answer for myself! Unhand that man.

GAL. Nay, patience, Cousin, patience.

SIR H. [*Advancing to Rylton*] Rylton!

GAL. [*Aside to Fleet*] Now, Fleet, be off. [*Fleet exit hastily*]

SIR H. [*Advancing to Rylton R.C.*] You here, you, Rylton, squabbling in a place like this! What does this mean, sir?

RYL. Uncle, I have been struck—struck by a low villain, whom I caught in the very act of cheating. [*Enter Teresa, in disorder, followed by Fernwood*]

FERN. Lady, respect yourself! Come back, come back!

TER. [*Aside to Galldove*] Oh, Galldove, are you safe? [*Crosses behind Sir Hugh and Rylton to L.*]

GAL. [*Aside to her*] Terry, have a care. Take your hand off me. What, in the name of all the fiends, brought you here?

GAR. Was there ever a row without its petticoat?

GAL. [*Aside to Teresa*] Now I think, I am not sorry. Go talk to Rylton.

TER. [*Crossing to Rylton*] I trust you are not hurt, Mr. Rylton?

RYL. Not in body, madam.

LORD R. [*Aside to Garnish*] How sweet she is on him!

SIR H. Countess, this wonderful! [*Crosses to R.H.*]

GAR. An angel in hell!

TER. How that 'tis over, it seems as wonder to me. My lodgings are just opposite.—You observe yonder window has been left open, through which I saw—you can forgive my woman's curiosity—all that was passing here. Mr. Fernwood too was with me, and no less eagerly watching everything. Did you not, sir?

FERN. I confess it. Captain Fleet you say? [*L.H. Aside to a man who goes out hastily*]

TER. We have friends here, dear friends—

GAL. [*Aside to her*] Keep your eyes off me, or by Heaven—look straight at Rylton. [*Turning up stage a little*]

TER. When this terrible tumult began, unable to distinguish who were engaged, and urged by a blind impulse, I dashed across the street; nor did I remember either my rank or sex, until I found myself among you all.—But some are friends, and all will pardon me. [*Lord Rew, Garnish and the others resume their game*]

Gal. [*Aside, advancing*] Excellent! the girl improves. [*Takes Sir Hugh apart*] Who can this happy friend be?

Sir H. Did she not say—friends?

Gal. Friend, I understood. The Countess is a dangerous woman, Uncle. Rich, beautiful, fascinating;—to sum all up, a belle, and therefore irresistible. Who can the friend be? She and Rylton seem to have much to say.

Sir H. Do you mean Rylton?

Gal. I mean no one, sir. I merely ask the question.

Sir H. Can it be possible this hapless boy so far forgets himself?

Gal. I hope not, Uncle, after all, he could not lose. The Countess is reputed very rich. What she is otherwise we know. Belles are sad witches; and can make the false true, the true false—ah! ah! [*Sighs*] You saw him kiss her hand this morning—a token of allegiance perhaps.

Sir H. Gods, no!

Gal. I am very sorry I mentioned it. Poor Mary—You know we spoke of her this morning.—Poor Mary! poor Lucy! [*Taking stage to L.H.*]

Sir H. Base villain! Would he play Lucy false? [*Calling Rylton*] Look you, Rylton, I asked what brought you here; you did not answer me; I asked an explanation of this quarrel; you did not answer me. I ask again.

Gal. [*Aside to Rylton*] Do not betray me, Cousin.

Ryl. I cannot explain without involving others.[51] My word, that I am not to blame in this unhappy business, must suffice.

Sir H. Indeed, indeed, sir! The word of a gambler who cries liar, scoundrel thief; then takes a blow—that must suffice me!

Ryl. I am no gambler, Uncle. I have been foully disgraced by yonder— What, has the coward fled?

Sir H. Ho! bully, would you rage again? You are a gambler, and worse for denying it.

Ryl. Uncle!

Sir H. Talk to me of truth and honor, after this scene? What would Lucy say, if she had witnessed the latter part of it?

Ryl. I am no hand at riddles.

Sir H. Cool hypocrite, your impudence shall not protect you.

Gal. [*Aside to Rylton*] Tell all; even if you ruin me.

Ryl. [*Aside to Galldove*] Generous man; never, to save myself.

Sir H. Nephew.

Ryl. Sir.

Sir H. I spoke to Mr. Galldove. Will you explain? Rylton, I would not do you wrong without a good reason.

Gal. Most cheerfully. I—

Ryl. Hold, Galldove! If you would not have me hate myself. Sir Hugh Blumer, it needs no witness to confirm my words!

Sir H. Address me thus for ever. What! do you hope to ride over me on your high horse? Away, sir, never let me look upon you more!

Gal. Indeed my cousin is innocent.

Sir H. Falsehood, so foul in him, looks well in you. You cannot save him.

Ryl. What, sir, do you think I cannot draw my breath without your aid?

Sir H. Graceless, disrespectful ruffian!

Ter. [*Aside to Galldove*] Oh, Galldove, can you—

Gal. [*Aside to her*] Peace! or I'll strangle you!

Ter. Take care!

Gal. [*Aside to her*] Nay, darling, you distract me from a game where all my skill is needed.

Sir H. Galldove, I have wronged you. My coming here is a dishonor to me. An hour ago I received an anonymous note, saying that I might learn much of one of my nephews at this detestable place.

Fern. Ha! [*Galldove starts and stares at him*] I see, I see. [*Aside*]

Sir H. I was weak enough to come; expecting to find you in some disgraceful act. How I have been deceived! Thank Heaven, I can be unjust no longer!

Ryl. For these noble words I can forgive all your injustice to me. [*Aside to Galldove*] What an escape you made!

Gal. [*Aside to Rylton*] Marvellous, marvellous!

Sir H. I want no forgiveness, sirrah. Get to your loathsome trade, con card and die, but never seek the company of honest men again. [*Crosses to L.H.*]

Ter. [*Aside*] Ah, Galldove, what a fall for you!

Sir H. As for you, madam—

Ter. Well, sir!

Sir H. Enough. No gentleman should turn his tongue upon a woman, though rigid justice may approve the act. [*Exit L.2E.*]

Gal. This is a sad matter, Mr. Fernwood.

Fern. How transparent a thing is rascality, when we look at it rightly! This sad matter is as clear to me, Mr. Galldove, as the sun at noonday.

Gal. [*Drawing Fernwood apart and aside*] Furies! Can I never walk but in your shadow? Fernwood, you have undertaken to be my enemy.

Fern. And a beautiful business I have undertaken.

Gal. You do not know me. You are in danger, sir.

Fern. What, from your tongue? Dare you use any weapon but the woman's? Poh! coward, back to your plots! I am sick of you.

GAL. You swore to Teresa.—

FERN. Back to your villainy, I say. My word is sacred.

GAL. Nay, sir—

FERN. By Heaven, I'll whip you to your game, if you do not obey me! Go, dog, go![52]

GAL. [*Taking Lord Rew apart*] Lord Rew, a word. Do you know Mr. Fernwood?

LORD R. Dark man, dark man, sir.

GAL. His complexion is dark, 'tis true.

LORD R. I mean, a green man.

GAL. He seems ripe enough.

LORD R. I mean, he has never shown—never started for a purse.

GAL. Is he a sporting character, a pedestrian, a modern Captain Barclay?

LORD R. Damn it, no! Don't you understand your mother English?

GAL. I left England before the delicacies of the stable had been introduced into society.

LORD R. Find your country on rising ground then. Running with a slack rein.[53] Don't enter against Fernwood. Know him like a book.—All bone and muscle. Come, Garnish; I want to get into my straw.

GAR. I say, Rew, this has been a jolly night. I have lost five hundred pounds, and seen a fight. [*Exit with Lord Rew, L.2E.*]

FERN. [*Aside to Galldove*] Galldove, this is no place for Teresa. Take her home.

GAL. I will, sir. [*Aside*] I'll try humoring you. Lady, shall I escort you to your door?

RYL. Oh, madness, madness!

TER. [*Aside to Galldove*] See yonder poor gentleman. We must not leave him thus. Ah, Galldove, Galldove, this is base indeed. I have dreamed bad things of you, for which I have blamed myself on waking, but never one like this.

GAL. Stop your romantic prate! Think you yon subtle wretch will play us false?

TER. He is no wretch, nor is there falsehood in him.

GAL. I hope, so, Terry. Everything looks fair. We may be married yet. You do not smile?

TER. That thought has lost its former joy.

GAL. Ha! so! well, well. [*Sighs. Aside*] Could I but get your shadow from my path. [*Exit with Teresa L.2E.*]

FERN. Rylton, my friend.

RYL. Have I a friend?

FERN. A true one.
RYL. How ungrateful in me! I have two friends left me yet—Galldove and you.
FERN. Be careful of your friend, Galldove.
RYL. Indeed I shall. While I have a heart, he shall divide it with all other loves. Fernwood, I am disgraced, ruined, beaten[54] by a rogue. That sits well on my pride, ha? What will Lucy think of me, so fallen?
FERN. Rylton, she'll love you more.
RYL. Your words are sunshine! But Sir Hugh?—No, no, I cannot crawl. Why, let him think his worst; the whole world does not lie within his park.
FERN. And you too think your worst, and then to better thoughts. There are two things on this earth whom I love, you and—and one other. By my life, I'd wade through more than blood to serve you! Cheer, my dear Rylton! When the sky looks black,

>The sun has not departed: No, oh, no!
>Abide one moment, and the prisoned king
>Will burst the hateful bondage of rude clouds,
>Making them subject to his royalty;
>As enemies, now threatening all our front
>With direful war, may serve to deck our triumph.
>Take heart. There now, I knew you had a smile
>In store for me. A philosophic man
>Should laugh in sadness, weep in joy; for who
>Can tell which way the wind may blow tomorrow. [*Exeunt L.2C.*]

ACT IV.

SCENE: *An apartment in Sir Hugh Blumer's house. Sir Hugh discovered at breakfast, reading the newspapers.*

SIR H. Every paper is full of it. Hints, innuendoes, references to me. All my friends may guess it at a glance. The Countess, too, figures; Galldove almost a martyr. Well that's one truth they have stumbled upon; the poor fellow has suffered badly. It's strange, that while there is so much truth in the world, a newspaper is the last place to look for it. Puff, puff, puff, where there is no desert, and scandalize where there is no demerit: One unending effort to help the lame, or to make the sound want help, by maiming them. 'Ods blood! what's this? [*Reads*] "Mr. R. who, as is well known in fashionable circles, has impoverished himself by a certain polite vice, is about to retrieve his fortune by leading to the altar a distinguished foreign lady of high rank. It cannot but afford our readers of quality—" Their readers of quality! A paper that has no circulation beyond beggars and fools! [*Reads*] "Regret to announce that the alliance between Mr. R. and the daughter of the late celebrated Lord W."—celebrated Lord W!—What a man may gain by dying! [*Reads*]—"has been broken off on account of—" The devil! [*Rings bell violently*] John—Mathew! [*Enter Mathew slowly L.2E.*] Why don't you come when I ring?

Mat. Hi comes when hi 'ears. Ha fust footman's legs haint telegrass, Sir 'Ugh.

Sir H. Silence, sir! Get me a paper that has nothing of Mr. Ryl—nothing in it!

Mat. Ha paper that hain't got nothin' hin hit! Hi must go to the paper mills then; fur they prints hall the papers ha week before 'and now, to get hin hadvance hof the hage. The news his stale, but the feelosofee his hexcellent.

Sir H. A paper with no Mr. — Here, sir, look here.—A paper with no damned dashes in it.

Mat. The cook used hall them, sir.

Sir H. Do you dare to open my papers?

Mat. Certain, Sir 'Ugh—we knows hour dooty hi 'ope. We halways reads 'em before they come hup: they might 'ave somethen himproper hin 'em.

Sir H. You impudent scoundrel, go get me a paper in Dutch, Hebrew, Greek—anything without this cursed R. with a dash to it! What are you grinning at? Go!

Mat. [*Aside*] Why, the hold feller's has rough has ha porkerpine with ha chill. [*Exit L.2E.*]

Sir H. What will Lady Willburg say? What will Lucy say? What will everybody say? What can I say? But I can do something. I'll disinherit the vagabond. I'll adopt Galldove—he will never disgrace me. Yes, as I live, I will. [*Enter Mathew L.2E.*]

Mat. Lady, hand Miss Willburg.

Sir H. Where shall I hide? Do you understand your business no better than to introduce company, without my permission?

Mat. They trod right hon my 'eels, Sir 'Ugh. Hi never see such people. The pos'man says the furren mails haint hin yet; hand so hi couldn't get no papers. The chambermaid give me ha book of Mr. D'Hisraheli's, 'owsomehever; haint that 'Ebrew enough fur you, sir? [*Offers a book*]

Sir H. What are you talking about? Get along, sirrah!

Mat. [*Aside*] Breezy mornen fur hall hof hus,—that's gospel. [*Exit L.2E. Enter Lady Willburg and Lucy*]

THE WORLD A MASK 35

Sir H. Good morning, ladies! A beautiful day, after the terrible night we had.

Lady W. 'Twas starlight when I left the Opera.

Sir H. Ah! I meant the night before. The weather has been atrocious of late. I am one mass of aches. [*Aside*] What shall I say next?

Lady W. Sir Hugh Blumer—

Sir H. [*Aside*] Mercy! here it comes!—Your ladyship.

Lady W. We have intruded upon you, to receive an explanation of certain offensive paragraphs which have appeared in the morning papers. [*Enter Mathew L.2E.*]

Sir H. The infernal papers!

Mat. [*Aside*] Furren mail must be hin hat last.—Mr. Galldove— [*Aside*] Cuss 'im!

Sir H. [*L.2E.*] Show him up. [*Exit Mathew. Aside*] Thank Heaven, here is some one to take them off me. [*Enter Galldove, L.2E.*]

Gal. Good morning, ladies!—Uncle, good morning. [*Bows*] What magnificent weather! Heaven must be nearer earth than usual, on a day like this. [*Aside*] They all look pleasantly distressed. [*Enter Betsy, violently, L.2E. Galldove retires*]

Betsy. Please, Sir Hugh, I just come up to make a complaint.

Sir H. Choose a fitter time, Betsy: I have company.

Betsy. Soonest said, soonest over. Please, sir, I was holdin' the door, while John run across to see Mr. Garnish's tiger—who they say's a girl in disguise—just to be romantic and pictersquee—when along comes Mr. Galldove, with his frightful face, and tries to squeeze and kiss me. [*Galldove goes down*]

Gal. You flatter yourself, my little Hebe.

Betsy. He-be yourself: I'm no He anything.

Sir H. Do you know no better, Betsy—

Betsy. Yes, I do, Sir Hugh, know better than to leave myself be kissed by ugly men.[55] And all I've got to say is, if any more nephews[56] comes into this house, I must leave it.[57] It's enough to be kissed by Mr. Fernwood and Mr. Rylton,[58] without—

Lady W. Unhappy chambermaid! Does Mr. Rylton?—

Betsy. Yes, he does, mam; and I ain't ashamed of it. He says he's only practisin' for his sweetheart.[59]

Gal. [*Aside*] How Lucy shudders!—Lady Willburg frowns! Of all the pack of women, Betsy's a trump!

Sir H. [*Aside*] More proof of Rylton's[60] perfidy! Run to your work, Betsy, run!

BETSY. I'm goin', sir. But all I've got to say is, that a delicate girl like me, can no more be expected to do the whole kissin' of a large family than the whole washin'.—That's all. And I give warnin'—I do. [*Makes a face at Galldove, and exit, L.2E.*]

LUCY. [*Aside*] Ah, Rylton, Rylton!⁶¹ to soil my lips with that girl's menial kisses!⁶²

LADY W. If I may be permitted, Sir Hugh, I should say that your establishment required the presence of a female head.⁶³

SIR H. Lord deliver me! if they all hold tongues like Betsy's. Though, to do her justice, my own indulgence has spoilt her. She nursed me faithfully through a long, long illness. In faith, I love her like a child. The only pity is she knows it.⁶⁴

LADY W. Before this unseasonable interruption, we were conversing, Sir Hugh—

SIR H. Ah—yes. Nephew, Lady Willburg has called on important family matters.

GAL. Perhaps I intrude? [*Going L.2E.*]

SIR H. No, sir; you are one of the family—my heir.

GAL. Your heir, Uncle! You certainly will not do Rylton the injustice—[*Crosses to Sir Hugh*]

SIR H. I do him no injustice. My property is in my own keeping. After what happened last night, how can I ever look at Rylton with any feeling but disgust.⁶⁵

LUCY. Sir Hugh—Mr. Galldove—is it, is it true? [*Galldove sighs*]

LADY W. [*Aside*] Miss Lucy, will you be obliging enough to remember your family, and not indulge in these fantastical feelings?

GAL. Uncle, you have certainly forgotten that trifle.

SIR H. Trifle, sir! If you ever speak to me in Rylton's behalf, I'll leave my property to a foundling hospital.

GAL. [*Aside to Sir Hugh*] Some of your relatives might get it among them even then.

SIR H. [*Laughing*] Ha, ha, ha! You disrespectful rogue.

GAL. [*Aside*] That's a jest that always tickles an old man. Ah, me, what a wicked world is ours!

LUCY. Is it all true?—about the Countess too? For Heaven's sake, answer me!

LADY W. Miss Lucy Willburg, I desire you to observe perfect silence on this occasion. My experience in matrimonial affairs should be sufficient guaranty that you shall have entire satisfaction. Sir Hugh Blumer, do I understand you to assert that Mr. Rylton is no longer your heir?

Sir H. You do, madam. [*Crosses to Lady W. Galldove sighs, Sir Hugh looks at him pityingly*]

Lady W. On your part understand, then, that the projected alliance of our families cannot be ratified, under existing circumstances.

Lucy. But, Mother—

Lady W. [*Aside to her*] Lady Willburg, if you have no personal objections, Miss Lucy. How often must I request you to control your exuberant emotions?

Gal. [*Aside*] Willburg and Company, Match-Brokers to the Nobility and Gentry!

Sir H. Certainly, madam, certainly. I have no desire to wed your daughter to a profligate.

Lady W. I may then expect to have an interview with you this evening. I shall receive at a small reunion; but will endeavor to obtain an interval for conversation with you.

Sir H. Assuredly, if you wish it.

Lady W. Mr. Galldove, we shall feel honored by your presence at any hour. [*Crosses to L.2E. Going. Aside to Lucy*] Miss Lucy, be good enough not to present your back to the company, without previously bidding them adieu!

Lucy. [*Aside to her*] For pity's sake, madam, do not speak so coldly to me.—Adieu! [*Exit with Lady Willburg*]

Gal. [*Aside*] How eloquently the old lady curtsies to the heir! Could I supplant Rylton there?—That were to gain a strong position—a goodly fortune, in her own right too. Then I might whistle at the old fool yonder. Besides, I think I love Lucy.—Yes, upon my soul, I do. By all that's fair, I'll try it! [*Enter Mathew L.2E.*]

Mat. Miss Garnish, Lord Rew, hand Mr. Garnish!

Sir H. At home. [*Exit Mathew L.2E.*] An hour ago I was sick of humanity; but now I should like to brave the whole world. [*Enter Miss Garnish, Lord Rew and Garnish*]

Gar. [*Precipitately*] Sir Hugh, have you seen the papers?

Sir H. Damn the papers, sir! [*Crosses to R.H.*]

Gar. So say I. Have you, Mr. Galldove?

Gal. Ah, Mr. Garnish, I fear I saw them before you; [*Aside*] for like a true author, I had the first peep at my own proofs.

Gar. Such whopping lies! You know he saved you from—

Gal. There, Mr. Garnish! this is a painful subject to my uncle.

Lord R. Galls him, ha?

Sir H. Gentlemen, I beg that you will drop the matter entirely.

Gar. Well, for all that, Rylton was right to show up a cheat. I saw it all. When the fellow struck him—my! wasn't that fine? He looked like the tiger, in the Zoological, when I punch him with my stick.

Lord R. Game to the backbone—blood will tell.

Gar. What if that foreign affair is in love with him? I see no harm in it; the girls all love him, and so do I. There's Hetty, now she'd give her new false teeth to kiss him. Wouldn't you, Hetty?

Lord R. Hold hard, Garnish! your tongue's getting away with you.

Miss G. Yes, your tongue is like a—like a—

Gar. Like a woman's, Hetty.

Lord R. Fills up the gaps nicely. [*Aside*]

Gar. Where's Rylton? I want to shake his hand.

Gal. [*Aside to him*] Mr. Garnish, Mr. Garnish, my uncle understands this matter fully. Every word you say pains him intensely. Have you no respect for grey hairs?[66]

Gar. Not when they cover empty heads.[67] It ought not to bore him. Mr. Rylton—

Sir H. Gods! Mr. Garnish, will you drive me from my own house?

Gar. Not if it suits you as it is.[68] As for the Countess, I like her well enough too; and if Rylton has a mind to slip old starchy Willburg's daughter, by gracious, I'll help him! But it's a funny thing.—Now she's in love with Fernwood, because she knew him years ago; then she's in love with Rylton, because she never knew him till yesterday. Now she's always talking with Fernwood; then she's always running after Rylton. Tomorrow she's to be married to Fernwood; next day to Rylton! By the big stick, I believe she means to marry both!

Gal. Do you bring your wit here for dyspeptics?

Gar. Why?

Gal. Because it is so stale.

Sir H. [*Aside to Galldove*] Galldove, you must entertain my visitors; I cannot. Excuse me, friends. [*Crosses to Garnish. Aside*] Shall I never hear the end of all this? [*Exit C.*]

Miss G. See what you have done.

Gar. What do I care? The ungrateful old dromedary! he should be proud to hear Rylton talked about.

Gal. Your pardon, Miss Garnish. Can I speak a word with you, Mr. Garnish?

Gar. To be sure. [*Goes up stage with Galldove*]

Miss G. How much did you win of Garnish last night?

Lord R. Five hundred.

Miss G. That completes the fifteen thousand.

Lord R. Yes. [*Aside*] What a good account she has kept!

Miss G. You know, when you had won the fifteen thousand—which you never could have done without my aid—we were to—to—to—

Lord R. Marry. All right. If I'm entered. I'll start.

Miss G. Have you lost nothing? I have heard that you lose.

Lord R. [*Aside*] Eyes like a lynx—No; invested profitably—trebled my winnings.

Miss G. Invested in what?

Lord R. Three hundred per cent stock.

Miss G. You astonish me!

Lord R. Yes; can show all the investments in my betting-book.

Miss G. Mercy! was that your stock?

Lord R. Running stock; what's better?

Miss G. When we are—hem!—you will give up betting, love?

Lord R. What! Rather give up—[*Aside*] Whew! Nearly made a false start.

Miss G. Oh, you monster! But we will not quarrel.

Lord R. Till we are yoked. Name the day, and distance; I'm in for any match, play or pay. [*Enter Mathew L.2E., Galldove and Garnish advance*]

Mat. The Countess di Crespo!

Gar. Show her up.[69] [*Exit Mathew L.2E.*]

Gal. Mr. Garnish!

Gar. I want to see her.

Lord R. The word is—go! [*Going to the door*]

Miss G. Without me, my lord? Come, Garnish.

Gal. Are you all deserting me?

Miss G. After the conduct of the Countess last night, how can you ask us, Mr. Galldove? The whole world has cut her.

Gal. Indeed!

Lord R. Dead as Saint Peter.

Gar. I'll stay. I'm fond of victims—show beef, soldier, and such things.

Miss G. You shall not on any account.

Lord R. Come, stupid. [*Exeunt. Miss Garnish takes Garnish's arm. Lord Rew takes hers and they drag Garnish off. L.2E. Enter Teresa*]

Ter. [*Looking after them*] Strange![70]

Gal. What brings you here?

Ter. I came to see Sir Hugh. Thank Heaven, you have forestalled me! Do you not feel happier, with that weight of deceit taken from your conscience?

GAL. What on earth are you so eloquent about?
TER. The affair of last night. Mr. Fernwood and myself—
GAL. So! you couple yourself with Fernwood—my enemy?
TER. My friend.
GAL. His friends are my foes. Beware, Teresa!
TER. I have no fear of you.
GAL. [*Aside*] So changed! then I must woo a little. Dearest, I have no desire to affright you.
TER. You do not.
GAL. [*Aside*] In love with Fernwood, or I know not woman! Good! Let me hold her but for today, and then farewell, in welcome. Teresa, why are you so cold to me?
TER. Am I? I did not know it.
GAL. [*Aside*] Ha! more proof.
TER. I came here on one business only; and it shall be done before I leave. Mr. Fernwood and I saw all last night's gaming scene through the open window.
GAL. Eavesdropping, how very honorable! [*Aside*] What fool left it open?
TER. With Mr. Fernwood's explanations, I was compelled to understand the whole, from first to last. The game—the impudent cheating, at which you winked—the bold exposure of it, for your sake—the brandished arms and angry controversy—the audacious blow. Ah, Galldove, what a wretched pantomime you played before me! Even then, fallen as I knew you, all my fears were but for you, not Rylton. Lest your poor body should receive some hurt; though I had seen you calmly stab your soul with more dishonorable wounds than man can give to man.
GAL. When I wish my wounded soul mended, I'll send for one of those men in petticoats who are licensed for the trade. That's bad enough, without having the poor thing stitched together with a woman's needle. My dear girl, take my advice, withdraw from this affair.—See what you have done for yourself already—cast your belleship out of society.
TER. What care I? 'Tis nauseous to me—loathsome, loathsome! I would not, for one day more, play in this tinsel masquerade of smiling misery, to lead the whole false rout into that fashionable paradise of which they dream over a velvet prayer-book. No; I am free as the wide air which brushes earth yet takes no strain from it. What! dance in golden fetters all my life, while even the unsettled doe and fearful chamois mock me upon my native mountains!
GAL. What a metamorphosis! The haughty belle, under full sail of ribbons flaunting silks, would be a naked doe or chamois on a mountain! But

pray you, gentle savage, do not forget the civilized amount of debts you have contracted—in your own name too. You may be obliged to dance a while longer in your golden fetters, here or in the debtor's prison. Bah! when did you take to thinking for yourself?

TER. When I awoke to find myself a criminal. Galldove, I have lost my self-respect; and with the knowledge of that loss the simple child departed. I am a woman, matured in a day. My self-respect I must and will regain. The first step is to throw off the duping mask, which I have worn to please you. The next, is to do Rylton justice; and if needs be, expose—I will not threaten, I would persuade you. These things I will accomplish! Then come, death, for I am sick of life![71]

GAL. 'Sblood! Would you cross me? Measure swords with me! Teresa Cespo, have more mercy for yourself.

TER. Threats again! Where is Sir Hugh?

GAL. Nay, Terry, but a day—grant me a day.

TER. What mischief may not a day do? A moment may commit a murder.

GAL. I will do nothing. All I ask is time for thought; to make some little refuge for myself, when you have pulled these ills upon me.

TER. I grant it. Keep this promise as your salvation. I have little faith in you.—

GAL. What!

TER. But here I will trust you, for the last time. See what a helpless thing is crime.—A feeble woman makes treaties with your powerful intellect. Oh, I beseech you, pray, adjure you, to leave the endless ways of guilt. Here, on my knees—[*Kneels*] These tears can wash your former sins, until they show like virtues.

GAL. Up, fool! Go show your precious tears to Heaven; to me they are but brackish water. Pshaw! will you preach? Get a congregation of Fernwoods, then, for I am an obdurate heathen. Keep faith, sweet Magdalen. Off, off! I want none of your handling. There is no need of empty shows of love between us now,[72] for, on my faith, the pageant grows dull by its weary length. Remember, saint, your holy word is passed. Go coo and bill with Fernwood. 'Sdeath, madam, I would be alone!

TER. Oh, Heaven, and I am alone; with nothing but a feeble clue of what is scarce yet virtue, to lead me through a dreary life! [*Exit L.2E.*]

GAL. Fair day to you and love! Now for a speedy marriage with dear Lucy—a sudden marriage. Yes.—When? Tonight, upon my soul tonight! I am too deep in love to wait a day. Lady Willburg? Hum, I can manage her. Sir Hugh?—Why, he is but another part of me. Where can Rylton be? This wedding must be private, quite private—secret. Even Fernwood—Did the sun go under a cloud just then? How dark it seems! Yes, Terry, true! What may not be done in a day? My plans cannot hold together long: the blow must fall at last. Then let me reap the harvest ere the storm. Wed Lucy, hold her wealth, and gag the world with gold. [*Enter Fernwood behind, L.2E.*] I must lead off this mountebank, this Fernwood, for today. What can he be designing?

FERN. Ask him; perhaps he'll tell you. Do not flinch. You might as well take your hand from your bosom. You have scarce courage to draw your dagger on a spider.

GAL. [*Aside*] Now shall I kill him? Nonsense! to let my passions get the start of me.

FERN. The hemp grows too long, and is too easily spun, for such tricks in England.

GAL. Marry, you did startle me, Mr. Fernwood. What a beautiful day we have?

FERN. Marry, now you startle me, Mr. Galldove. Do you ever look in nature's face, and call it fair? Remember, in her angry eyes the lightnings lodge, and the great storms are gathered up, to sweep the base from her insulted presence.

GAL. Well, sir, is my face a book; and would you read my answer?

FERN. The fairest book in your whole catalogue.

GAL. Oh, thank you! [*Aside*] The lizard's playful!

FERN. In your face I read none of the hateful sins which you have printed, line by line, throughout the unshown volume in your breast. No, all is white—an album for the world to write its fair name on. But even your heart I can turn over, leaf by leaf, and read such matters as would set the world aghast. Still fumbling in your vest? Give up the thought; there is nothing heroic in you. Galldove, you'll never hang: a gaol can hold all your most daring guilt.[73]

GAL. Mr. Fernwood, I cannot endure this insolence. Leave the house; or I shall call the servants.

FERN. Call them. There is not one, who would not lose an arm for me. How go the plots? Well, I hope.

GAL. Gods, sir, you'll drive me frantic!

FERN. I wish no harm to even you. You did not violate Teresa's sanctity, when she was in your power. Although, even there, perhaps I overcredit, as virtue, what issued from cold policy. I'll think the best, however. You are in my power now. Make fair amends to Rylton, and Sir Hugh, give up Teresa, brew no more mischief with your wily tongue, and there shall be no voice louder in your praise than mine.—

GAL. Take her, in Heaven's name! She's a clog, a fool, a—

FERN. Lady, and under my protection.

GAL. Then make what you please of her. Make her your—

FERN. Had that word come out, I would have torn your tongue out with it! Wretch, have you no latent goodness in your nature? Then smother in your crimes!

GAL. You have sworn—

FERN. Not to you, devil. Teresa holds, Teresa can unbind. Look, look for ruin, when I slip my leash!

GAL. Oh, could the furies of the yawning pit spout up their flames, and sear you to the bone!

FERN. That's right! The fiends you call for, show what help you use. [*Enter Rylton, followed by Mathew. L.2E.*]

MAT. Ho, sir, hi 'ave perooosed the papers, with tears hin my heyes has big has the cook's pestle. Ho, Mr. Rylton, what would your mother 'ave said, hif she 'ad seen this 'eavy mornin'? Ho, Mr. Rylton—

RYL. [*Gives money*] There, Mathew, there! Get some cordial for your grief.

FERN. His last shilling perhaps.[74]

MAT. Ho, sir, not puppies, nor mandragons, nor hall the boozy surrups—has Hihago says—

RYL. Peace, Mathew. You may not have another chance to obey me.

MAT. Ho, now furhever then farewell the—

RYL. Go, sir! [*Exit Mathew, weeping, L.2E.*] Where is Sir Hugh?

FERN. [*Aside to Galldove*] Play out your game. I will not, like Rylton, cry "cheat" to save a friend: you have given too shrewd a lesson. [*Crosses to R.H.*]

RYL. Galldove, where is my uncle?

GAL. Bless me, Cousin, how wild you look! You must not see Sir Hugh, in this state. Have you been drinking?

RYL. No! Do you think I cannot bear my griefs without the coward's opiate? Where is Sir Hugh?

GAL. Out, Rylton, out.

FERN. [*Aside to Galldove*] A most decided lie.

RYL. Galldove, Fernwood—[*Crosses to C.*] my old dear friend—What is there in me so detestable that even Lucy should shun me? Am I not the same as yesterday? What limb has crooked, what thought has gone astray, what deed dishonored me? Even now—a moment since—a lackey, who has bowed his powder to the dust before me, with the slammed door hurled me upon the pavement of her mother's house.

Fern. Her mother's house, not hers.

Ryl. True, true. What does this mean? Since yesterday fate has wantoned with me. Yesterday I awoke rich, happy, loved;—today, poor, miserable, despised! Yet all this change without one act of mine. An invisible net of destiny catches me within its toils, and draws me here and there, as if I were a straw—as if I lacked the common power of motion. What is this? Speak, Fernwood; you are wise and strong. Speak Galldove; you have a subtle mind.

Fern. Speak, Galldove, speak; I am sure that you can fathom it.

Ryl. By Heaven, I begin to doubt the presence of the immortal ones who help our limping virtue: or have the devils taken the upper hand, and made their kingdom stable?

Gal. Rylton, Rylton, this is sheer frenzy. Sir Hugh is angry, Lucy in a pout, and all this bluster for such trifles.

Ryl. Trifles! I tell you I am knit heart, mind and soul to her;—all else are trifles. Take wealth, station, power and I will smile at you; but leave me her, or life is bankrupt!

Fern. Your fall from these robs you of Lucy. Her mother—

Ryl. Curses upon the shallow souls that bound man's worth within a guinea's compass. I see it now; and feel far nobler in my misery, than Lady Willburg could, even if her narrow brows were aching with a diadem.[75] Here, Fernwood, here the immortal part of me can hold me up against a sneering world for ever!

Fern. Well said! Why are you quiet, Galldove? Do you mark how starving virtue towers and sings among the clouds, while pampered vice, o'ergorged with its foul feast, rolls silent in the filthy mire?

Ryl. I will see Sir Hugh; explain my conduct, without involving you, my Cousin. I have been rash, headstrong; have I not?

Gal. No; you have acted as I would have you.

Fern. [*Aside*] Galldove's first truth.

Ryl. That is cheering. I hoped that I had not been very wrong. But Sir Hugh is my father, or stands so near my heart, as to seem one. My silly pride makes me ungrateful. I will abide his coming.

Gal. That would ruin you. Have you no honest spirit? I would not cringe thus. Let me smooth your way. Tomorrow come; and, on my life, you shall be reconciled. Now go! [*Aside*] What if Sir Hugh return?

FERN. [*Aside*] I see there is something to be done between now and tomorrow. You must work darkly to escape my eyes. Come, Rylton; you have had advice.

RYL. Just one word more with my good cousin. Tell Sir Hugh—

FERN. Poh! I am much safer company than your "good cousin."

RYL. Why? What is the purport of your hints, your keen glances towards him, your shrugs, and scornful smiles? Fernwood, you are a man to whom I'd trust my soul with the same confidence as I commit it to the wide arms of sleep. Ha! that look again!

GAL. Liar! Liar!

FERN. [*Looking around*] At whom can he be railing?

GAL. Beware of your confidant, Rylton. He who betrays one, will betray all. [*Crosses to R.H.*]

FERN. [*L.C. stopping Rylton as he goes over*] Remember that. We are in a maze. [*Aside to Galldove*] You, Galldove, cower behind your mask, lest your own act destroy you. Come, Rylton, come! [*Getting round to Rylton's L.H.*]

RYL. Look you, Galldove, could I believe that you were playing me false, by Heaven—here where we stand—I would tear you into shreds. [*Seizes him*]

GAL. Cousin, Cousin! Will you kill me? 'Sdeath! man, you use me harshly.

RYL. No, no, it cannot be.

GAL. Would Fernwood suffer it? Ha, ha! [*Laughing*] See how he frowns at the bare thought—your friend—your true friend. Fernwood!

FERN. [*Aside*] He catches at a straw.—Of course not, Mr. Galldove. I have much to say to you—Come, Rylton, come. [*Exit with Rylton, L.2E.*]

GAL. Oh, liar—torturer!—ha, ha, ha! [*Laughing*] Honorable Mr. Fernwood! This is no fancy; I am mad—stark mad! [*Falls into a chair L. of table*]

ACT V.

SCENE: *A sumptuous and brilliantly lighted saloon, in Lady Willburg's house, filled with company. Music. As the curtain rises, a fashionable dance is seen, which presently ceases. Sir Hugh Blumer, Galldove, Lord Rew, Garnish, Lady Willburg, Lucy Willburg, and Miss Garnish are discovered among the company. As the music and dancing cease, Miss Garnish, Lord Rew, and Garnish advance.*

MISS G. The Countess not here! Has Lady Willburg cut her?

LORD R. Without giving her a show.

Gar. Well, Hetty, you don't care; it rather tickles you. I don't know why you women like to see each other trip; but you do though. Don't they, Rew? [*Crosses to C.*]

Lord R. Can't make a dead heat of the whole field. Somebody must win, somebody must lose.

Gar. A week ago, nobody would go to a ball where she was not, and now, nobody will go to a ball where she is. That's fashion, is it? Hang fashion in its own garters then, say I!

Miss G. Will you never learn, you thirty-years-old baby?

Gar. Fiddle faddle, Hetty! You look as wise as an owl in the day time, and, whip me, if I think you can see any better. Now the Countess is down, I begin to like her. I am going to call on her. Where's my hat!

Lord R. Rather late for a morning call.

Gar. Well I'll be there early enough tomorrow.

Miss G. She is engaged to Fernwood, 'tis said.

Lord R. No; matched against Rylton. That's what started Lady Willburg.

Miss G. Ha, ha, ha! [*Laughing*] So Rylton has jilted his poor little Lucy!

Gar. What a good-natured laugh you have, Hetty! A hyena would blush to hear you. I have heard in this ball-room, that the Countess is engaged to Fernwood, to Rylton, to Rew, to me, and to fifty others. That all the old maids in town—you included, Hetty—are to be bridesmaids; and that the whole bench of bishops is to marry her. I suppose she intends to start something new—a he harem, perhaps. The women are getting on, Rew.

Miss G. How abominably you talk! 'Tis reported, that Fernwood used to sigh for her behind the orange-trees, in her father's Italian park, before she had ever seen him. How pretty! [*Laughing*]

Gar. Fudge! So you and Rew are about to get married, on my losses, are you? That's some more news I picked up.

Miss G. Oh, Garnish, your sister's blushes.

Gar. Why did you not blush when you were putting Rew up to win my money? That was something to blush at.

Lord R. [*Aside*] Bit's in his teeth—Never stop till his heart breaks.

Miss G. You astonish me!

Gar. I have no doubt I do. Do you think I would have let him win, if I hadn't known for what you wanted it? I am no fool at piquet, I can tell you, Miss Garnish.

Miss G. Brother, Brother, you talk too loud.

Gar. Well, as Rew says, trot out. Kneel down, both of you; I want to bless you. Hetty, I'd as lief marry into a racing stud.

LORD R. Might cross with a worse stock. I'd have you to know, sir, a horse is a gentleman!

GAR. There! he'd fight if I called the beast a blackguard! Marry away, drybones—it's nothing to me. Only you'll be so damned miserable—that's a comfort; and that's all I let you win for, old boy.

LORD R. Look here, Garnish, I'll draw with you.

GAR. Can't do it, it's too good a thing. The money's up.

MISS G. If you have no feeling, have you no politeness, gentlemen?

GAR. As for me, Hetty, you always called me a fool; and as for Rew, Galldove says his creditors entered him at the last cattle-show, and he took the prize from all the other horses. So don't expect too much from us!

LORD R. [*Aside*] If this is not a fast family, founder me!

MISS G. They are walking this way. I shall be happy in one thing, Brother; I shall be rid of you.

GAR. Ditto, Garnish!

MISS G. Is there no kind devil to fly off with you? [*They retire, R.H. Lady Willburg and Galldove advance*]

LADY W. [*L.H.*] But so precipitate an affair would justly subject us to scandal.

GAL. On the contrary, 'tis your only method of escaping it. The world will say, tomorrow, that Rylton jilted Miss Lucy for the Countess; but marry her tonight, and you gain every advantage of him. The world may wonder, but it cannot sneer.

LADY W. There is sufficient plausibility in what you observe, Mr. Galldove.

GAL. It would be a bold stroke—a grand, a magnificent stroke! The whole Court will marvel at your delicate tactics. Indeed, I shall envy you your reputation.

LADY W. Mr. Galldove, you are the only sensible man I ever conversed with. If Sir Hugh will ratify the conditions, I agree without hesitation. Shall I endeavor to procure a license and a priest?

GAL. I will spare you that. I have a license in my pocket.

LADY W. Brilliant diplomatist!

GAL. There never was a party without a priest, since the days of Rabelais. Priests have an instinctive sense, by which they discover beauty and good living.

LADY W. Sir, your observations on abstract human character, are only surpassed by the happy use to which you apply them. There is indeed a clergyman present.

GAL. Miss Lucy's consent is still wanting.

LADY W. You are mistaken, sir: I perform all my daughter's mental operations. While you are conversing with Sir Hugh, I shall instruct Miss Lucy. [*Retires, L., and talks with Lucy*]

GAL. Bravo! Galldove, bravo! The game is mine, Mr. Fernwood, though you held all the cards. What a gloss the guineas put upon a man! I'll have myself plated with pure gold and set up for an idol!

SIR H. [*Advancing*] Tired of dancing, Nephew?

GAL. No, my dear Uncle. Lady Willburg wished to speak with me.

SIR H. What about?

GAL. She proposes that I shall marry her daughter.

SIR H. The old ghoul! She seems determined to feast on my remains.

GAL. Nay, Uncle; a proposition so joyful to me, should not be met harshly.

SIR H. Do you love Lucy? Why, it appears to run in the family.

GAL. Madly, Uncle, madly! [*Aside*] I believe that is the style in which the lovers say it.

SIR H. It seems rather hard for poor Rylton.

GAL. Ah, Uncle, I am delighted to see you relenting towards him.—

SIR H. 'Sdeath, sir! I am not relenting. What do you see in me, that looks like it, pray?

GAL. Ah! [*Sighs*] But you know he is about to marry the Countess di Cespo, and has therefore no further use for Lucy.

SIR H. "No further use!" You talk of Lucy as if she were a door-rug.

GAL. Has he not treated her so?

SIR H. Yes; hang him!

GAL. Then you have no objections?—

SIR H. None, none. Get married instantly.

GAL. Instantly?

SIR H. The sooner, the better you will please me.

GAL. Lady Willburg wishes us to be married tonight.

SIR H. Tonight!

GAL. Only to secure poor Lucy from the scandal of being jilted.

SIR H. Sensible old fool! Tonight? What says Lucy?

GAL. She is ready.

SIR H. There, damn it! I always said so. Women have no hearts. They are all buckram outside, and all cotton within. But it is nothing to me. That I ever could see Lucy marry any man but Rylton! Why, they grew, and bloomed together, like twin buds, until this blight fell upon him. Well, well, there is no use of weeping, at my age; but, upon my word, I feel something like it. [*Aside. Retires up*]

GAL. Excellent, excellent! I' really begin to feel proud of myself. Now, Fernwood, where are your Argus' eyes? [*Fernwood appears at back of scene. Looks around keenly and retires. Lady Willburg advances R.*]

LADY W. Have you obtained Sir Hugh's consent?

GAL. He is charmed with the idea.

LADY W. In that respect Miss Lucy rivals him.

GAL. Indeed?

LADY W. Of course, of course! Do you suppose for a moment, that my child would presume to differ from me in opinion?

GAL. Certainly not, my lady. Your system of education is perfect. Shall we proceed at once?

LADY W. I have already contrived to have it whispered among the company, that I have invited them to a nuptial.

GAL. Your ladyship is ever thoughtful, ever skilful. The priest?—

LADY W. Occupies a living of mine, and therefore is not influenced by any ridiculous scruples. We will proceed. Miss Lucy [*Lucy advances L.H.*], Mr. Raby, be so obliging as to commence the ceremony. [*Aside to Galldove*] Mr. Galldove have you provided a ring?

GAL. [*Aside to Lady Willburg*] A dozen of them. I have one to fit each finger.

LADY W. I am overwhelmed with admiration! Mr. Raby, we are prepared.

LUCY. [*Rushing, crosses to Lady Willburg*] Mother, I cannot, I cannot!

LADY W. This insane behavior is preposterous.

LUCY. I would make any sacrifice for you—you know I would; but I cannot murder my heart in cold blood.

LADY W. Your vulgarity is unpardonable. I almost believe that you have been silly enough to fall in love with the reprobate to whom you were betrothed.

LUCY. Was it wrong, madam?

LADY W. Wrong! Supremely absurd. How, in the name of wonder, could you have managed him?[76] Lord Willburg—Heaven bless him!—was a most dutiful husband; yet he would have blushed to confess that I was enamored of him. Do not disgrace your parentage.

LUCY. Oh, madam, this heartless marriage will disgrace my nature, degrade me, kill me.[77] I will try to love Rylton no longer; but I cannot marry this Galldove.

LADY W. If you do not comply instantly, my mansion will no longer be a welcome habitation for you. Come, Miss Lucy: I will be obeyed. [*Forces

Lucy to join hands with Galldove] Mr. Raby, the bride and bridegroom would feel indebted, if you would omit all unnecessary supplications.

RABY. Assuredly, madam. "Dearly beloved—"

LUCY. Begin the burial, not the marriage-service; for though I die, I will not marry him!

LADY W. Proceed, Mr. Raby.

RABY. "Dearly beloved, we are—" [*Enter Teresa to L.H.*]

TER. [*Coming down between Galldove and Raby*] Hold, priest, I charge you! Stain not the livery of Heaven with this atrocious crime!

GAL. [*Aside*] Earth, gape and gulf her! Woman, are you mad?

TER. Shameless traitor, are you the first to speak?

GAL. The trick is plain, your ladyship. Her love for Rylton has driven her to this fantastic act.

TER. Love Rylton, yet seek to keep his promised bride from your polluted clutches? How the lie blushes upon the face of what you say!

SIR H. [*R.H.*] There's truth in that.

GAL. [*Laughing*] Ha, ha! She will say she loves me next; and call this scene a sample of her feelings. [*All laugh*]

TER. Never again. But had your oaths been worth the breath that shaped them, you were bound to me as man was never bound to woman. Sir Hugh, Lady Willburg, I shall endeavor to be calm. This whole affair—Rylton's disgrace—his supposed love for me—all, all is a contrivance of yon man, or Heaven desert me!

LUCY. I knew it!

GAL. A pretty lie, with a train to it—in full court dress!

LADY W. Countess—

TER. Do not address me by that hateful name. I am no Countess; I am Teresa Cespo;—once weak with guilt, now strong with dear repentance. [*All start and look at her*]

GAL. Mark, how she confesses her deceit, then turns to you for credit.[78] Who told you this? [*Apart to Teresa*]

TER. Fernwood.

GAL. Destruction! in his toils again! [*Aside*] Madam, Sir Hugh, sweet Lucy, I hope the ravings of this creature have no weight with you.

LADY W. [*Looking enquiringly at Sir Hugh*] None whatever. Countess— Miss Cespo, be kind enough to depart; your presence is offensive.

TER. Madam, I will not!

GAL. [*Aside*] Oh, for one hour to call my own!

GAR. I believe the Countess: hang me if I don't stand by her! Look you, Galldove, I'm no fighting man, but if I can't flax you out, right in the middle of the next quadrille, my name is not Sam Garnish!

GAL. Poh! Mr. Garnish. [*Turns his back on him*]

GAR. There's the curse of being thought a fool. I can't get up even a sensible fight. [*Aside*]

MISS G. Garnish, you are making a fool of yourself.

GAR. To be sure: I'm always at it. [*Retires up L. with Miss Garnish*]

LADY W. [*Aside to Galldove*] Mr. Galldove, how shall I dispose of this lunatic?

GAL. [*Aside to Lady Willburg*] Call in the servants—there is the door—a little gentle force—then, on with the marriage!

LADY W. Miss—I have forgotten your name—if you do not take your departure, my domestics—

SIR H. No, no, you shall not! Lady, for your own sake, I beg you will leave. Your confession of the false part which you have played, shakes all faith in your word. I would believe you, if I could.

TER. Galldove, your hour has come.—Fernwood, take back your promise! [*Enter Fernwood and Rylton, L.2.E.*]

GAL. Mercy, Teresa! I will—

TER. Stop, Fernwood, stop!

FERN. Too late; the word is spoken. I pronounce yonder trembling wretch a trickster, swindler, villain; and dare him to the proofs!

GAR. Fifty to one on Fernwood, Rew!

GAL. Lies, lies, all lies!

FERN. Bring in the prisoner. [*Enter two officers with Captain Fleet, down L.H.*] Speak, and be free.

GAL. An escaped convict—a galley slave—I swear it! Is this your proof?

FLEET. There's no use, Galldove, in calling a comrade ugly names. Mr. Fernwood is too deep for us. Gentlemen and ladies, I am not used to fashionable society, so excuse my manners—All Mr. Fernwood says is true. Mr. Rylton never turned a card with me. Indeed I may say—without being thought vain, I hope—that all the nice little trick was mine and Galldove's.

FERN. That will do. Release him. [*Exit L.H.W.E. Fleet and Officers*] One look at Galldove overproves his guilt.

RYL. [*Advancing*] It does, or innocence assumes the felon's scowl. Then, wretch, take the blow which you had put upon me! [*Strikes Galldove*]

GAL. Nay, Cousin, you are deceived.—You cannot mean to disgrace me?

RYL. Lest you should doubt it, take another.

TER. [*Crosses to Rylton and falls at his feet*] Oh, pity, pity! He is so weak, so fallen!

FERN. Teresa, back! [*Passes her over to L.H.*]

TER. Ah, sir, I loved him once so dearly.

RYL. For your sake, lady, I let him go: But I hold him no worthier of pity than a wounded serpent, whose remorseless fangs are deadly to the last. Pardon my haste: for there are wrongs that burst our customary bonds, and loose the natural man. Dear Lucy, the clouds are past, the sunshine comes again. [*Crosses to Lucy; embraces her*]

GAL. [*Going to each*] Dear Uncle—

SIR H. Away! Do not defile me with your touch.

GAL. [*Going to Lady Willburg*] Lady Willburg—

LADY W. Detestable dissembler!

GAL. [*Going back to Fernwood*] Fernwood—[*Fernwood turns his back upon him. Galldove draws a dagger. Raises it and as Fernwood turns slowly around he drops it*]

ALL. [*Starting*] Ha!

FERN. Be not alarmed. 'Tis but a piece of pointed steel;—in Galldove's hand, 'tis nothing. Well, sir, what shift is left?

GAL. The curses of a blasted life lie on your soul, burden your latest hour, and hale you to perdition! Oh, good Heaven—good Heaven! Teresa! [*Going up C.*]

TER. [*Crosses to him followed by Fernwood*] Galldove!

GAL. A little nearer, by the love you bore me.

TER. Had you but prized it. [*She approaches him*]

GAL. Take my last curses!—Death and damnation. [*Exit L.2.E.*]

TER. Oh! [*Faints and is supported by Fernwood*]

FERN. Look up, Teresa. Stand back, I pray—you keep the air from her. [*Teresa recovers and retreats, looking at Fernwood in a bewildered manner*] Teresa, here is one who claims you by a higher, purer right.

TER. Who?—Where?

FERN. Oh, blind, blind nature! Here, in me—Marco, your brother!

TER. [*Rushes into his arms*] Ha! my heart half knew it.

FERN. How I escaped the wreck, how landed here,
    And built a fortune out of my mischance—
    Why I withheld the knowledge, hoping some day
    To make a joy like one raised from the grave—
    How, when the time was ripe, I sought our home,
    And found the roof-tree fallen, the walls decayed,
    The very ruins almost overgrown

THE WORLD A MASK

With the luxurious herbage of the south—
Our father dead, our mother—you, ah! you,
(So said the neighboring peasants) worse than dead,
Fled with gross shame upon you;—all these things
Shall form the stories of our winter nights.
Think me not cruel that I withheld the truth,
While you were helpless in a villain's snare.
There was but one way of escape for you—
That way I found. For it were naught to free
Your body, sister, yet leave your heart in pawn.

GAR. There, Rew, I told you so!
SIR H.   Your pardon, nephew.
Lucy, Rylton, my blessing be upon you. [*Joins their hands*]
GAR. Step up, Sister, and get a part of it.
Your marriage will need it.
LORD R.   Hold hard, Garnish!
Your tongue will throw you yet.
MISS G.   Forgive us, Brother.
GAR. Certainly; I feel in a forgiving mood. [*Joins their hands*]
Children, my blessing!
TER.   Marco, we will back
To Italy. There is no balm on earth
For a sick heart, like our own native air.
Have patience with me; I may yet become
Something far better than a countess.[79]
RYL.   Fernwood,
We too feel grateful, but your richer deeds
Made our best thanks seem poor.[80] Besides, my friend,
You have taught me, in a day, what a whole life,
Of joys and cares, teaches in vain to many.—
Uncle, my lady, Lucy, gentlemen,
Has he not proven all the world a mask?

CURTAIN

NOTES

THE WORLD A MASK

[1] MS III shows a slight variation throughout, in the names of the characters. Garnish is changed to "Garrish," Teresa Cespo to "Teresa Crispo," and Willburg to "Willbury." The character of Betsy is omitted from the *Dramatis Personae* of MS I.

[2] Omitted in MS I.

[3] The three preceding speeches are omitted in MS II.

[4] In MS I, "Going."

[5] "for it" omitted MS III.

[6] MSS II and III read: "Poor Lucy! Isn't it dreadful, Hetty? So young too!"

[7] MS I omits "Rylton."

[8] MSS II and III read: "Garnish [Garrish]! Your tongue grows worse as you grow older."

[9] For "your funeral" read "it" in MSS II and III.

[10] The four preceding speeches are omitted in MS II.

[11] MSS II and III read "If Lady Willbury did steal her wits; I am sure no one would accuse her ladyship of having them now."

[12] This speech omitted in MS II.

[13] MS III reads "men's hearts."

[14] The preceding four speeches, not in either the original or the acting version, appear in MS III.

[15] MSS II and III omit "simply."

[16] MSS II and III read "Shakespere."

[17] "I pulled our stock . . . and adore" omitted in MSS I and II.

[18] The first sentence of this speech and all of the two preceding speeches omitted in MSS II and III.

[19] This sentence and the entire preceding speech are omitted in MS II.

[20] MS III reads "mistake."

[21] MSS II and III read "zounds."

[22] The speech is cut to this point in MS II.

[23] MS I reads "Enter Teresa and Galldove."

[24] MS I interpolated at this point, "perhaps a morbid influence of moon's, fallen upon him with his other ills"; but this is crossed out in ink and not retained in the later MSS.

[25] "and should . . . that you win," omitted MSS II and III.

[26] "Bah! . . . them" omitted in MS II.

[27] This speech omitted in MS II.

[28] Omitted in MS II.

[29] Not in MS I. Included in MSS II and III.

[30] "Have you seen Rylton? . . . while I wither—" omitted in MS II.

[31] This phrase omitted in MS II.

[32] This speech and the preceding omitted in MS II.

[33] This sentence omitted in MS II.

[34] This speech and the preceding omitted in MS II.

[35] This speech in MS I read only "A gentleman. Who could say more?" It was expanded to present form in MSS II and III.

[36] This sentence, and the four speeches preceding, are omitted in MS II.

[37] This sentence is omitted in MS II.

[38] This and the preceding speech are omitted in MS II.

³⁹ MSS I and II read "For he is my cousin."
⁴⁰ "He is . . . to aid him," omitted MS II.
⁴¹ This speech is omitted in MS II.
⁴² This and the preceding speech are omitted in MS II.
⁴³ This and the preceding speech are omitted in MS II.
⁴⁴ MS I added "while my tongue wags;" omitted in MSS II and III. The whole speech is scratched out in MS II and may have been omitted in the acting.
⁴⁵ This speech omitted in MS II.
⁴⁶ This sentence is omitted in MS II.
⁴⁷ This and the preceding speech are omitted in MS II.
⁴⁸ This sentence is added in MSS II and III.
⁴⁹ This sentence and the preceding speech are omitted in MS II.
⁵⁰ From "Can you leave," above, to this point omitted in MS II.
⁵¹ This sentence omitted in MS II.
⁵² This, and the two preceding speeches are omitted in MS II.
⁵³ This sentence is omitted in MSS II and III.
⁵⁴ MS II inserts here "—think of that—beaten."
⁵⁵ MS II inserts "I hope!"
⁵⁶ MS II reads "plain lookin' nephews."
⁵⁷ MS II inserts "I must."
⁵⁸ MS II inserts "every time they pass me."
⁵⁹ MS II adds "and there's no harm in that."
⁶⁰ MS I reads "of his perfidy."
⁶¹ MS II reads "Impudent!" for "Ah, Rylton, Rylton!"
⁶² In MSS II and III this speech appears before the three preceding speeches.
⁶³ MSS II and III omit "the presence of."
⁶⁴ MSS II and III add "too well."
⁶⁵ This speech, an interpolation in MS I, is deleted from MS II and omitted from MS III.
⁶⁶ This sentence is omitted in MS II.
⁶⁷ This sentence is inserted in MS II as if in revision, and does not appear in MS I.
⁶⁸ This sentence was added in MSS II and III.
⁶⁹ MSS II and III add "by gracious!"
⁷⁰ This speech is inserted in MSS II and III.
⁷¹ All but the first sentence of this speech is deleted in MS II and does not appear in MS III.
⁷² The remainder of the sentence is deleted in MS II.
⁷³ The first three sentences of this speech are omitted in MSS II and III.
⁷⁴ This speech is omitted in MS II.
⁷⁵ The remainder of this speech is omitted in MS II.
⁷⁶ The remainder of this speech is deleted in MSS II and III.
⁷⁷ The remainder of this speech is deleted in MSS II and III.
⁷⁸ From this point to "Madam" in Galldove's next speech is omitted in MSS II and III.
⁷⁹ MS I bears a final note written in Boker's hand: "When the character of Teresa is the chief feature of the piece, the play may end with her last speech. [signed] G.H.B." This arrangement would cause the play to conclude at the point noted.
⁸⁰ In MS II the remainder of this speech is struck out and an alternative ending is written in pencil. It is likely that this second ending is the one which was employed in performances of the play, although it is impossible to be certain of this. It is this second ending which has been followed by the typist in making the typescript of 1886 (MS III). Since it seems unlikely that Boker would prefer the second ending, which is inferior, I have preserved his first ending, that of the original MS I, in the text. The second ending, following directly upon Rylton's line "Make our best thanks seem poor," is as follows:

LADY W. Count—madame,—miss—
          Miss Cespo—Fernwood—
LORD R. [*Aside to Garnish*] The old girl is mixed.

GAR. Straighten her with a string.
LORD R. She's off again.
LADY W. Miss—Miss—Et cetera,—I have this to say,
   That Mr. Fernwood's sister, socially,—
   Setting aside some foibles, to forget,—
   Must ever hold an unexceptionable
   Position in our set.
LORD R. Not a bad finish.
TER. I thank you, madame.
FERN. Lady Wilburg, thanks!
   Your generous courage moves me. For I know
   'Tis no light matter for that woman who
   First takes a censured sister by the hand.
   Teresa, now your coronet is cast
   Among the rubbish of our social lies,
   Is not your forehead lighter? Turn your brow,
   Now pure with truth, and resolute for right,
   To us who love you; but do not forget,
   The hardest and most painful part to play,
   Even in this feigning theatre of life,
   Is one of false pretences. Bear it all;
   Bear all the penance that your fault deserves:
   Only thank Heaven that you no longer breath
   The stifling air of fraud under a mask.

                              CURTAIN

THE BANKRUPT[1]

DRAMATIS PERSONAE

Edward Giltwood, *A merchant*

James Shelvill, *His former friend* (Passing under the assumed name of Shorn)

Paul Tapeley, *A wealthy lawyer*

Mr. Elton, *A banker*

Pike, *A police-officer*

Dreggs, *A creature of Shorn*

Amy Giltwood, *Wife to Edward Giltwood*

Mrs. Startle, *Her mother*

Betsy Crum, *Housemaid to Amy*

A Citizen, Policemen, Servants, etc.

TIME AND SCENE—THE PRESENT.

ACT I.

Scene 1: *A street. Enter James Shorn.*

Shorn. Ten years ago, city of sin and misery, you drove me from you for a crime of which I was guiltless; now I return to you, after a career that would make your early charge seem lenient.² Ten years ago, I left you poor, persecuted, yet innocent; now I return to you rich, powerful, yet guilty. I will make you sob in your houses, and lament in your streets! I will cram you with new grief, until it equal my old sorrow! Woe! to you who trampled upon my heart! There was but one man, among this multitude of men, who raised a voice in my behalf when the world disowned me. Now, Heaven, hear me swear! If need be, over his ruin, over all he holds dear, over his very corpse, will I stride to my revenge!—[*Enter Dreggs*]

Dreggs. Why, Captain Shorton!—

Shorn. [*Interrupting him*] Fellow, don't captain me. I know you, Dreggs. You were in the Texas Bank affair, and in the Isthmus-gold business.—

Dreggs. Oh! yes; and in waylaying the Ohio drovers, and in the lift from the silversmith's in New Orleans, and—

Shorn. There! you need not brandish your crimes, as if they were virtues.

Dreggs. Well, I was in the check business, on the Charleston bank; and I was nabbed by the beaks for it; and I've never had my share of the shiners.

Shorn. I told you, then, that you were a fool, and I see no reason to change my opinion; or you would not be howling my name out in the streets. Dreggs, you were, and you are, a poor, miserable, womanish, leaky idiot; and I only wonder how you ever got among the men. The next move you would make—if it were not out of your power—would be to betray us. Don't you know that you must not be seen talking with me? That, here, I am Mr. James Shorn, a rich Californian? All this was in the last general order.

Dreggs. I haven't seen it. I've been shut up, for priggin' wipes.

Shorn. Served you right, you contemptible devil! You, who have seen service under gentlemen, to be caught stealing handkerchiefs! For shame! I thought a little better of you than that!

Dreggs. I was starving, sir.

Shorn. Why the devil didn't you starve, respectably, before you became a pickpocket?

Dreggs. Did you ever starve, sir?

SHORN. No.
DREGGS. Then you don't know how hard it is to do.
SHORN. You might have written to your officer, if you were suffering.
DREGGS. I didn't know where he lay; besides, I can't write.
SHORN. Either reason will do.
DREGGS. I got astray from the men, and didn't know where to go.
SHORN. You have drunk away the little wit Heaven spared you. Go!
DREGGS. I can't.
SHORN. What? [*Offers to strike him*]
DREGGS. Oh! don't hit me, dear Captain! I want money, I do, indeed!
SHORN. For what?
DREGGS. I'm starving.
SHORN. For liquor. It's your own helpless drunkenness that ruins you. There is not a man in your company who cannot live, and spend money, as a gentleman, if he choose. Have you received nothing for the last quarter?
DREGGS. No, indeed.
SHORN. Here is an order on the paymaster, and a hundred dollars in cash. [*Gives a paper and money*] Now, be off to Galveston. They have use for you there. Report yourself to Lieutenant Ruff. Do you hear?
DREGGS. Yes, sir.
SHORN. Go by the first train to the south tomorrow.
DREGGS. I'm off, sir. [*Going*]
SHORN. Stop! Do you see that man, coming round[3] the corner? I have seen him, somewhere, before—where?—where?
DREGGS. That's a police.
SHORN. The devil! Hush! Stand still, you infernal fool! [*Enter Pike carelessly*]
DREGGS. Oh! Lord! I wonder if he's after me?
SHORN. Silence, coward! My poor man, I pity your misfortunes, and will do all I can to relieve you. Where did you say your family lives?
DREGGS. [*Imitating the whine of a beggar*] In the streets—Lord bless you, and be merciful to you, good gentleman!—Not a morsel has passed these lips—
SHORN. [*Aside to him*] Save rum.
DREGGS. For two whole days.
SHORN. I will call, and see your family; and, perhaps, send my pastor to you. In the meantime, here is a shilling, to buy bread. [*Gives money*]
DREGGS. Heaven bless you, sir! [*Exit Shorn*]
PIKE. It won't do, Peter!
DREGGS. Could you, kind gentleman, give a poor man—
PIKE. I said it won't do; and when I say it won't do, I mean it won't do!

DREGGS. Sir!

PIKE. Come, Dreggs, my boy, I know all about it. You're Pete Dreggs; and that charitable gentleman has only lately come to his benevolence; hasn't he, Peter?

DREGGS. For all I know, sir. I only know he's a good, kindhearted gentleman, to a poor man who has lost—

PIKE. You'll make me angry, Peter, indeed you will, if you don't stop your nonsense.

DREGGS. Sir?

PIKE. I'll lock you up, Dreggs—upon my soul, I will! I saw you take a young swell's wipe, not half an hour ago.

DREGGS. What, this? [*Produces a ragged handkerchief*]

PIKE. No, Peter; a ragpicker would break at that business. Cambric, Peter, all worked over with hearts, and darts, and rosebuds, by his girl. You have it, in your left-hand pocket, now. I shall be obliged to pull you, my indigent friend.

DREGGS. I found a handkerchief, sir—

PIKE. Yes; I know. Sticking out of a gentleman's pocket; and so you picked it up. That's the story. I know all about it. I wasn't after you, Peter; but, as you come so handy, I guess I'll just take you along, for the sake of your delightful company.

DREGGS. [*Eagerly*] Who was you after?

PIKE. No! you don't say! Who told you I was a fool? When you scatter chaff, Peter, you must look up younger birds. Come along. Walk straight, Mr. Dreggs. You've made me angry, and I'm going to lock you up. [*Takes hold of him*]

DREGGS. No!

PIKE. Yes! strange as it may appear to so virtuous a person. You must retire awhile to the seclusion of the City Prison where you can think over your few slight sins. You'll be a sort of an involuntary hermit, St. Peter,—a very holy man, no doubt. Come along, Mr. Dreggs. [*Exeunt*]

SCENE 2: *A parlor in Giltwood's house. Betsy Crum, discovered, dusting the furniture.*

CRUM. I wish there was no dust in the world. It seems to me, that everything on earth is dusty all the while, and I'm called on to get rid of the whole of it. There's dust in the parlor, dust in the drawing-room, dust in the chambers, dust in hall, dust on the doorsteps, dust on the pavement, dust on the winder-glass, dust on the master's boots and mistress' bunnet; dry dust on every air that blows, and wet dust, well rubbed in, on the faces of all the master's little ones;[4] dust on the bride's veil, and on the deadman's pall; and, at last, it's dust to dust, and there's an end of it! Hang you! Will you ever get dusty again, you awful old sofa? I'll rub the soul out of you! [*Rubbing fiercely*] I believe you are stuffed with dust; for as soon as I rub one side of you clean, the dust is flying out on the other. If I owned you, I'd have the carpet-men beat you to death with rattans, you frightful, ugly, hard, mahogany old maid![5]—Ugh! but I'm tired. [*Sinks upon the sofa panting. Enter Amy Giltwood. Crum rises*]

AMY. Why, Betsy, my poor girl, what is the matter with you? 'Tis not yet nine o'clock, and you look as if you had passed through a hard day's work.

CRUM. Some folks can't look as pretty as other folks always. I suppose, it's because I'm not a lady, that I'm red and ugly. Lord bless me, no! I've got no o'-de-colone and milk-'er-roses, to make my face pink and smooth. I've got no Frenchified bunnets, and shawls, and frocks, to set me off like a doll-baby. If I'm glad, I mustn't laugh—if I'm sorry, I mustn't cry—if I'm sick, I mustn't faint; 'cause that 'ud be ridickellous in a servant-gall!

AMY. I had no intention of raising such a storm of words. What has put you into this passion?

CRUM. That old, four-legged, quadderped of a sofa!

AMY. Indeed! [*Laughing*]

CRUM. Yes, mam; and I give you warning, Mrs. Giltwood, if you don't have that sofa sent out 'er the house, I must go—that's all, mam!

AMY. What is the sofa's fault?

CRUM. I hate it! and I ain't a-going to pass my life a-dustin' it, and a-slighten' its betters. It has broke my heart, it has; and I won't stand it any longer!

AMY. Betsy, if the sofa really makes you unhappy, I will send it from the house. A good servant is a rare thing, in this part of the world, and I would not part with you for so trifling a cause. You have been a kind, faithful nurse, in my hours of pain and illness, and—

CRUM. [*Interrupting her*] There! You're always a-makin' fun of me, and a-throwin' the children's births up to me, as if they was my own. Well, I suppose, you brought the naughty little provokins home. And I suppose, Neddy has been a-playin' marvels in the sweeps, while you held your sunshade over 'em. And Amy has tore her best new frock, a-runnin' after a beggar gall; and they're both dirt, from head to foot, and want scrubbin', like two little, rusty, old iron pots—drat 'em!

THE BANKRUPT

AMY. No such calamity has happened. We only went to the flower-garden, to buy bouquets for their father. Each of the children is armed with a nosegay, as big as its little body; and they are now waiting, to waylay Mr. Giltwood, as he comes from his room. Has he been down yet?

CRUM. No, mam, I wonder what's the matter with him too? He don't sleep well. I know it by the awful state his bed's in. Then, he sets a-starin' at the fire, as if he could tell his fortun in it; and he's always after the nusepapers—he had 'em to bed with him this morning; and often he comes to breakfast with his slippers on wrong feet; and often he don't hear you when you speaks to him; and often, when I speaks to him—

AMY. [*Interrupting her*] That will do, Betsy; this is no concern of yours.

CRUM. Oh! yes; I suppose, I'd better mind my bizness! I suppose, I ain't got no heart—not I!

AMY. Yes, you have; a large, kind and faithful heart too.

CRUM. Then, I suppose, I'd better swaller my "large, kind and faithful heart," and keep it to myself! Well, things ain't right about this house—I know that; and they don't go on as they ust to. Well, I suppose, you think, Mrs. Giltwood, I'd better go scrub, and dust, and scour my fingers sore; and earn my daily bread as I oughter? I know what you're thinkin'—I know what you're thinkin'!—Betsy Crum's a idle, good-for-nothin' vagerbone, and I mus' change her—I mus'!

AMY. [*Smiling*] I assure you, I have no such remarkable thoughts.

CRUM. You may do wus, Mrs. Giltwood—you may do wus—you may do wus—[*Exit*]

AMY. Poor creature! her whole inner life is one unending ferment. She never drew a dispassionate breath. Her very sleep is a sort of frenzied nightmare. That which she said of Edward is true, however. There is something upon his mind which I might lighten perhaps. Ah! men, men! if we, simple women, were permitted to share your dark counsels, at least one half of the secret misery of your toiling lives would vanish before our smiles. But so it is; the pursuit of wealth seems to be a sacred and dangerous mystery, which woman's weak service would profane. [*Enter Giltwood hastily with two bouquets which he flings upon a table*]

GILT. Is my breakfast ready, Amy?

AMY. Nearly.

GILT. I must to business. There seems to be a miserable want of punctuality about this house. Whenever I am in it, I am continually waiting for something. Where have you been so early?

AMY. To a flower-garden. Did you not see the children?

GILT. Yes, yes; they gave me some flowers or something.

Amy. "Some flowers, or something!" Are those your best thanks for their beautiful bouquets?

Gilt. It was very kind in them, no doubt. But, really, I cannot approve of this mode of dribbling away money.

Amy. The happiness which they enjoyed would have been cheap at any price. They have talked of nothing, but their pretty presents to you for the last hour. I hope, you did not receive them coldly.

Gilt. I believe not. I might have kissed them, to be sure—

Amy. Did you not?

Gilt. No; I had not time. I tell you what, Amy, when a man's head is as full of important business, as mine is, he has something better to do than kiss his children.

Amy. Something else, perhaps, Edward; but not something better. The kiss of a parent, laid on the forehead of a child, is as holy as the invisible benediction of Heaven.—

Gilt. There, there! You are about to repeat some sentimental stuff from your everlasting poets. What has the nineteenth century to do with poetry?

Amy. Too little perhaps, for its own good; but poetry will have much to do with the nineteenth century. It will either embalm the years in a cloud of immortal fragrance, or hand them down to wondering posterity in a gloom as dense and odious as that which horrified our childish fancies at the bare mention of the Dark Ages. Edward, shall I never convince you that poetry is a substantial thing: That its curse is worse than death, it is infamy, and its praise is eternal fame?

Gilt. This is very fine.

Amy. It is very true. It seems disagreeable to you, however; therefore, let us talk of other things.

Gilt. Yes; just now, of breakfast.

Amy. What is your hurry?

Gilt. It is not mine; I am hurried—very much against my will, I assure you. Do you know that the best paper is offered, in the market, at two per cent a month, with no buyers at that rate? that stocks are as flat as poetry? that grain is down, cotton down, shipments of gold enormous? the Californian steamer not in; and the banks grinding us to powder, in order to save themselves? Do you know that a monetary plague, worse than the cholera, is passing over the land; and that it threatens to sweep us all into nothingness? Is this not enough to hurry the devil?

Amy. Is there no hope?

Gilt. Hope! What has hope to do with dollars and cents? Their motion is like that of an inflexible machine, crushing all before them. Talk of rigid fate, or immutable law, or any horrible and uncontrollable power you can fancy; but never whisper hope in connection with "the almighty dollar!"

AMY. Tell me of your own connection with it.

GILT. Pshaw! you could not understand me.

AMY. Am I incompetent?

GILT. No, no; you women have brains enough for your own affairs; but, when you come to business, why—I'll leave the sentence unfinished, for the sake of my gallantry.

AMY. There it is! You judge without a trial. If you come home careworn or ill, and I ask the cause—it is "business"! If your thoughts wander, when I try to amuse you—it is "business"! If you smile sadly on the children, while they use their pretty arts to attract you—it is "business"! If you toss in your sleep, or wake⁶ with a frightful dream—it is "business"! If you put me from you, a little quickly, when my loving arms would hold you longer—it is still "business"! This dreary spectre haunts you forever, it pervades all things—oh! Edward, it is pushing me from your heart!

GILT. [*Embracing her*] No, no—Heaven bless you!—not so bad as that. I love you as well as ever; only—well, well, you must not perplex your foolish little head with such ideas. Leave me alone with my disease. The crisis has come, and a few hours will make or mar me forever. After that, you shall suffer no more from business, my sweet wife.—I wish to Heaven the *Occident* were in. [*Enter a servant*]

SERV. Mr. Shorn.

AMY. Who is he? At such an hour too!

GILT. I do not know; I never heard of him. Show him in, however; he may have some news. [*Exit servant. Enter Shorn. Amy walks apart*]

GILT. Good morning, sir! Be seated. [*Offers a chair*]

SHORN. By Jupiter, Edward, this passes belief! Do you not know me?

GILT. I have not that pleasure.

SHORN. We were not strangers once. I am James—

GILT. [*Interrupting him*] James Shelvill! Why bless your soul, how you have changed! But, my dear fellow, this is a sort of premature and unauthorized resurrection. You were reported to be dead long ago, years before my marriage. You are welcome to life again, however, James Shelvill—

SHORN. [*Interrupting him*] Not as James Shelvill, Edward. If you retain the slightest trace of friendship to me, forget that disgraced and painful name. A whisper of it, in this city, might expose me to new persecutions. I dropped it, when I left you, into the grave where I am supposed to lie; and I have not returned to take it up again.

GILT. Don't let that old affair dash your spirits. You are not the first man, Shelvill—

SHORN. [*Interrupting him*] Shorn, if you please. Edward, you are the only possessor of my secret; if you should mention it to any one, under any circumstances whatever, you shall never see my face again.

GILT. It is a slight thing to do for you, and I promise to observe your wishes most religiously. Shorn, Shorn, Shorn! I must not forget that name. I must not forget that name. Well, Mr. Shorn, what is your present condition? Prosperous and rich, perhaps; honest and generous always, to that I'll swear.

SHORN. Yes, to your first two statements; the latter two are a matter of opinion.

GILT. Not with me. Oh! James, I have so much to tell you. I have been married, since we parted, to the sweetest little mortal—Here, darling! [*Amy advances*] Let me present you to my old friend, Mr. Shel—hang it! Mr. Shorn.

SHORN. [*Starting. Aside*] Ha! Amy Startle! Is that lady your wife?

GILT. Yes. Should I not be proud of her?

SHORN. [*Aside*] Proud! You should be the most wretched of men.

GILT. Well?

SHORN. Excuse me, madam.

GILT. Pshaw! No "madams." Call her Amy! I call her Amy.

SHORN. [*Aside*] Better for you had you never breathed her name.

AMY. Where have I seen that face, and heard that voice? Mr. Shorn, have we not met before?

GILT. Hang it! Call him James; his name is James. Look you, good people, I shall not permit any ceremony between you two. Where are you staying, James? You must come straight to us.—Must he not, Amy?

SHORN. Perhaps, Mrs. Giltwood does not desire the intrusion of one who is a perfect stranger to her, if not to her husband.

GILT. [*Laughing*] Ha! ha! ha! Speak your mind, Amy.

AMY. [*Aside*] A stranger! I was mistaken then. It has been a rule of my life, Mr. Shorn, to extend my welcome to all whom my husband calls friends. On this occasion, I shall not depart from it.

GILT. Boo! Amy, you are preaching; and as coldly, too, as if your sermon were a written one. Come, my dear, you must warm up some room in your heart for my old friend, even if he occupy a part of mine.

AMY. My house is more under my control than my heart; and I will endeavor to make it look cheerful to Mr. Shorn, if only for your sake, Edward.

THE BANKRUPT

SHORN. Mrs. Giltwood, I beg that you will offer no hospitality to me, for your husband's sake. Under the roof where I lodge, I must be received for my own sake, or not received at all.

GILT. Come, come, James! you are too proud. Amy means well; it is only her manner to strangers. Amy, I am ashamed of you. [*Apart to her*]

AMY. [*Aside*] So am I of myself. My duty urges me to be hospitable, yet my heart shrinks from the office.

SHORN. To prove to you, Edward, that I am not proud—at least with you —I accept Mrs. Giltwood's equivocal invitation. If I should find myself positively unendurable, I can beat a retreat at any moment.

GILT. That's right! But you mistake Amy altogether. Does he not, my dear?

AMY. I hope so. Mr. Shorn shall have no reason to complain of me again while he remains with us.

GILT. Well said! Now shake hands, and be friends. You are the most difficult pair to introduce, entirely, I ever undertook. It has taken me a quarter of an hour, only to get your hands together. [*They shake hands: she reluctantly*]

AMY. [*Starting. Aside*] Good Heaven! his long, cold fingers closed around my hand, as if they were governed by a spring of steel; and the stern pressure numbed my arm, and sent my blood back, half frozen to my trembling heart! If I were superstitious, I should say that I had shaken hands with the dead.

SHORN. [*Aside*] Oh! Heaven! what memories crowded back on me, with the light touch of that warm palm! I should relent, and play the waterish fool, had I not felt that marriage ring turn, like a serpent, beneath my finger's tip! What devil prompted her to offer me her left hand, when the right is dedicated to such uses?

GILT. You are the most romantic couple I have had the pleasure of meeting for some time. You hardly shake hands, before you both start aside, and begin mumbling to yourselves like the patchwork heroes of a high-strung tragedy. What in the deuce—to come down to simple prose—possesses you?

SHORN. Dismiss this matter, my dear fellow. When two inharmonious natures join hands, for the first time, it is no ordinary action for either party. You may account for the emotion on chemical principles.

AMY. Or on the mechanical principles, Edward. Mr. Shorn shakes hands as if he were a hand-shaking machine.

SHORN. I prefer the chemical; they are more hidden and subtle.

AMY. And I the mechanical; they are more evident and honest.

GILT. Well done, both! Wits should be friends.

AMY. No; wits should be foes, or wit loses its edge.

GILT. What say you to that, James?

SHORN. When two edges meet, the softer must suffer.

AMY. I shall refine my wit to your temper, if I stand in danger.

GILT. Then it will be "diamond cut diamond."

SHORN. [*Bowing*] Mrs. Giltwood is, doubtless, that royal jewel: as for myself, I am content to be baser glass; and only beg that she will write her fair name upon my very heart.

GILT. Bravo! gracefully turned! Amy, you can say nothing to that. Now that you begin to banter each other, I am sure that you will end by becoming friends.

SHORN. I have no higher ambition. Edward, you questioned me regarding my worldly affairs; how do you stand yourself?

GILT. Upon the unstable foundation of a man in business. To be circumstantial; I have a heavy payment to make this day, and the means to meet it are all in that tardy steamer, the *Occident*. She is now overdue by a week or more. You know the financial blight that rests upon[7] the market. A man who was begged to borrow thousands, at common interest, scarce a month ago, can hardly obtain hundreds, at any interest, now.

SHORN. I have always held, that the way to break a man is by giving him plenty of bank credit.

GILT. Sound doctrine, as I know to my cost. If I get out of this scrape, I promise you to hoard my money in an old stocking, and abjure bank credits forever.

SHORN. Then there is still hope for you. But do not trouble yourself about these payments. I have enough for you, and something over.

GILT. At what interest?

SHORN. Fie! you inveterate trader! at no interest.

GILT. James!—

SHORN. What is the matter with you?

GILT. What a weight passed off with that breath! I will be frank with you. I was on the verge of bankruptcy.

AMY. My husband!

GILT. It is too true, Amy. Had not the *Occident,* or James Shorn, arrived today, I should have been a bankrupt.

AMY. And I in utter ignorance of your situation! Oh! had I known it, I would have sold my last garment—I would have starved myself, I would have starved my children, I would have starved all my family, save you Edward—to rescue you from your peril. And here I have been inventing wants —hunting the town down for silks, laces, India shawls, jewels, plate, horses,

THE BANKRUPT

carriages—I have rivalled firmly settled millionaires in extravagance—I have made my establishment the wonder and envy of the vulgar rich—I have wasted on vanity more than would have supported a hundred families—while you were struggling against the ruin which I was making inevitable. I humbly ask your forgiveness, for I shall never forgive myself. [*Weeps*]

GILT. [*Embracing her*] My poor wife, you are not to blame. I urged you to all that you did; I fostered your fine taste. It made me proud, to see upstart wealth quail before your severely critical eye. I delighted in seeing you courted and feared by the touchy fashionables. It was weak, perhaps, to wish you to be the idol of a class, whose chief claims to eminence are that they are rich enough to be ostentatious, and insolent enough to set their feet upon the poor man's neck. Like you, I am cured of such desires; but while they lasted, I was content to toil like a slave, so you might reign like an empress. It was very silly, I confess.

AMY. Yet its lesson shall be fruitful to both of us. Mr. Shorn, you think that I have been discourteous to you.—Away with courtesy! it has no laws for a grateful heart, and no language for its feelings! I could embrace you, as a brother; Heaven knows that I will pray for you every day!

SHORN. Really, madam, you overwhelm me. I merely offer to lend Edward a few dollars, and straight your heart is in my hand. If such hearts as yours can be purchased, at so low a rate, I shall go into the business, at once, with a large capital.

AMY. You treat your virtues lightly. It is not the money which you lend, but the noble spirit which dictated it, that awakens my enthusiasm. I know what it is for so proud a man as Edward Giltwood to fail; and I also know what a service is done him by the man who saves him from it.

SHORN. Enough, and more than enough! Edward's bright face outshines my miserable gold, and makes me ashamed of the poverty of my offering.

AMY. And you are happy now, Edward? Will you kiss the children for their pretty flowers? Will you always confide in me; and not put me off with a mere word, when I ask you about your mysterious "business"?

GILT. Yes, indeed, Amy, to all your questions. Come, let us go to breakfast. Hand Amy down, James. All things look hopeful again.

AMY. Get, you bad philosopher, you said there was no hope in dollars and cents. Oh! yes, there is hope in everything! Hope is the omnipresent voice of Heaven, crying aloud through the dark chambers of the human heart.[8] It sings a glad song to us, from the cradle to the crutch; and, as the grave opens to receive us, its voice rises from the depths—as when a chapel's doors are swung out before the rejoicing organ—into a thunderous anthem of joy and thanksgiving!

SHORN. [*Aside*] And fate has doomed me to spread desolation through so glorious a nature!⁹ [*Exeunt*]

ACT II.

SCENE 1: *The breakfast-room in Giltwood's house. Giltwood, Shorn, and Amy Giltwood, discovered at the table. Giltwood reading a newspaper. Servant-in-waiting, etc.*

AMY. My dear, do put down the newspaper; your tea will be quite cold.

GILT. In a moment, Amy. Very interesting money article. More fires, more burglaries! It seems that we are suffering under an epidemic of crime. For the last week, the town has been infested by incendiaries and thieves. But I suppose you know that. How long have you been in the city?

SHORN. About a week. Your tea is excellent, Mrs. Giltwood.

GILT. A whole week, and this your first visit to us!

SHORN. I was prevented by business from—

AMY. That will do, Mr. Shorn. Business is Edward's final excuse for everything. If he cannot take it, he should not offer it.

GILT. Really this is becoming alarming. I fear the insurance offices will all break. Here is a string of fires, half a column long, and the rest of the column is made up of burglaries. This, added to the financial panic, will cause great distress in the city.¹⁰ Why let me see: full a million of property must have been burned up or stolen during the last week. There is no doubt, besides, that it is the work of designing villains.

SHORN. Particularly the burglaries, Edward. Mrs. Giltwood, I should myself feel inclined to fire a house, if there was no other way of boiling your teakettle. Another cup, if you please. [*Passing his cup*]

AMY. Edward, dear Edward, please to drink your tea. You hear how flatteringly Mr. Shorn speaks of it.

GILT. Directly, Amy. Well, the police—

SHORN. Are very active, of course. They are always so, if you believe their own reports.

GILT. No; they are completely at fault.

SHORN. They are always at that, too, if you believe your own senses.

GILT. Some few arrests have been made.—

SHORN. Of the wrong persons doubtless.

GILT. [*Reading*] "Yet the work of devastation goes on unabated: nay, with steadily increasing fury." So says the newspaper.

SHORN. In its own grand style. The editor has emptied the false orthography of Webster's whole dictionary over a few petty accidents, and fancies that his readers will be horrified by his big words and bad spelling. Truly, so far as the spelling goes, I am horrified indeed.

GILT. [*Throws down the newspaper*] Now, Amy for your tea.

SHORN. By the way, Edward, when will you require the money for your notes?

GILT. Now, today, before three o'clock.

SHORN. Indeed!

GILT. Yes.

SHORN. Then, I hope the southern mail may be in; for I expect my funds by it.

GILT. Or the *Occident*. I have still hope that her arrival may spare an appeal to your generosity.

AMY. What a precarious condition you men of business live in, when the arrival of a steamer, or a mail, may settle your fortunes for life!

SHORN. It is almost like trusting one's fate to the turn of a card.

NEWSBOY. [*Without*] Herald!—Herald!—Extra *Herald!*—latest news of the *Oc-ci-dent!*

SHORN. What's that?—the *Occident*? [*They all rise*]

GILT. Thank Heaven! she's in, and I am safe! [*Laughing*] Ha! ha! Amy, don't you feel like dancing a polka with me?

AMY. No, Edward; but I feel like showing my gratitude to Heaven in a more sedate and becoming manner.

SHORN. [*To Servant*] Here is a shilling. Run down and get the extra. [*Exit Servant*] If the steamer be really in, one half my plans have come to naught. [*Aside*]

GILT. My dear little Saint, you are always preaching when you should be rejoicing. I respect your religious feelings; but, indeed, they seem to come in very much out of place at present.

AMY. They can never be out of place. Our smiles and our tears are alike from Heaven. I am not about to preach again, however. Let me rail at Mr. Shorn for his sins.

SHORN. If you will permit me to kneel at your shrine, I shall bear any kind of penance patiently.

AMY. Fie, Sir! you are an habitual flatterer. Awhile ago, you sneered at the newspapers; and, almost before your words die away, the voice of the poor little newsboy rings in my husband's ear, as if it bore the august tidings of an angel of mercy. Hark!

NEWSBOY. [*Without*] Herald!—Extra *Herald!*—Loss of the Steamer *Oc-ci-dent!*

GILT. Oh! Heavens!—[*Staggers*]

AMY. Sit down, my dear. [*Helps him to a chair*] You did not understand, perhaps. Besides, the steamer may be lost, you know, yet the cargo saved. [*Re-enter Servant with paper*] Read the paper, Mr. Shorn—in Heaven's name, read the paper!

SHORN. [*Reading*] "Telegraph from Portland. The fishing-schooner *Shark*, just arrived at this port, reports that, on the fifteenth of the month, she fell in with a boat, and pieces of a wreck, supposed to be parts of the spars of a large steamer. No doubt can exist that these fragments were fragments of the steamer *Occident*; as the boat was marked"—

AMY. Dear Edward, be a man! You must bear up, for my sake and the children's, if not for your own. Despair is an idle, whining idiot that helps no one. Come, come! this trial was ordained for a wise purpose. You must look to Heaven, Edward, when there is no light upon earth.

GILT. I have no strength for anything.

AMY. Heaven will help you, if you ask its aid. Besides, love, we are not so helpless; here is Mr. Shorn.

GILT. True: the blow took away my senses. Now, James, my only hope is in you.

SHORN. And mine in the southern mail.

AMY. Do not depress him, sir, by suggesting doubts. What fear can be there? The mails come in, as the tides rise, with unerring punctuality. Cheer up, Edward! I will ask nothing for household expenses. I have money and jewels enough to support us for a twelve-month.

GILT. But I want money now—this instant.

AMY. Raise it on the house and furniture; not to forget my ridiculously large wardrobe and the children's trinkets.

GILT. Nonsense! they would not bring a tithe of the sum which I must have; and have it I will, by Heaven, if I wring it from some usurer's heart!

AMY. Do not talk so, Darling! You are beside yourself—Heaven forgive you! Even if I cannot aid you, as I would, surely the house is worth something.

GILT. It is mortgaged. Furies, madam! why do you force me to this indecent exposure of my condition?

SHORN. Edward!

AMY. Don't notice it, sir. He is well-nigh crazed. Indeed, Mr. Shorn, it is the first harsh word he ever spoke to me, and—Well, I have no right to play the fool now. [*Wiping her eyes. Enter a Citizen hastily*]

CIT. Mr. Giltwood, your warehouse is afire! [*Exit*]

GILT. By Heavens! I shall go frantic! Amy, you dunce, why do you hang about me? My hat, my hat! [*She runs to a table for his hat, and returns*]

THE BANKRUPT

AMY. Here it is, Edward. What else can I do?
GILT. James, keep her at home. She'll be running to put out the fire next. [*Exit*]
AMY. Edward, dear Edward, good bye! Heaven bless you!—bless you!— [*Faints*]
SHORN. A hand of iron and a heart of steel, these are the things affliction gave to me; or such a scene would melt me into man. Out! tempting mercy! I but equal my vengeance to my wrongs. [*Bends over Amy*]

SCENE 2: *A street before Giltwood's house. Enter from the house, Shorn.*

SHORN. Shall I renounce the purposes of years—the ends for which I toiled and sinned—because I feel some twinge of humanity at the sufferer's agonies? Was it for this I organized such a scheme against society as the world never saw before? Was it for this I plunged myself in crime to the eyelids, subdued the last trace of Heaven in my nature, went downward, step by step, until, now, Satan might ask me to share his rivalled throne?[11] Tears! what are tears? Have I not shed them too?[12] Who felt for me?[13] Heaven knows, Giltwood, I would not willingly call you foe, had not your fatal union with Amy made you so; for through your sufferings only can I reach her heart, and make her feel the pangs that never die in me. I have sworn—I have sworn. [*Exit slowly. Enter Tapeley and Pike*]
PIKE. There, Mr. Tapeley, that is Captain Shorton.
TAP. Why do you not arrest him at once?
PIKE. [*Laughing*] Because I don't wish to make a fool of myself. I have followed him, like a dog, for three mortal years, in all kinds of disguises, and I never yet thought of laying my hand upon his shoulder.
TAP. Why?
PIKE. Because I could never bring a shadow of proof against him.[14] To-day, I caught a poor, rum-soaked hanger-on of his gang, one Pete Dreggs; but I let him run; there was no use in questions. That's what makes me want the rack and thumbscrews revived; for his gang will never talk till they are brought to such a pinch. Hang it! I am as much fettered by the law as he is.
TAP. He must be a strange man to inspire such fidelity.
PIKE. I tell you, Mr. Tapeley, he's a genius. The mind he has worked up in rascality would have won half the world for him, honestly.
TAP. But you must have discovered him in something, after three years pursuit.
PIKE. Never in person. He does nothing with his own hand. He is the brains—the moving power, of his gang, and no more. If I arrest the whole of

them, what does it amount to?[15] I tell you, sir, there is not one in a hundred of his own people who could swear that he has anything to do with them.

TAP. This is very curious.

PIKE. Curious! I[16] think it is. The whole thing is managed by grades. For example: say, Shorton is chief, Ruff second in command, Johnson third. Well then, Ruff must know Shorton, and Johnson must know Ruff; but there is no need of Johnson knowing Shorton, do you see?

TAP. I understand.

PIKE. So they go down, through a hundred grades; each man knows the one above, and the one below him, but that is all. Then, when you[17] consider that the whole infernal association is organized thoroughly, disciplined like a society of Jesuits, supplied with secret signs, and a telegraphic language, you may have some notion of its vast power for evil. Isn't it ingenious, Mr. Tapeley?

TAP. Fearful, Mr. Pike, fearful!

PIKE. Why, sir, it was a year before I discovered that there was such an organization; it was another year before I discovered that it was moved by one man; and it took a third year to trace who that man really was.[18] Once, I got superstitious, thought the devil was at the head of it, and nearly gave up the chase. But three years—every minute of which was spent on this thing—has done the business; and now I know more about the association than any man alive, except the Captain himself.

TAP. You deserve a rich reward for your perseverance, Mr. Pike.

PIKE. I shall get it, if I bring Shorton to justice.[19] Today will be my last chance for a year. By the southern mail he will receive the yearly reports of his officers; he will read them; and five minutes afterwards they will all be smoke and ashes. If I can get those papers, he is gone.

TAP. But, I hear, the southern mail has been robbed.

PIKE. Oh! yes; but he robbed it; for what reason I can't tell. He has run a great risk for nothing; so far as I can see; for the mail contained but little plunder. Now, sir, I'm bound to get the papers, unknown to Shorton.[20] If he knew that I am on his trail, Lord! what a dance he'd lead me!

TAP. Good day, Mr. Pike!

PIKE. Strict confidence, Mr. Tapeley?

TAP. The very strictest.

PIKE. And promise to appear against him?

TAP. Yes, I would go beyond my profession to bring so sublime a scoundrel to justice. My friend, the district attorney, is very anxious about these continual fires in the city; do you know anything of them?

PIKE. All Shorton's, sir. They puzzle me as much as the mail-robbery. I never knew him to be engaged in anything that didn't pay before.

TAP. Good Heaven! that such things can exist in the midst of us! [*Exit*]

PIKE. "Sublime scoundrel!" Great genius! that's the name for Captain Shorton, alias James Shelvill, alias Mr. Shorn! Upon my soul, I admire you, Captain! Yours is the greatest mind that ever busied itself with the philosophy and practice of crime. Here you live, hey! with your friend, a rich and respectable merchant? You sit down at his breakfast table, and by signs, as rapid as the telegraph, you order his storehouse to be burned to the ground; and, before you have swallowed his tea, it is done. Oh! you are a great man —a very great man—and I am about to take a look at your premises. If I am further from you than your shadow this day, laugh at me for a fool. [*Goes to Giltwood's door, and takes out a bunch of lock-picks*] Number one? you won't do. Five? that looks more like it. [*Picks the lock, and opens the door*] All quiet. [*Listens*] Now, Captain, I'll pay your rooms a short visit. [*Exit into house, cautiously*]

SCENE 3: *A parlor in Giltwood's house. Enter Pike stealthily.*

PIKE. I shall be fit to join the Captain's men shortly: I have such a quiet way of moving through another man's house. Lord knows, I've tried hard enough to get into the Association; but it was no go. I'm a baby to Shorton; and the little I know I learnt by watching him. Well, I've been through his rooms; but there is nothing in them.[21] However, I must do something; I can't be idle; and who knows but this time—Ah! here comes some one. That closet? No; people open closets. Behind this curtain? Yes, this place will do. [*Hides behind a curtain. Enter Amy, followed by Crum*]

CRUM. Oh! mistress, mistress!—[*Weeping*]

AMY. Now, my poor girl, do not go on so. Mr. Giltwood's storehouse is fully insured, and he will suffer no loss; Mr. Shorn assured me of that.

CRUM. Oh! mam, how can a house burn all up to nothin', and nobody lose nothin' neither?

AMY. It would be tedious to explain, Betsy; but you may be confident of one thing; Mr. Giltwood will only suffer a temporary inconvenience.

CRUM. A tenpenny inconvenient! Well, ain't that somethin'? A tenpenny inconvenient must be a dreadful thing; or Mr. Giltwood wouldn't 'er took on so. I was a-washin' the steps when he run out; and he trod in the bucket, and tripped over the brush, and fell flat; and then he got up agin, and put the house-rag in his pocket, and rushed down the street like mad. Don't tell me, mam; it ain't in natur. A man can't have his store burnt over his head, and ony suffer a tenpenny incon—something or other mam. [*Weeps bitterly*]

AMY. There, Betsy! Your tears are both foolish and useless.

CRUM. They ain't! my eyes is my own, and I'll cry 'em out if I choose. I tell you what, Mrs. Giltwood, if a body can't cry when they please, why I want to quit the house—that's all!

AMY. Really, Betsy, you should not trouble me at such a time.

CRUM. "At such a time!"—There! I knowed it! You're a-tryin' to fool me. We're all ruined, and you want to hide it. Oh! dear! dear! you'll have to take in sewin', and Mr. Giltwood'll have to work at a trade, and the children'll have to beg cold victuals, and Betsy Crum'll have to see you do it—oh! dear! —oh! dear!—and that'll be wust of all—oh! gracious! [*Weeps. Bell rings*]

AMY. Hark! there is some one at the door. The house is in confusion, the servants are all at the fire, and there is no one to answer the bell. Pray run down, Betsy.

CRUM. I hope, I know my dooty, without bein' minded of it, Mrs. Giltwood. I guess, it's only Mr. Shorn, anyhow. He's been a-runnin' in and out all day, and a-trackin' his dirty boots all over my steps and carpet. I suppose, I'm to clean after him, too, am I? I don't like your company, no how, Mrs. Giltwood. He's snaky, very snaky, mam; and ought 'er have a hole in the ground, to stick his ugly flat head in; instid of a-pokin' it into a decent house —he ought. [*Bell rings*] Oh! I'm a-comin', I'm a-comin'—when I get quite ready—drat you! [*Exit*]

AMY. One should have the patience of Penelope, to bear with that creature's disposition. Her good qualities appear only in moments of extreme trial; and to such occasions no one would willing look forward. Poor Edward! why has he not returned? If it had not been for the kind counsels, and inspiring cheerfulness, of Mr. Shorn, I should have followed him to the fire. [*Enter Shorn*]

SHORN. Mrs. Giltwood—

AMY. Go on, sir, go on! You look sad. For mercy sake, what is the matter? Edward is not well?

SHORN. Yes; and striving as becomes a man. But the office, in which his property is insured, has been so crippled with losses occasioned by the numerous fires of late, that it has closed its doors.

AMY. My poor, poor husband! Is there—oh! tell me, sir—is there a way in which I can serve him?

SHORN. I fear not. He requested me to tell you to remain at home.

AMY. In that matter, I must judge for myself. Edward would keep me at home, because he thinks me unable to assist him. He misjudges me, sir. The energies of even a feeble woman, when empowered by the strong arms of love, may achieve something heroic.[22] Never talk of weakness to a loving heart. The will to do is the thing; the power we all possess.

SHORN. [*Aside*] Disobedience! She takes her first downward step!

AMY. But the southern mail, by which you expected your remittances; is it in?

SHORN. Alas! I forgot to tell you. Between the railroad station and the post office, the mail was stolen, by some adroit villains, and there is no clue to its whereabout.

AMY. Stolen! what next?

SHORN. Heaven only knows! My loss is nothing; but poor Edward!—

AMY. What would you advise?

SHORN. I would advise you to listen to something which I am about to tell you.

AMY. This is strange!

SHORN. Not so strange as my words will be. Mrs. Giltwood, I am about to relate to you something that has given me more pain than any event of my life.—

AMY. Pray, stop, sir. If this matter relates only to yourself, we can postpone it until some fitter time. At present, I feel that it is my duty to devote all my thoughts and energies to my unfortunate husband. Come, sir, let us talk of him; and cheer him, on his return to us, by laying before him some unerring plan for his deliverance.

SHORN. It is of his happiness that I would speak. That which I have to say, concerns him more vitally than the safety of his goods, or even of his mercantile credit: it is of his honor, as a man, that I would talk.

AMY. Be plain then. Speak to the heart of the subject.

SHORN. Just before the fire broke out, a person, resembling your husband in every respect, was seen to steal from the back part of his warehouse, and walk rapidly in the direction of your dwelling. At least a dozen people saw this; and the strange circumstances is public talk. More; there was one man, among the lookers-on at the fire, who boldly says that he saw this same person enter the back alley which leads to your house. Edward's goods were fully insured; and, but for the breaking of the office, he would have suffered no loss. Under all circumstances, it is better, perhaps, that the office failed; otherwise, Edward would be in danger of prosecution.

AMY. Pshaw! Mr. Shorn, this is idle scandal. We can account for every moment of Edward's time this morning.

SHORN. For all but about fifteen minutes. You remember that he left us, on our way to breakfast; returned, in a hurried manner, after a quarter of an hour's absence, and busied himself with the newspapers.

AMY. True.

SHORN. There was ample time to walk to and from his warehouse.

AMY. Very true. Where could he have been?

SHORN. Now, that I think of it, I requested him to bring his balance-sheet to me. He returned without it, to be sure; and made some excuse about his bookkeeper not being at the office, or something of that kind: sufficient to prove, however, that he had been to his warehouse or to his office, at least.

AMY. Did he?—

SHORN. Yes; and don't you remember that, after waiting breakfast for sometime, you said, "Why, there is Edward coming up the yard?"

AMY. I believe I did.

SHORN. I know you did.

AMY. Sir!

SHORN. All these things, taken together, go—

AMY. [*Interrupting him*] To make up one infamous lie!

SHORN. I hope so, sincerely.

AMY. You know so, beyond doubt, or you do not know Edward Giltwood.

SHORN. Why, really, madam—

AMY. [*Interrupting him*] Mr. Shorn, if on weighing this matter, with the severest eye of justice, you harbor in any corner of your mind the slightest suspicion of my husband's entire integrity, there lies your path—through yonder open door; and, let me tell you, sir, you are the first man who ever crossed its threshold—were he the most grovelling worm that crawls—with such a doubt in his false and degraded heart! Begone, sir!

SHORN. I only looked at the matter with the eyes of the multitude.

AMY. Then go mingle with the multitude; for you have no right to the hospitality of this house.

SHORN. Your suspicions of my faith in Edward are more unjust to me, than my worst thoughts of him. I believe him to be wronged and slandered, but, not the less, in danger. I have known innocent men, before his time, who have been hunted to death by lies. There was an unhappy man of this city, who died broken-hearted in California, one James Shelvill—

AMY. [*Interrupting him*] He was an inbred villain. Dare not compare my husband with that man!

SHORN. [*Aside*] She strengthens me against herself. I shall not falter again. You knew James Shelvill then?

AMY. Too well.

SHORN. Yet not enough, if you believed him guilty. Your maiden name was Amy Startle—excuse me—Miss Amy Startle?

AMY. It was.

SHORN. Your native place was a small town, some miles from this; there Shelvill saw you first—long before your husband heard your name?

AMY. Yes.

SHORN. James Shelvill loved you?

AMY. No; he was incapable of love, or any noble passion.

SHORN. At least, he loved you in the best way he could; even as the base may love and worship Heaven, and from that Heaven gain mercy, if no more.

AMY. Perhaps.

SHORN. You did not show him even mercy. No! You rejected his heart with scorn—[23] you degraded him beneath his self-contempt; you turned his face towards hell, and drove him downward! You have this upon your hands —this ruin of a human soul—to answer for; how can you answer it?

AMY. 'Twas in the days of my girlish folly, when we think lightly of the time to come. I confess that I acted with little wisdom, but with no cruel design.

SHORN. You talk well, madam; but, for all your talk, the issue was the same to him: a life of misery, and a death of horror!

AMY. I sincerely pity him.

SHORN. Pity! he asks it not. You insult his memory with your pity.

AMY. Mr. Shorn, this Shelvill, in whom you take so much interest, was—

SHORN. [*Interrupting her*] He was my friend—a bold and trusty friend— the best, and only one, I've had through life.

AMY. He was a bad man.

SHORN. He was that which you made him. Until you spurned him, he was an honest man. But you set up the hunt; and all the human pack, whom you call fellows, joined the chase, and drove the hapless wretch to desperation. At the first shout of scorn, he paused in innocent amazement; but the yell grew loud and near; he turned and fled, like Cain, without Cain's crime. Now hear the words he whispered in my ear.[24] He lay dying upon the California plains, with nothing but the sailing clouds 'twixt him and Heaven, as thus he spoke: "James Shorn, that woman is the death of me.[25] I do not ask just Heaven for vengeance on her head; I only ask for justice on her deed— such as its law metes out to sins like hers. Swear to repay the deed."[26]

AMY. And you?—

SHORN. I swore.

AMY. Hear me!—

SHORN. Wait, wait! Even as I swore, a whirlwind eddied round us, and snatched up to Heaven—for so it seemed to me—his prayer and my oath.

When I looked on him, the sharp touch of death had fixed his features on eternity!

AMY. Oh! horrible! Dark and mysterious man, the oath you swore was more than sinful.

SHORN. I am neither dark nor mysterious; it is my function makes me seem so. I am—as you now know me to be—but the cold minister of justice; in all else, a feeling man, I trust. It is the dead that haunts you, and your own guilty soul that makes you feel his presence.

AMY. Then do your worst! I am a woman, feeble as I know, with many ties, as husband, children, home, through which I may be struck. Strike here—here at this heart—and let its riven shield protect the sacred beings whom I love, and before whom I cast myself, a willing victim!

SHORN. No, madam; I have thought it over. You must not die, but suffer—suffer until the scales of justice, which Shelvill now drags down, be balanced equally between you, pang for pang.

AMY. Fie! sir, I am awake. You have been playing on my fancy, oppressing me with a wicked dream. In this land there are laws that curb the powerful, and protect the weak. The sense of right is strong within the people; and twenty[27] millions of courageous hearts are guardians of mine and of my country's liberty.[28] Lay but a finger on my free-born limbs, and you shall see a spectacle of steel rise, like a harvest round you! I defy you!

SHORN. Your patriotic fire were well, if you were free; but you have ensnared and bound yourself in chains more oppressive than those of slavery—in the chains of guilt. The work of vengeance was ready to my hands before I entered on it.

AMY. Go on then! There is not a word of our conversation which Edward shall not hear, and make you answer for.

SHORN. He shall not hear one.

AMY. I am about to seek him, and we shall see. [*Goes to the bell*]

SHORN. Hold! you are pulling ruin on your head, and on your husband's. For his sake, I have paused thus; and may the dead forgive me! Before James Shelvill died, he put this paper in my hands. [*Produces a paper*] It is a police report. A certain country maiden was arraigned, before a magistrate for pilfering. Her name—so runs the print—was Amy Startle.

AMY. Gracious Heaven! has the old shame, that poisoned half my life, returned to craze me? Mr. Shorn, I was as innocent of crime as—

SHORN. [*Interrupting her*] As Shelvill was: I grant it. Yet you have kept it, as a loathsome secret, from your husband.

AMY. Only for shame, only to spare his noble mind the stain of such disgusting memories. I'll tell you all. I was an unknown country-girl. I came to town, to make some purchases. Leaving my father in a neighboring street, I walked into a store, bought some small goods, turned from the counter—then my brain ran around. I knew no more, until I found myself arraigned for theft, with my poor father sobbing at my side. It seems, a piece of costly lace caught to my sleeve-hook; and, as I put my hand within my muff, I drew the lace in after. It was an accident, such as might have happened to any lady in the land. But I was alone and unprotected; so the base shopman had no mercy on my youth and evident innocence.

SHORN. Yes, yes; and yet your father purchased silence, at any price, rather than bring the matter to trial. The same event, with all your innocence, exposed you to the hints, and taunts, and slights of your whole village; drove you from your native town, and made you seek this city, as a refuge from disgrace.

AMY. I own all that; but I assert my perfect innocence.

SHORN. How? On your husband you have palmed a fraud. He married you, spotless, as he thought; to find you—

AMY. [*Interrupting him*] Spotless still at heart.

SHORN. But most deformed and tainted in your history. Madam, you cannot evade the fact. You should have told your story before your wedding. You did not. There lies your crime; and my plain duty to Edward, as his friend, is to inform him of it.

AMY. I will confess it to him at once.

SHORN. Dare, and you will drive him mad. Add this infamous affair to his present troubles, and, before tonight, Edward Giltwood will rave in a madhouse. I am more merciful: I pause for pity towards him. No; when the blow comes, it shall come from me; or, rather, from the cold, relentless hand of him whose spirit hovers 'round us now.

AMY. Have mercy on my poor children and my careworn husband! I am guiltless; yet I ask nothing.

SHORN. Not of treachery to Edward.

AMY. Oh! I was thoughtless. A false shame closed up my lips to him. I feared that it might have cost me his love: I could have sacrificed all else.

SHORN. "It might!" it would have cost you his love and him; you know it. You know his touchy honor too well to doubt a moment.

AMY. Sir, you have found some virtues in me, you have praised them too; I assure you, they all spring from that unhappy accident. It humbled me, it brought me to my knees, and from my knees I looked toward Heaven. Hear me! I could not treat James Shelvill, now, as I did in my haughty girlhood. I was a village belle, a silly hair-brained child.—I tell you, sir, that all my little goodness dates from that day. You will not spoil the charity of Heaven, by turning its mournful blessings into curses? You will not wring the heart of your best friend, at such a time, with such a history? Wait till his mind is at rest; and, then, I promise you that I will not shrink. If, after hearing all, he cast me off, I will depart in peace. Think of my children!—of the downcast man who staggered from you, all aghast, this morning, with ruin staring him in the face—oh! think! [*Shorn is slowly departing. She clings to him*]

SHORN. Think of James Shelvill, of his wrongs and grief! Think of my oath, that pity cannot touch!

AMY. Oh! spare poor Edward!

SHORN. I promise nothing. Are you humbled?

AMY. Yes; beneath the dust! [*Shorn tears himself from her, and exits. She falls upon her face. Pike comes from behind the curtain; and exits thoughtfully*]

ACT III.

SCENE 1: *The private office of Elton's banking-house. Enter Giltwood and Elton.*

ELT. Mr. Giltwood, there is no necessity for prolonging this conversation. After your notes have been protested, your creditors may grant you an extension; at present, I cannot.

GILT. But it is the protest I wish to avoid. The idea of failing fills me with horror.

ELT. I have nothing to do with feelings. A bank is a mere machine, for the more convenient transaction of business. You know that, as well as I do; and I am really astonished that a man of your understanding, can expect us to depart from our established rules.

GILT. But there are certain cases which, I hoped, might touch the feelings of even a banker. I have been particularly unfortunate, Mr. Elton. I should have had ample means to meet my engagements had the *Occident* arrived; or had the southern mail, which contained the funds of a friend, not been robbed on the way hither. Today, my storehouse has been burned to the ground; and the office that insured my goods failed before the fire was extinguished. You see to what a combination of mishaps I owe my present position.

ELT. Very well; what have I to do with all this?

GILT. Mr. Elton, you are unfeeling. Six months ago, when money was a drug in the market, you came to me, hat in hand, and begged me to borrow a portion of your idle funds. I refused. You persevered; you filled my head with speculations; you decoyed me into my ruin!

ELT. Sir!

GILT. Aye, I repeat it. You talked of shipments to California, of the immense returns which they had made; you opened before me schemes of sudden wealth. I relied on your experienced judgment; I was fool enough to believe you; and this is my return.

ELT. I cannot control the money-market.

GILT. Then you should not base your promises upon it. You prophesied an easy money-market for the next twelve-month. You bankers have much to answer for. When money is plenty, you entice us into speculation by begging us to borrow; and then, at the least change in the prospect, you call in your loans, before we have reaped the benefits of them, and crush us at a blow. This is the history of my case, and it has been that of a thousand others.

ELT. Really, Mr. Giltwood, I have no time to waste on this discussion.

GILT. Circumstances, of a private nature forbid that I should ask a favor of the holder of my notes, Mr. Tapeley. You refuse to do it for me. My case seems desperate. What would you advise me to do?

ELT. Break.

GILT. Good Heaven! Mr. Elton, can you look me in the face, in that cool way, and offer such advice? It is a proverb that banks have no heart; I fear that some of their officers are in a like predicament.

ELT. You are impertinent, sir!

GILT. No; you have taken away the spirit to be so.

ELT. Go to your creditors. Your notes are with me for collection only. I have no interest whatever in them.—Though, after the rumors that are flying about, I fear your creditors will show you but little mercy.

GILT. Rumors regarding me?

ELT. Much to your discredit.

GILT. How!

ELT. It is reported that you know more about the fire at your warehouse than anyone else.

GILT. It is a base lie!

ELT. Hum! hum!

GILT. What, do you give credence to the falsehood? Confess that belief, if you dare, and I will offer you such an insult as no gentleman can receive!

ELT. Come, this is no place for your theatrical rages. Mr. Giltwood, I have the honor of wishing you a very good morning! [*Bows*]

GILT. Mr. Elton, do you know what is the greatest curse of this perverted world? Do you know what it is that blinds man to nature, and blocks up the pathway between earth and Heaven? Do you know what can turn the heart to marble, and the eye to lead? Do you know what can still the bounding blood of youth, and dry up the narrow veins of age? Do you know what can make the intellect and education lick the dust from the feet of folly and ignorance? Do you know what can make the most delicate refinement servile to the most brutal vulgarity? Do you know what can load the scales of justice, and blunt her sword? Do you know what fills the hospital, the almshouse, the jail, and stretches the accursed cord of the gallows? Do you know what can break all the Decalogue, create every crime forbidden in Holy Writ, and invent new ones too numerous and too odious for language? Do you know what draws tears from the angels, and peals of laughter from the fiends? Do you know what keeps Heaven empty, and makes Hell groan with its myriads? I can answer all these terrible questions, and in one word—Money! [*Exit*]

ELT. Upon my soul, a very excitable young man, and no bad hand at an oration. Really, he should go into politics which, I believe, was invented by some humane individual as a sort of general charity, a refuge for those who have proved themselves unfit for all other kinds of business. [*Enter Amy with a basket*]

AMY. Mr. Elton?

ELT. At your service, madam. Pray be seated.

AMY. No, I thank you: I shall detain you a moment only. The gentleman who just left you, Mr. Giltwood, was he successful in his mission?

ELT. If you consider his mission to be that of an anti-monetary declaimer, he was very successful indeed. I never heard such a tirade against everything that was, is, or may be, in the whole course of my life.

AMY. Excuse me, sir; but I would rather listen to no jests regarding that gentleman. I remained outside your office, for purposes of my own, until I saw him depart; and now I simply wish to know whether he accomplished his object?

ELT. His business with me was to postpone the payment of certain notes, placed with us for collection.

AMY. And you?

ELT. I could not grant it.

AMY. You "could not grant it?" Weigh your words, sir.

ELT. Under no circumstances. Before we go further, in another man's private affairs, I should like to know what relation you bear to him?

AMY. I am his wife.

ELT. I supposed as much.

THE BANKRUPT

AMY. I came here with no purpose of appealing to your feelings. This is a matter of business, and should be so treated.

ELT. A very sensible view of the affair.

AMY. Mr. Giltwood's notes are due today. His funds are, as he has perhaps informed you, in the missing steamer, *Occident*. I am quite ignorant of business etiquette, but if the payment of any moderate amount, or the pledging of some not valueless property, would be a sufficient inducement for you to grant him a little time—say, a week, or two or three days—I am ready to offer you security. [*Uncovers her basket*] See, sir, here are my jewels—quite superfluous, I assure you—and a small package of trinkets which I will place in your hands. At home, I have other costly property—such as laces, India shawls, robes, furs, plate, and so forth—which I have written down in this schedule. [*Offers a paper*] They are all entirely at your disposal, on condition—

ELT. [*Interrupting her*] Good Heaven! Madam, I am not a pawnbroker! You are, doubtless, quite innocent of wrong; but, really, you are wounding me very deeply.

AMY. There can be no insult in intentions as earnest as mine.

ELT. Mrs. Giltwood, I shall offer you the advice which I lately gave your husband: Go talk to the holders of the notes. Both you and Mr. Giltwood seem to forget that I have no power over them.

AMY. Who are the persons to whom you refer me?

ELT. The owner of the bulk—nay, when I come to think of it—the owner of the whole of them is a large capitalist, to whom they came in the course of business. But, I fear, your labor will be lost; for Mr. Tapeley is not a man to surrender—

AMY. [*Interrupting him*] Mr. Tapeley?—an old gentleman?—a lawyer?

ELT. The same.

AMY. He is saved! He is saved! Heaven bless you, for your kindness in mentioning that name! Why, sir, Mr. Tapeley was an old friend of my father: I grew to girlhood under his eye. To be sure, my marriage with Edward offended him a little, on account of some differences between them; but when he understands our misfortunes, he will certainly relent.—Why do you shake your head?

ELT. Because, madam, you do not appear to know how little such things enter into a man's ideas of business.

AMY. Oh! sir, his heart enters into everything he does. You do not know Mr. Tapeley as I do, or you would not suspect his generosity. You still doubt? Well, I can try, I can try. If I fail, I shall at least feel that I have done my duty.

Elt. Mr. Tapeley's office is in—

Amy. [*Interrupting him*] I know where it is. I have not lost sight of him, though he seems to have forgotten me. Good day, Mr. Elton! I owe you the blessing of a bright hope, and I am not ungrateful for it.

Elt. Good morning, Mrs. Giltwood! Heaven speed you! for you deserve success.

Amy. Oh! thank you! thank you! [*Exit*]

Elt. By Jupiter! that's a noble creature! If she had said a few words more, I should have felt inclined to take up Giltwood's notes myself. Well, well, a banker has no business with feelings. If I helped all the cripples that come to me, I should soon need crutches for myself. [*Enter Shorn*]

Shorn. Mr. Elton, I believe?

Elt. Yes, sir.

Shorn. My name is Mr. Shorn.

Elt. Mr. James Shorn of California?

Shorn. I am he.

Elt. [*Shaking his hand cordially*] Why, my dear sir, I am delighted to see you. Sit down, Mr. Shorn, sit down. [*Offers a chair*] Really, sir, this is an unexpected pleasure. To what do I owe the honor of your visit, Mr. Shorn?

Shorn. To our common idol, Mr. Elton, the golden calf.

Elt. [*Laughing*] Ha! ha! very good, very good! You, who have such a slice of the idol's carcass, can afford to laugh at us poor fellows who pick at its bones. Allow me to take your hat, sir. Upon my word, I am glad to find you looking so well.

Shorn. I called to inquire with regard to some notes of one Edward Giltwood. When are they due?

Elt. Today, at three o'clock. [*Aside*] Those cursed notes again!

Shorn. This Giltwood is a poor devil, I fear, Mr. Elton.

Elt. A very poor devil, Mr. Shorn.—I beg your pardon: you were about to observe?—

Shorn. It is currently reported that he set fire to his own warehouse, in order to obtain the insurance.

Elt. I have no doubt of it, not the least.

Shorn. And that he has not a penny in the *Occident,* even if she should arrive. All humbug, to gain time.

Elt. All humbug, Mr. Shorn; I never had a doubt of it. His wife is the only valuable thing in his possession.

Shorn. And she—ha! ha! [*Laughing*] But we'll not be scandalous.

Elt. Ha! ha! [*Laughing*] She just left me, Mr. Shorn.

Shorn. Oh! Elton, Elton, you sly old villain!

THE BANKRUPT

ELT. Come, come, you'll say nothing, Mr. Shorn. She made nothing by it, I swear.

SHORN. I'm not sure of that. Oh! Elton, Elton! [*Laughing*]

ELT. Mum's the word.

SHORN. Honor bright, upon my soul! Well, then, the end of the matter is that Giltwood's notes are not worth a copper.

ELTON. Not worth a single farthing.

SHORN. I'll tell you why I wish your opinion, Mr. Elton: I have a notion of buying them.

ELT. Hey!—indeed? Well—if you come to their market value, they are not so bad as you may suppose.

SHORN. You must let me have them, Mr. Elton.

ELT. Why, really, Mr. Shorn, you know that this is entirely out of my line of business. The notes are put with us for collection only, and—

SHORN. [*Interrupting him*] Mr. Elton, by the next packet, I shall receive one hundred and fifty thousand dollars, in gold, which I would as leave deposit with you, as with anyone; provided I have Giltwood's notes at, we'll say, a quarter off.

ELT. Well, I think we can manage it. Tapeley is a friend of mine, and I'll take the responsibility of selling the notes, if we can agree on terms.

SHORN. It would be doing Mr. Tapeley a service.

ELT. I really think so.

SHORN. Further, my name is not to appear in this transaction in any way. The notes are to be protested, as if they belonged to Mr. Tapeley; though I pledge myself to pay them afterwards. If Giltwood should redeem them in time, the whole matter goes for nothing. These notes are of no use to me, unless they be protested. I desire them for an after purpose, to have a certain hold upon this Giltwood. You see, Mr. Elton, I am talking you into my confidence.

ELT. Upon my soul, sir, I see nothing of the kind. This is a very curious and incomprehensible affair, Mr. Shorn; and it places me in an extremely awkward situation. Really, sir, I must decline having anything to do with it.

SHORN. Indeed? I'll tell you why you will oblige me. You will oblige me, because you said that Giltwood was an incendiary and a swindler; because you said that his wife was a wanton, and plainly hinted at your own share in her infamy. Because Edward Giltwood, being a gentleman of an exceedingly fiery disposition, on acquaintance with our conversation, would not hesitate to add another ounce of lead to the already weighty number which you carry upon your shoulders. I have a close personal friendship with that dangerous character, and shall feel it my duty—

Elt. [*Interrupting him*] Good Heavens! Come into the front office, Mr. Shorn. I have no doubt that I shall be able to satisfy you. Walk in, Mr. Shorn, walk in. [*Bows Shorn off, and exeunt. Aside*] Upon my word, this Mr. Shorn is rather a sharp man of business.

Scene 2: *A street. Enter Giltwood, hastily.*

Gilt. Why should I hurry from street to street in this frenzied manner? I cannot borrow a dollar on my word, and I have nothing else to offer. I see men's answer in their faces, before I open my lips. My credit is gone; and my character too, I should judge, from the way in which I have been treated. There is no course left but to break—Oh! Heaven! that such an alternative was ever offered to me—unless my friend, James who seems to bear full half my suffering, has been able to effect something. [*Enter Shorn*] Well, James what success? You need not answer: I see my ruin reflected in your features.

Shorn. Not all, my poor friend!

Gilt. What more?

Shorn. What? Ah! there is the sorrow! I will out with it, if he kill me; I have no right to conceal the dishonor of my friend, of his children, from him who—Oh! I cannot, cannot get further.

Gilt. You have heard how the town slanders me.

Shorn. Has it got abroad?

Gilt. I refer to the miserable falsehood about the fire at my warehouse. Let them bring it to trial: I court, and defy investigation. Have you seen Amy?

Shorn. Have I?

Gilt. What, in the name of mercy, are you driving at?

Shorn. Hear me, Edward, but be patient. Nothing but the sacredness of friendship, could compel me to the task. I spurned the faithless woman—I swore to reveal her baseness—and, by Heaven, I will!

Gilt. Her!—Who?

Shorn. Of course, you know that your wife is fearful of losing her position in society?

Gilt. That is quite natural.

Shorn. If you fail, she must lose it.

Gilt. Undoubtedly; I know that.

Shorn. Would you believe that the frivolities of fashion have taken such a hold on her?

Gilt. They have not. You heard what she said, this morning, about selling out her establishment.

SHORN. A mere ruse. Her plan, as she confessed to me, was even then formed.

GILT. Her plan for what?

SHORN. To save your credit.

GILT. Heaven bless her for it!

SHORN. Peace! Peace! your blessing is blasphemy.

GILT. You seem to possess some painful secret—something that may affect my good opinion of Amy—something discreditable to her.

SHORN. Ah! me!

GILT. Speak out, and speak quickly; or as she lives, and I love her, I'll strangle you in the open street! [*Seizes him*]

SHORN. Before I speak, I can promise full and sufficient proof of all I say. You requested her to remain at home; do you know that she is even now running about the streets—paying visits, and so forth?

GILT. Most disgraceful!

SHORN. This morning, when we were alone together, although she must have known that I was using all my power in your favor, she offered me—indirectly, Edward, with proper and lady-like delicacy, I must say that—she offered me—on condition that I would save your credit—

GILT. [*Interrupting him*] What?—what?

SHORN. Her honor.

GILT. Ha!

SHORN. What do you think of it?

GILT. Think! I do not think at all. I know, James Shelvill, that you are a scoundrel and a liar!

SHORN. I was prepared for this, Edward. I should have said the same to a third person. I know that my life is in your hands, and I am willing to yield it to you—

GILT. [*Interrupting him*] But you spoke of proof, proof.

SHORN. You shall have it, if you consent to overhear a conversation between us—conclusive proof. I swore to reveal the matter to you, and she is in fear lest I should do it before she can conveniently desert you. Doubtless, she thought that I would be unable to resist her beauty—

GILT. [*Interrupting him*] Damn her beauty! I'll not leave a vestige of it!

SHORN. Look, she comes. Promise me to treat her kindly, until you are convinced of her perfidy?

GILT. James, you act as a generous man, who has been persuaded against your will, but you are deceived.

SHORN. I would beg in the streets, to believe so.

GILT. Has this, too, fallen upon me? Lend me your arm; for I have scarce strength to stand alone. How dare she meet me, after I ordered her to keep at home? [*Enter Amy*]

AMY. [*Aside*] Edward! If he send me home, I shall not see Mr. Tapeley after all.

SHORN. [*Apart to Giltwood*] Mark her confusion.

GILT. [*Apart to Shorn*] I can see nothing else. The world seems filled with treachery, all centered on myself. [*To Amy*] Mrs., I desired you to stay at home.

AMY. But, Edward, I thought proper to—

GILT. [*Interrupting her*] What right had you to think anything, madam, after my message to you?

AMY. If I have displeased you, I will return. Only, dear Edward, please allow me to run over to Mr. Tapeley's for a moment; will you not?

GILT. Tapeley! my old enemy, the niggardly usurer who holds my notes, and who opposed our marriage! Would that his schemes had all been successful! I wish no worse fortune, and myself no better.

AMY. Edward! what does this mean? [*Aside*] Ha! Mr. Shorn has betrayed my secret. If Mr. Shorn has—

SHORN. [*Apart to her*] Hush! you will destroy yourself. I have not revealed your secret. Spare him the pain; he is mad with excitement.

GILT. [*Aside*] By Heaven! They are whispering—before me too! Go home, Mrs. Giltwood, go home!

AMY. Will you not soon be there? Our children—

GILT. [*Interrupting her*] Fie! fie!

AMY. Edward, what excites you thus? Have you not found means to meet your notes?

GILT. What are my notes to you? Go home!

AMY. I am going, Edward. You are ill? I know that you are, or you would not speak thus to your poor wife. I am a woman; I have that claim, at least, on your forbearance; and no man can ill-use our defenseless sex without deserving rebuke. You are ill, are you not?—Speak to me, my dear husband!

GILT. I shall speak enough before long. Why do you loiter there like a beggar?

AMY. Oh! Heaven! my heart will break! [*Exit weeping*]

GILT. There, James, I kept my promise: I treated her with forbearance, did I not?

SHORN. With perfect kindness.[29]

THE BANKRUPT

GILT. The proof! The proof!—I'll have the proof!—or one of us shall face his doom before yon sun goes down! [*Exeunt*]

SCENE 3: *Shorn's apartment in Giltwood's house. Crum discovered making up the bed.*

CRUM. I ain't a-goin' to make up beds twice a day for nobody—that's flat.[30] Oh! What a lookin' bed! I tell you what, Betsy Crum, the man as sleeps in that bed has a orful conshunce.[31] Lor' me! If there ain't a place where he's rolled the sheet up in a wad, and bit it half through! Well, I never! My, a hungry wolf wouldn't 'er done that. Me! Me! I'd as leave be Pontus Pirate, hisself, as have that man's dreams. The good-fur-nothin', bed-spilin', lining-eatin', nightmare-rudden Judas! Oh! if I had 'im, I'd learn 'im to be a commin' inter respectable houses, and a-eatin' up all their beds!—I'd show 'im —[*Enter Pike, disguised as a porter, with Shorn's trunks, etc.*] Oh! Lor!—Oh!

PIKE. Hush! don't make a fool of yourself! I won't hurt a hair of your beautiful head, Miss Crum.

CRUM. Dear me! Mr. Porter, don't flatter yerself; I'm not afeared of a dozen like you. Ony, the next time you come inter a body's room, if you don't knock, I'll know why—that's all!

PIKE. Why, Lord bless you, my lovely creature, I'll tell you why, now: my hands were full.—Ha! by Jupiter! there's the tin box upon the table! [*Aside*] My sweet girl, couldn't you get a poor fellow a drink of water? If you put something in it, I won't swear—that is, if you make it strong enough to take away my breath.

CRUM. No, sir! I'm a-goin' to stay in this 'ere room till you leave it.

PIKE. Very well. Now, Betsy Crum, I just want to speak a word with you. I'm about to open that tin box, and take something out. If you make a noise, I'll be angry with you; and if I get angry with you, Betsy, I'll lock you up, Betsy—upon my soul, I will!

CRUM. You'll lock me up, will you? I'd like to see you make a beginnin' at that. Now, I jest want 'er speak a word to you, Mr. Porter. If you tech anythin' in this room, I'll wallup you over the head with this brush, Mr. Porter; and I'll raise the house too, you, you—oh! you ugly man!

PIKE. No, you won't, Betsy, my darling. You're too sweet a temper to do such naughty things. Come, come! I've no time to lose. My name's Pike, of the police; and I came here, in this disguise, for the express purpose of opening that box; and I'm going to do it, straight. Sharp's the word!

CRUM. Well, Mr. P'lice Pike, you can't come a-disguisin' about here, I tell you. And the sooner you git out of this, the wholer'll be your skin.

PIKE. I must open the box, you know, dear.

CRUM. You can't, beauty. Besides, it's locked. [*Trying the box*]

PIKE. Now, my love!—

CRUM. Do you know what "humbug" means? [*Takes down the box and sits upon it*]

PIKE. I'm sorry to disturb you; but, really, you must find another seat, Miss Crum. [*Endeavors to draw her off*]

CRUM. I'm quite comfurtable, thank you! [*Sitting firmly*]

PIKE. Pshaw!—Oh! by the by, Miss Betsy, you have a brother—Joseph Crum, Esquire?

CRUM. I'm not ashamed of 'im. He's a hard-workin' man; and what he eats he earns, honestly, with the lims Heaven gave 'im; and not with the crookid brain that the devil's always a-creepin' inter.

PIKE. He's so fond of hard work, that he don't get enough of it in his regular business, so he runs with the fire-engines. And that's not enough for him either; he's so industrious that, last Tuesday night, he must hit a man over the head with a spanner—only to keep his hand in, I suppose. Well, now, Betsy, as much as you admire all this in Joseph, the law don't like it: and so the mayor put a warrant in my hands, which I shall serve, on the aforesaid Josephy Crum, Esquire, if you don't get off that box. Here it is: read it. [*Gives paper*]

CRUM. Lors a mercy! what'll you do with 'im?

PIKE. Nothing, Betsy, if you'll be a good girl.

CRUM. But I can't be a good girl. My dooty—[*Sobbing*]

PIKE. Nonsense! If you're obliging, you may make curl-papers of that warrant, when you're going to bed; and they'll become you so too; and you'll sleep so much easier, with your head dressed in that fashion, won't you, Betsy? [*Gradually draws her off the box*]

CRUM. But it's locked, Mr. Pike.

PIKE. See here: it may be interesting to you. [*Takes out lock-picks*] You observe, Betsy, that's too large, and that's too small, but this is just the thing! [*Opens the box*] By the great United States, here they are! [*Takes out papers*]

CRUM. No!

PIKE. Yes! Did you ever have a love-letter?

CRUM. He! he! [*Simpering*][32]

PIKE. And you felt like kissing it, you jade?[33]

CRUM. Oh! go 'long!— [*Simpering*]

PIKE. Do you know, I feel like kissing these just as much? As it is, I'll put them next my heart. Then, we'll lock up the box again, you see—[*Locks*

THE BANKRUPT

it] And, maybe, nobody, but you and I, will know anything about it: And we'll say nothing, will we, Betsy, for poor Joe's sake?

CRUM. Dear me! but you're a queer man! You ought 'er be sent to the World's Fair in a glass case.—

PIKE. Hist! [*Sits upon the box, and whistles. Enter Shorn suddenly. Pike rises, and bows*]

SHORN. Well, man, what do you want here?

PIKE. [*Bowing and scraping awkwardly*] Gentleman's porter, sir—Brought over the gentleman's baggage from the hotel, sir.—Like a little porterage, if the gentleman pleases.

SHORN. You did not bring that box; what in the devil are you doing with it?

PIKE. No, sir; gentleman brought that over in his own hand. Just seein' if it's all right.

SHORN. Ha! ha! you are? Get up! [*Pike rises*] I'll take a look at it myself. [*Tries the box*] All safe. [*Aside*] My schemes of revenge are making me neglect my other affairs. The contents of this box should have been destroyed an hour ago. Here is your pay, porter. [*Gives Pike money*] When you carry my luggage again, you will please to remember that you must not meddle with things which do not concern you.

PIKE. No offense, I hope? [*Apart to her*] Not a word, Betsy! Good morning, Captain Shor—[*Aside; and exits hastily*] What a fool I am!

SHORN. What's that? Call the fellow back! Quick, you hussy!

CRUM. Hussy! I'll set you up with hussy!—

SHORN. Call him, I say!

CRUM. Porter! porter!—

SHORN. From the window! [*Snatches up the box*] Is this an old scratch near the keyhole? [*Feeling for his keys*]

CRUM. [*Running to the window*] Here, porter, porter! There go his coattails round the corner, sir!

SHORN. [*Opening the box*] Gone, by hell! Who was that man?

CRUM. I know I've acted wrong, sir; but poor Joe—

SHORN. The devil take poor Joe! Who was that man?

CRUM. I'd have you know, Mr. Shorn, that the devil's not as likely to take Joe, as some other folks I know—

SHORN. Look you, woman, I am a man of few words; speak to the point, or, by the Lord, I'll choke the truth out of you! [*Threatens her*]

CRUM. Mr.—Shorn—I hope—[*Sobbing*]

SHORN. Speak!

CRUM. Well, then, that man was a-disguisin' about—[*Sobbing*]

SHORN. Ha!
CRUM. That man was no porter, sir.
SHORN. No porter!
CRUM. No, sir; he was—he was—[*Sobbing*]
SHORN. Who?—who?
CRUM. P'lice Pike!
SHORN. Oh! Heavens! an officer! I am a ruined man! [*Sinks into a chair*]
CRUM. Lors a massy! so am I! [*Sinks into another chair*]

ACT IV.

SCENE 1: *The drawing-room in Giltwood's house. Enter Shorn.*

SHORN. In three hours I must depart; but, by that time, my vengeance will be complete. The papers are all written in a difficult cipher: that must delay discovery. I have stationed my spies in every part of the police office, to give me early warning. No! I will not be frightened from my designs by a stupid policeman. But I am suspected; that is clear. How can it be that plans, which have baffled the world for years, shall be discovered in a day? Poh! I terrify myself with shadows. [*Enter Giltwood*]

GILT. I have come home, according to my promise, a miserable, heartsick man. In a few hours, the public voice will declare me a bankrupt. It has already whispered that I am a criminal; and, in truth, I am so broken down and wretched, that I begin to doubt my own honesty.

SHORN. You must not give way to fancies. You should face destiny, nay, trample upon it, as I have done.

GILT. You counsel with pride of Satan, another, with the humility of a saint; yet the issue of your counsel is the same: I must bear up.[34] Test your philosophy in your own life, before you prescribe it to another. Well, what of Amy? I suppose I must bear that, too, with a placid face? I must smile at my own dishonor; I must laugh at it, as the world will laugh at it? This is all very beautiful in theory—it is happiness made easy upon paper; but it is not human; and I, abject and down-trodden as I am, have not ceased to be a man.

SHORN. Poor fellow—

GILT. Peace! You have wasted sympathy enough on me. Give me the proof of Amy's falsehood, which you pledged yourself to do; and if I do not meet it with manly fortitude, I will grapple it with fiendish rage. Something shall be done. I will not sink into this lethargy of mind and body, without a struggle, if I die in the effort.

SHORN. I will, Edward. That much I owe to your honor.

GILT. Honor!—pish! The word seems strange and unnatural to me. Honor flew to Heaven long ago; it was washed out of the world by a flood of gold more destructive to man than the first deluge.[35] Away! with your wordy virtues, that only live in terms! I, for one, will henceforth be a natural man.[36] If Amy prove false in the trial, I'll drive her from the door of this house, as I would a thief. If you have even erred in judgment, take care, and fly betimes. I'll hear no explanation of your course, no cry for mercy, no appeal to the remorseless fire that burns within me; but, on this spot, I'll tear you limb from limb!

SHORN. And I will offer no resistance. Edward, Edward, it wrings my heart, to think that we two have seen the day when such words can pass between us! You need forgiveness, and I forgive you.

GILT. You see that I am not moved by your words. Grief has fallen upon me, drop after drop, until I am hardened into stone. Take back your friendship! From this day,[37] I will neither call man friend, nor woman wife. I am disgusted with you, one and all!

SHORN. Your wife is coming: I heard her chamber-door close.

GILT. What will you do with me? Is she so bold in crime that she will speak before me?

SHORN. You must secrete yourself.

GILT. That's thievish; and, in your catalogue of terms, might be called dishonorable. Well, man, why do you stare at me with such perplexity? I am ready for your contemptible purpose. You must not be too nice with a bankrupt incendiary; it is but little more, to prove him a wittol.

SHORN. Edward, you will kill me with your bitterness.

GILT. Fie! sir; you are faint-hearted. Come, begin!

SHORN. Conceal yourself within this closet. [*Opening a closet*]

GILT. What if I steal the things within? They are not mine; they belong to my creditors. Ha! you can trust me? That's fair, but hardly wise. [*Enters a closet*]

SHORN. Just so I suffered.—Now, wit, be present! [*Enter Amy*]

AMY. Has Edward returned?

SHORN. Not yet.

AMY. That is strange: I thought I heard his voice.

SHORN. He was here awhile ago, but—

AMY. [*Interrupting him*] Well, well, what news? Is the *Occident* in? Has he raised the money? Are we safe? Say yes, Mr. Shorn, for today at least.

SHORN. I am sorry—

AMY. [*Interrupting him*] Ah! you are sorry! and that means all you can say? I want a word to express the misery I suffer. Can you do nothing?

SHORN. Nothing.

AMY. Not for the offer which I made? It was all I had to give. Here, sir. [*Takes him apart, and whispers*] I would not be overheard. Edward hates Mr. Tapeley so much, that he would not forgive me, if the act saved him. But do you take this note, and all the useless jewels and finery, to Mr. Tapeley; and see if such a spectacle of misfortune do not move his feelings. I know that it will, more than words could.

SHORN. I cannot, madam. What do you take me for?

AMY. Oh! you men are so proud, so foolishly proud. Now I could beg, in such a cause, and feel no qualm of pride.

SHORN. I believe it. You have such abject thoughts to struggle against, that pride could hardly find a refuge in your heart.

AMY. You are severe. But I will not quarrel with you; because I wish this thing done.

SHORN. You ask in vain. Had you an angel's tongue and graces, I would not be concerned in so dishonorable an affair. Think of my friend Edward's reputation.

AMY. But neither he nor anyone need know, if we are prudent.

SHORN. Your humiliating proposal would be worse than bankruptcy.

AMY. You mistake. Only save his credit, and I am willing to suffer almost any personal humiliation. You will not do it?

SHORN. No!

AMY. Pray, Mr. Shorn—

SHORN. [*Interrupting her*] You waste your words.

AMY. [*Kneeling*] Heaven knows, such service is its own; yet here, upon my knees, I beg you to relent! [*Giltwood rushes from the closet*] Oh! I am lost!

GILT. Stay there, fixed upon your knees, as a living monument of woman's degradation! Oh! you vile hypocrite, who, through a life of dissimulation, have dared face the man who loved you! Out! I cast you from my house, as from my heart!—Out! to the world, and steal your daily crumbs, till your vile plunder choke you!

AMY. Steal! Good Heaven, Mr. Shorn, have you betrayed me?

SHORN. I swore to do it to yourself.

GILT. Ay! you hit upon a man at last, too honest to conceal your loathsome secrets. You have made deceit the practice of your life, until the world seems tinged to you with your own baseness![38]

THE BANKRUPT

AMY. Listen, Edward, listen! 'Twas for your sake—

GILT. [*Interrupting her*] Oh! wretch, to make me the excuse for your guilt!

AMY. Indeed, dear Edward—

GILT. [*Interrupting her*] I will not hear a word. And, though I am a ruined and degraded man, I will not suffer the further insult of being "deared" by you.[39] Go! you will lose nothing by separation. I have not a farthing, to clothe your proud back with silken finery, not one to pander to your luxurious appetites. Go! you may earn this splendor in the streets, by your own natural ways.

AMY. You reproach me with your own gifts, with the kindness which, I thought, came warm from your heart!—

GILT. Silence! I would not hear you speak. The sound of your voice offends my ears.[40]

AMY. You judge, not only without mercy, but without trial. Is this just, Edward?

GILT. Have I not heard enough? Your crime, under the rigor of the ancient law, would have exposed you to the populace. Such things as you, were in the old days stoned to death beyond the city's walls.

AMY. Has Mr. Shorn told you all?

SHORN. All.

GILT. All! ay, he made excuses for you, madam;—Talked of your pride in me, your love, and Heaven knows what! He is one of those rare moralists who make one virtue the excuse for a thousand vices. What, now! you'd have me take her to my bosom—forget my wrongs—Heaven—bless her—and what not? Would you not, Cato?[41]

SHORN. Yes, indeed I would.

AMY. Heaven be as merciful to you as you have been to me!

GILT. I knew he would; he is so soft of heart; but I am flint. Oh! you might talk yourself to death, upon this theme, and I would never relent. By Jove! it amazes me, to see you stand so long beneath my eye, and not dry up to dust! Madam, your impudence keeps at full pace with your crime.

AMY. And it amazes me, to see you so very passionate about a crime of which, as Mr. Shorn has told you, I am quite innocent.

GILT. Innocent perforce. Was your deceit to me innocent?[42] Is black white? or can you make it so, to my sight, by persisting in it? Have you looked upon your guilt until it seems pardonable in your own eyes?[43] Away!

AMY. Oh! Edward!—husband!—[*Approaching him*]

GILT. Touch me not, or I shall forget my manhood. Begone! your touch would defile a leper!

SHORN. Go, madam, go! You cannot help yourself by staying here. Time may do much. [*Apart to her*] Edward will feel the loss of you, and then—

GILT. [*Interrupting him*] Promise her nothing. If her sobs and tears move you to pity, or you breathe a hope of our reunion, in the sight of Heaven, I'll curse you.[44]

SHORN. Might I but say a word in her behalf?

GILT. Say it, and I will strike you!

SHORN. You hear, madam.

AMY. Edward, I beseech you to pardon me! I do not ask to be your wife again; I only beg to be allowed to remain near you—to wait upon you—to toil for you—to be your slave. Lest you should think my humility beneath me, it is not for your sake, alone, I ask it. A mother's heart cries through my lowly prayer. What will our young and helpless children do when I am far away? Whose hand shall smooth their pillows; or allay our little sufferers' agonies when sickness withers them? Whose hand shall join their rosy palms in prayer to the great power whom we so much offend? And if Heaven's wisdom should remove them hence, as it has done with one before their time—the child we buried in the spring, my husband; among the violets and early flowers, dropped like a severed bud—oh! then, what hand would not desecrate the dead, if it performed those offices of love which Heaven has sanctified to me alone? Think of it well. I only ask to live beside my children. I promise you, I will not vex your thoughts, by keeping my poor person in your sight.

GILT. Your female eloquence is lost on me. I prepared myself for these tricks of the tongue.

AMY. Edward, you are not yourself. I know that trade has hardened you, day by day, and that the absorbing lust of gain has slowly usurped the place in your heart which belongs to your family by right; but I never thought that you would so far forget your better nature, as to resist a plea such as this, even from the lips of a stranger. I am not weeping to make you pity me. I do not wish to soften you by any but rational means. These tears are shed over the disgrace which is about to fall upon our children. You have no right to forget them in your passion. You have no right—Oh! Edward, if my heart breaks down, and I am so choked with sorrow, my silence does not prove my cause unjust. [*Weeps*]

GILT. Have you done?

AMY. Never! While I can speak, I will raise my voice for my children—our children, Edward; and when my utterance fail me, nature shall echo me, in the stillness of your bosom, with tenfold power. You will regret this. I am of little value in your thoughts, perhaps; but when I am gone, there will be an empty chair ever before you, a familiar voice lost from your house; and in the dead of night, you'll stretch your arms out, in forgetful sleep, and start awake to find me gone. Better for you if I were dead—oh! would to Heaven I were!

GILT. Amen.

AMY. Oh! misery! Grief has quite worn me out. I would speak, if I could; for I am sure I might say more. There yet must be some slumbering warmth within your heart, which my faint breath might blow to flame. The children, husband—Edward and Amy, our repeated selves—what shall you say to them, when they turn up their innocent faces, and ask you for their mother? Answer me! I will be answered. Why, the thought of them could reconcile me to a felon—could make me gentle to him—if I heard their tender voices call him "father."

SHORN. Dear madam—

AMY. [*Interrupting him*] Sir, you interpose 'twixt man and wife; there is no power, save one on high, that has a right to whisper in their counsels! Speak, Edward Giltwood, speak! How has your unjust wrath provided for your children?

GILT. Take them along with you. How can I know if they are mine?

AMY. Ruffian! you have insulted me, and cast stain upon your guiltless children! Here, the pride of my poor, trampled sex can rise sublime against you! Till you spoke those words, the gates of love were open wide between us: now they have closed, forever, with a clash that startled those above us. Heaven grant, that its pity stopped the ears of our departed child against its father's voice, so that its saintly joy may not be marred! I will not ask you, sir, to seek our Nelly's grave, and keep it clear of weeds. No, no! the weeds, and noxious things, would sprout beneath your eyes. I will do all that duty, and such love as never entered in your callous heart, can do for Nelly's memory. Never, if you have any sense of shame, never dare meet me by that little grave!

GILT. Amy!—

AMY. Peace! I bore the foulest and most unjust taunts man ever heaped on woman, calmly, from your lips—I bore your brutal manner, when you cast me from you almost with a blow; but, now, you dare despise your offspring, soil the glittering links that Heaven let down to us—and in Heaven's name, and with Heaven's dread authority, I say to you that you, Edward Giltwood, have committed sacrilege! I, who have neither power nor will to judge you here, shall see you judged before all-powerful Heaven! Farewell! May some good spirit come to you, and bend your stubborn heart to better ways! My influence over you is gone forever. Look!—look in my eyes—and see my innocence! Look!—for you've taken your last gaze on me! [*Exit*]

GILT. Amy!—[*Falls*]

SHORN. Vengeance is mine, forever! [*Exit*]

SCENE 2: *A room in Mrs. Startle's house. Enter Mrs. Startle.*

MRS. S. Dear me! these dreadful reports about Edward Giltwood frighten me to think of. I always said that Amy should not have married him.[45] I wonder if she's really happy? Fashionable life is too often a refuge from domestic misery. Ah! me! rich dresses, and bright jewels, cover as many aching hearts as the rags of the beggar. When the heart of a refined and educated person once begin to ache, it aches indeed! I'll put on my bonnet, and run over to Amy; for it is in vain for me to try to be easy here. [*Going. Enter Amy, with her two children, followed by Crum*] My dear daughter, I am so delighted to see you! I was about to pay you a visit. You have brought the children, I see: then, you mean to spend the day with me? Why, here is Betsy, too!

CRUM. Yes, mam; I follered her, and I ain't done a-follerin' her yet. If I foller her fur enough, I'll foller her to Heaven; I know that, Mrs. Startle; and I'd jest like to hear anybody gainsay it.

MRS. S. Amy, what has happened? My child, you have been weeping!

AMY. I have had reason for more tears than my eyes could yield me. Mother, I will not pain you with doubts and surmises; I will tell you at once.

MRS. S. Then, speak, speak!

AMY. You remember the disgraceful charge that was once brought against me?

MRS. S. The old affair about the lace?

AMY. Yes.

MRS. S. Too well; yet you were entirely without blame.

CRUM. There! there! I knowed it! Her own mother says so! and if her own mother don't know, I'd like to know who does?

AMY. Pray, be quiet, Betsy.

CRUM. I'm a great, red blatherin', ugly fool—I know I am, Mrs. Giltwood; but unfortunately for me, and other folks, I've got a heart, Mrs. Giltwood, and it's always a-bustin' out—oh! dear! [*Weeps*]

MRS. S. Betsy, Betsy, you must be quiet.

CRUM. Well, I'm a-bein' quiet, as hard as I kin. I wish you'd send me where I kin cry in peace and happiness; and not be a-scoldin' me when—when—[*Weeps*]

MRS. S. Go into the little parlor, and take the children with you.

CRUM. Oh! I'm a-goin', I'm a-goin' I suppose, I've got ears; and, I suppose, they're a leetle too long for this company? Come along, darlin's! Betsy Crum's a jabberjaw and a gabbler—mind that! Your nuss can't be trusted, she can't. She's the wust woman you ever seed—she is—she is—[*Exit with children*]

AMY. Poor Betsy! she has been most kind to me in her own strange way! Mother, would you believe that when the whole world seemed against me, yonder uncouth creature broke into such a passion of indignant love, that my accusers fairly quailed before her? Ay, and she brought me all her little hoardings, and vowed to leave me if I did not take them. Oh! gracious Heaven, what I have endured! [*Weeps*]

MRS. S. My dear child, you must calm yourself, and tell me your troubles.

AMY. Yes, Mother. I have come to your bosom again for refuge, as I sought it many a time in my childhood. Alas! It seems to be the only refuge, next the grave, that is left to me.

MRS. S. You shall never ask shelter from me: I will give it, unasked[46] and bless you for receiving it.

AMY. Thank you, my own true mother!

MRS. S. Your thanks shame me: I can do so little. You are a mother; how would you act, if one of those weak beings who just left us, sought your protection from the storms of life?[47] Now, speak.

AMY. I have but little to say. The unhappy occurrence of my youth I never confided to my husband.

MRS. S. That was very wrong.

AMY. I know it. Say no more. I have been punished far beyond my fault. I meant to inform Edward of it a thousand times, but my heart always failed me.

MRS. S. Well?

AMY. A friend of Edward's, Mr. Shorn, became acquainted with my history, and under some dreadful vow, made to a dying man, he told my husband all.

MRS. S. Mean tattler!

AMY. No; I cannot judge his motives, nor can you; let Heaven arraign them.

MRS. S. Go on.

AMY. Edward grew furious at my deceit, and so—[*Pauses*]

MRS. S. And so?—

AMY. I came to you.

Mrs. S. For my advice, you mean? Well, then, let us go back to him. I will explain the matter to his satisfaction.

Amy. No; we cannot.

Mrs. S. Why?

Amy. He drove me from his house! [*Weeps*]

Mrs. S. Inhuman villain!

Amy. Hush! dear mother, hush! Edward may be passionate, unjust, even cruel; but he is no villain, on the word of one who has suffered the most from him.

Mrs. S. But all this cruelty for so small a thing!

Amy. So small! Mother, to me it seems the greatest sin a woman ever did.

Mrs. S. Amy, this is not all: you deceive me.

Amy. Indeed it is.

Mrs. S. In solemn truth?

Amy. Yes, by my father's soul, the only grave fault I ever committed towards my husband. Do you, too, doubt me?

Mrs. S. No, my child: But there has been some villainy afoot. Who is this Mr. Shorn?

Amy. An old friend of Edward's; I saw him this morning for the first time.

Mrs. S. Trust me, your husband thinks you guilty of some worse offense, than a piece of shamefaced concealment. Did he accuse you of nothing else?

Amy. No.—Why, Mother, deceit to him seems monstrous in my eyes. He made no charge save that. He only railed at me, and ordered me to quit the house.

Mrs. S. Amy, I believe, your husband is in error, and supposes you guilty of some other sin. Men do not turn their wives from their doors for such a woman-like fault as you committed.

Amy. Do you think so?

Mrs. S. Yes.

Amy. Bless you, Mother! I should so love to forgive him!

Mrs. S. Do not go back at once; but write to him, and ask a full explanation.

Amy. I will be guided by you. If that which you hope be true—

Mrs. S. I have no doubt of it.

Amy. No doubt! are you in earnest?

Mrs. S. Never more so.

Amy. [*Embracing her*] Come to my heart! You feel, dear Mother, how high it beats with your hopes! But Edward—Good Heaven! do you know that he is on the brink of ruin? and I might save him even now! What is the time?

Mrs. S. Just two o'clock.

Amy. Then, I must hasten: but one hour remains. Oh! what a faint-spirited wretch am I, to forget his necessities in my selfish griefs! Run, run!—order a carriage!

Mrs. S. But—

Amy. [*Interrupting her*] Oh! do not speak. I will explain when I return. I am not going to Edward. But, now, be quick, if you would save us both! [*Exit Mrs. Startle*] How slowly she walks! Oh! had I wings!—[*Enter Shorn*] Ha! Mr. Shorn, you enter unannounced!

Shorn. But not unwelcomed, I trust.

Amy. Has Edward—

Shorn. [*Interrupting her*] No! nor does he deserve to feel the blessings of forgiveness. A man who casts his wife off, on so slight an occasion, deserves no pity. I kept my painful vow to Shelvill: I told your husband all, most circumstantially; yet while I did it, I hoped it might have no effect. I even pleaded for you; but when I saw how he still raged, I thought him mad, and I left him.

Amy. You did not act the friend.

Shorn. Not I, by Heaven! I left the bankrupt beggar to his fate!

Amy. [*Aside*] Let me keep calm, and hear.

Shorn. A man who, in his passion, would renounce the only blessing of his life, is like a drunkard in his cups, who spills the precious wine that gives him joy. Pshaw! I consider him beneath my anger, the hollow, weak-brained ingrate! You squandered love upon a fool who thus repays you.

Amy. I fear you speak too truly.

Shorn. Do you know that he has already made you infamous throughout the town?—that he has whined his wrongs into every ear unmanly enough to listen? Not content with his first insufficient charge, he has tried to establish it by a lie.

Amy. How?

Shorn. He has accused you of infidelity, spread the base slander far and near, and set the whole world hissing at your name.

Amy. Villain!—You, you, I mean! [*Aside*]

Shorn. Damned villain! I, too, am wrung into his obscene fraud. He charged me with being the partner to your guilt.

Amy. Shame! oh! shame!

Shorn. Does he deserve the least remnant of your love?

AMY. How can you ask? Now this secret fiend begins to unfold himself. I must be patient, and lure him on. [*Aside*]

SHORN. But were there one who really loved you?

AMY. No one could love a woman so traduced.

SHORN. Oh! yes; and love you better for that cause. One, whom the world has wronged, as it has you—one, whose innocence was no protection from obloquy—one, to whom you seem a being marked out by Heaven as his only mate.

AMY. Is there my equal in misery?[48] Oh! I would weep away my wretched life with him, if I might discover him, sitting in tears, amid his realm of grief!

SHORN. Behold him at your feet! [*Kneels*]

AMY. You, you, James?

SHORN. Yes, Amy. The false world has already coupled our names with infamy; let us mock the slander with our mutual happiness.

AMY. Happiness! Oh! where is happiness?

SHORN. It exists, even for us. There is an island of the southern seas, once visited by me, long years ago;—a piece of Paradise, which Heaven's relenting hand severed from Eden, and, with jealous care, hid from mankind in the wide waste of sea. A place all balm and sunshine, where rude winds are laid in heavy slumbers; while, above the palms, waved on by gentlest zephyrs, fan to life odors that mock the Persian's[49] mimic arts.[50] There fruits, that seem as if they drew their birth from the thick golden veins beneath the soil, hang from each bending branch their mellow offerings to the thirsty lip. There all is peace. The jarring foot of trade can never break harmonious nature's music.[51] Oh! could you tread that fair oasis of the seas, its charms would find a voice in you; and nature, speaking with your lips would say, this place was surely formed by Heaven, and, with its grand solemnities, forever consecrated to undying love!

AMY. How beautiful! And I may be the goddess of this wondrous isle?

SHORN. It's only one. The goddess of the isle, of all things in it, and of me. Fly, dearest, fly! for even now, perchance, the hungry minions of man's impious laws are on your lover's track.

AMY. Yes, in a moment I shall fly.—But, while I gaze upon your face, strange memories reassemble. My fond heart whispers me that your too winning voice was heard before; and that your features have, in times long passed, looked, like a cloud-girt star, upon my dreary path of life, then vanished again, and left me desolate.

SHORN. True, true! Know me for one, changed in all things but this, a deep and passionate love for you; at once the curse and blessing of my life.

I am the old made new, the abhorred made lovable, the dead returned to life —know me as James Shelvill!

AMY. As a despicable and shallow rogue! Oh! I could laugh, till echo answered me, to think how all your arts and snares have fallen to naught before the simple craft of woman's love!

SHORN. Traitoress!

AMY. I read your black heart like an open book. Now there is not a word of yours, an act of my husband's, not a point in my own history, that is not clear to me. I see it all. Lies, lies, and only lies, have brought about this monstrous nothing. I thought it out, while you described your gorgeous islands of the southern seas. Ha! ha! [*Laughing*] You silly trickster! Now, I will rebegin my sunny life: your clouds have blown away. I'll save my husband, win his love again, bring the old peace back to my frightened home, heal every wound inflicted by your hand—so that not even a scar of malice shall remain; and, as for you, let Satan do his will,—you are beneath my punishment. [*Going*]

SHORN. Where are you going?

AMY. I will answer you; I have received such blessings at your hands. First, Mr. Shelvill, I go to save my husband's credit; then, straight to his heart, to make it bound with joy.

SHORN. [*Drawing a pistol*] Another step, and I will fire!

AMY. [*Advancing toward the door*] Lo! it is taken!—fire! [*Crum steals behind Shorn*]

SHORN. Dare you!—[*Points the pistol. Crum seizes him, behind, around the arms*]

CRUM. Yes, fire, fire, if you can! Run, mistress, run! [*Exit Amy*] Ho! tug your fill! If I can't hold you, Betsy Crum's big arms have scoured pots and pans to no purpose. Ugh!—ugh! It's pull Dick, pull devil!

SHORN. Let go, you she beast, or I'll shoot you!

CRUM. Blaze away!

SHORN. Take that! [*He strikes her down. As he rushes toward the door, enter Pike*]

PIKE. [*Tapping Shorn on the shoulder*] I beg your pardon, Captain, but you can't pass there. [*Other policemen appear at the door*] How's Joseph, Betsy?

CRUM. Why, bless my eyes, if that ain't the P'lice!

PIKE. Yes; you see I make myself at home wherever I go. By the by, Captain, I'd rather not have that revolver pointed at me. Not that I care at all—because there are others, just like me, at the door—only I fear, you may get yourself into trouble with it. It might go off accidentally, you know; and that would be dreadful. That's a good, sensible fellow, now. [*Takes the pistol*]

SHORN. Sirrah, you are insulting. What is the meaning of this?

PIKE. Well, now, that is gamey! Why, Captain Shorton, you are arrested.

CRUM. Is he?

PIKE. Yes, indeed!

CRUM. By the lore?

PIKE. By the law, my dear.

CRUM. [*Sings*] Forward two!—ballinsay!—up and down the middle! [*Dances up to Shorn*]

SHORN. Silence, scullion! Officer, am I to be outraged in this manner?

PIKE. You must be decent, Betsy, indeed, you must. I've seen as fine a girl as you dance on nothing, with nobody for her partner; and she began by being only a little cruel. You must move along, Betsy,—as much as I desire your company. [*Points to the door*]

CRUM. Oh! you're all alike—you're all alike! Everybody must have a snub at Betsy Crum,—they must. I jest might as well be a lobster, in a kittle, as try to be happy in this world 'er hot water—I might—I might—[*Exit*]

SHORN. Officer—

PIKE. [*Interrupting him*] Why, don't you know me, Captain? Don't you remember the old French gentleman who played billiards with you, in New Orleans, for weeks together?—That was Mr. Pike! Don't you remember the black-faced ruffian who tried so hard, and so often, to get into your Association,—though you wouldn't have him?—That was Mr. Pike! Don't you remember your roommate in the crowded hotel, at San Francisco, whom you caught looking through your trunks, in his sleep, only in his sleep, I assure you?—That was Mr. Pike! Don't you remember the young swell who got drunk with you—I did, but you didn't—in Charleston?—That was Mr. Pike! Don't you remember the gentleman's porter, [*Bows, scrapes, and mimics his former character*] who carried over the gentleman's baggage this morning, and would fancy a certain tin box that didn't belong to him?—That was Mr. Pike!

"Oh! don't you remember young Alice, Ben Bolt?"

In short, I am Mr. Pike; and I hope, for the future, you will remember me.

SHORN. [*Laughing*] You seem to be a jolly sort of a treacherous dog, Mr. Pike, and I admire you.

PIKE. [*Bowing*] Oh! I admire you, too, Captain, if you come to compliments. You gave me my education, and I ought to.

SHORN. In what, pray?

PIKE. In villainy. Now, Captain, I have made you a study, for three interesting years; and I should like to know why you were so imprudent as to leave that tin box in your room. It was a great pity, indeed it was. I fear, you have let your feelings run away with your usual caution. Haven't you been in love or in hate, or something? If you had carried the cool head, for your peculiar affairs, that distinguished you so long in California, I should not be here with this warrant. [*Shows a paper*]

SHORN. I am completely ignorant of your meaning.

PIKE. Prudent at last! The cipher, in which the papers were written, was no go. We got hold of a poet—a great genius people will say, after he's dead—and he read off the cipher, as if it had been[52] printed. Mr. Poe is waiting at the office to explain his system to you.

SHORN. Look here, Pike! [*Produces a pocketbook*] Here are twenty thousand dollars in—

PIKE. [*Interrupting him*] In good money?

SHORN. See, for yourself. [*Gives the pocketbook*]

PIKE. Well, I'll just put it into my pocket. You might try this trick on some weaker brother of mine. I tell you, it's no use, Captain: a shipload of gold wouldn't bribe me. The pride I feel in taking you is more than all you can offer. If you have any reasonable wish, I'll grant it, before I lock you up; for I admire you, Captain,—upon my soul, I do!

SHORN. You shall repent this usage, when my innocence is established.

PIKE. I shall be ready to repent then. Let me tell you, I've got you pinned to a board, like a beetle in a museum; and all your wriggling won't alter it. —So come along!

SHORN. On my way to the magistrate, I demand to see my friend, Mr. Giltwood.

PIKE. For what?

SHORN. To procure me bail, if necessary.

PIKE. Cool as January! You're a great man, by Jupiter! For how long?

SHORN. About five minutes.

PIKE. Granted! Now let us be jogging; his honor, the mayor, is waiting for us. You shall see Mr. Giltwood; but you mustn't try to run, or talk, or to make signs. Pop's the word, if you do. Here, Bill and Jim! [*The other Policemen advance*] You walk before the Captain, and you behind; I'll enjoy the pleasure of his society. If he makes a motion, you know what: and keep your hands on your pistols. Step on lively, Captain!

SHORN. [*Aside*] Infernal fate!—Now for my last move on the board of life! The game is up with me; yet they who won shall rue their victory yet![53]

[*Exeunt*]

ACT V.

Scene 1: *Mr. Tapeley's office. Tapeley discovered writing at a table, surrounded by books, papers, etc.*

Tap. Here's my last will and testament. I, who have made so many for other people, should needs set about one for myself. Perhaps, it would be better, if there was some one, by the name of Tapeley, to leave my money with; but, as there is no one near me in blood, I'll even leave it to one near me in heart. Amy Startle—or Giltwood, as they call you now—you shall have every dollar of it.[54] Amy will employ my wealth to good purposes, I know. By the by, I'll go over and make friends with her again; and if she seem pleased to see poor old Paul Tapeley, once more, why, by Jove, I'll stick to this will. I was all wrong about Giltwood, it seems; and hang me, if I don't beg his pardon for my opposition to his marriage. By the way, I had some notes of his, that fell due today. I wish they had not been sold to this Mr. Shorn, as Elton writes me in confidence—Why, in confidence, forsooth? I should like to make Amy a present of those notes. Elton was a fool for selling them, without permission. I'll withdraw my account from him. The numbskull! not to know—[*Enter Amy*] Why, Amy Startle—Giltwood, I mean; but I'm always forgetting—bless your pretty face! let an old man kiss it! [*Kisses her*] I have been thinking of you, for a long time past, and I was about coming to see you.

Amy. It was very kind in you, Mr. Tapeley.—

Tap. [*Interrupting her*] Booh! Mr. Tapeley! Call me Uncle Paul, as you used to. You must forget the coldness there has been between us. I was in fault; and I'll ask your husband's pardon, frankly; and—There, there! read that paper. [*Offers the will*]

Amy. Excuse me—Don't you know—[*Bursts into tears*]

Tap. What is the matter with my darling? Quit, Amy, quit! You're a naughty girl; and I'll cry, like a fool, if you don't behave yourself. [*Wipes his eyes*]

Amy. Uncle Paul!—Oh! you are too good! [*Embraces him*]

Tap. Hey! Heaven bless you!—there it is!—Uncle Paul, just as you used to lisp it!

Amy. Edward is in trouble. I fear he cannot pay the notes you hold against him.—

Tap. [*Interrupting her*] He need not. Lord bless me! I'm not so badly off as that. 'Twas all in business—business, Amy.—But, by the by, they have passed out of my hands; or I'd give them to you, to make little soldier-caps for your thumbs, as you used to in old times. Ah! Amy, Amy—

Amy. [*Interrupting him*] Where are they?

Tap. They were bought by some Mr. Shorn, a stranger to me—

Amy. [*Interrupting him*] But not to me. Alas! Edward is lost, and all my labor in vain!

Tap. Lost!—hey!—how? What do you mean?

Amy. Shorn is a villain, bent on our destruction.

Tap. He is?—well?

Amy. If he has the notes, Edward is ruined.

Tap. Can't they be paid?

Amy. No; Edward's misfortunes—

Tap. [*Laughing*] Ha! ha! ha! You little goose! Can't Paul Tapeley pay them?

Amy. Can that be managed, if Mr. Shorn refuse?

Tap. Why, you helpless, sweet know-nothing! we'll see if it can't be managed. [*Writes*] Here, Jacob! [*Enter a Servant*] Run over to Mr. Elton's with this—quickly too. [*Looks at his watch*] My stars! 'tis nearly three o'clock! If you are not there before three, don't come back to this house. Do you hear?

Ser. Yes, sir. [*Exits hastily*]

Amy. But if Mr. Shorn will not take—

Tap. [*Interrupting her*] My little lady, I advise you, as a friend, not to be tying your silly brains up into such hard knots. Shorn can't refuse: because it is not in the way of business to do so.

Amy. Business! Oh! that's enough! I never wish to hear that word again. But are you now sure that Edward's credit is safe?

Tap. Has he other obligations?

Amy. I believe not.

Tap. Then he is entirely safe.

Amy. Uncle Paul!

Tap. What, Amy?

Amy. I wish to kiss you.

Tap. I'll not flinch. [*She kisses him*] Oh! you sweet, little wretch! This is the way you crawled into poor, old Paul Tapeley's heart, long before you could walk alone.

Amy. And, then, Uncle Paul, I wish to lay my head on your dear, kind bosom, to have a good cry; and, then, I have something so terrible to tell you,—all about Edward, and me, and the children—[*Enter Pike suddenly*]

Tap. Go away, man!

PIKE. I have him, sir—I have him; and you promised to appear against him, you know? I took him, so pat, in Mrs. Startle's house—

AMY. Mrs. Startle!

PIKE. Yes, mam.—Oh! Mrs. Giltwood, your servant. [*Bows*]

AMY. You seem to know me.

PIKE. I know pretty much everybody. My name is Pike, of the police; and it's a part of my business to know everybody.

AMY. By whom did you arrest at Mrs. Startle's house?

PIKE. Captain Shorton.

AMY. Captain Shorton! Who is he?

PIKE. Well, there is a poser? I couldn't tell you in a week. However, he was your guest of a day, Mr. Shorn.

AMY. Indeed!

PIKE. Yes, mam. Shelvill, alias Shorton, alias Shorn. That's the order of his names. I've got him all straight at last.

TAP. And he has been your guest, Amy?

AMY. It seems so.

TAP. Why, he is the most consummate scoundrel on the face of the earth!

AMY. For what did you arrest him?

PIKE. For every crime on the statute books, for every sin in Holy Writ; among other things, for frightening a certain lady with that old lace affair.

AMY. What do you know of that?

PIKE. Why, bless your soul—

TAP. [*Interrupting him*] Mr. Pike, I wish you distinctly to understand that Mrs. Giltwood's soul does not require blessing.

PIKE. Oh! well, I beg your pardon, mam. But, as I was saying, I arrested you, on the shopkeeper's oath, who was pushed forward by this same James Shelvill. I saw it all.

AMY. That man has been the bane of my life. But I was innocent, Mr. Pike; you know that?

PIKE. As a lamb unborn. I knew it, as soon as I put my eye upon you.

TAP. Poh! Amy, don't trouble yourself about that ridiculous business. If anybody doubts your innocence, let him come here, and I'll hammer it into his head with my cane.

AMY. It has been a cause of much recent sorrow to me, Uncle Paul. To think that Shelvill was received as a friend by Edward!

PIKE. They were old cronies, long before your marriage, Mrs. Giltwood. Shelvill is with your husband now.—

AMY. What?

PIKE. He wished to speak with Mr. Giltwood, and I granted it.

THE BANKRUPT

AMY. Madness!

PIKE. He is quite safe: I have a guard of armed policemen 'round him. Trust Pike, mam.

AMY. He is now with Mr. Giltwood?

PIKE. Yes.

AMY. What imprudence! Who may tell of what diabolical scheme he is now making Edward the victim!

PIKE. By Jupiter! I never thought of that.

TAP. Pike, you are something very like a fool, I fear.

AMY. Come, Uncle Paul!

TAP. Where are you going?

AMY. To Edward. I am in agony. Come, come!

TAP. But I can't come without my hat. [*Looking about him*]

AMY. Yes, yes, you can. [*Dragging him off*]

TAP. But I won't!—Oh! there it is. [*Picks up his hat*] Now, Amy! come Pike!

NEWSBOY. [*Without*] Herald!—Herald!—Extra Herald! 'Rival of the steamer *Oc-ci-dent!*

AMY. Hark! [*Pauses*]

PIKE. Yes, mam; the *Occident's* in at last, dismasted and crippled, but all safe. Another thing, mam: the fellow who set fire to your husband's warehouse, one Pete Dreggs, has been arrested. He confessed it, too, while laboring under his old complaint—a rush of rum to the stomach. But not a word of his Captain—not a word—for love, rum or money. Ain't it queer, Mr. Tapeley?

AMY. Mr. Pike, despite your stern office, you are a messenger of good to me.

TAP. Yes, Amy; even the law has its bright side.

NEWSBOY. [*Without, and more distant*] Herald!—Extra Herald! 'Rival of the *Oc-ci-dent!*

AMY. Hear that, Uncle Paul! Its music will cheer us on our way.—Dear Heaven! it seems to me as if the angels were singing all together! [*Exeunt*]

NEWSBOY. [*Without faintly*] Herald!—Extra Herald! 'Rival of the steamer *Oc-ci-dent!*

SCENE 2: *The drawing-room in Giltwood's house. Giltwood discovered sitting on a sofa. A clock strikes three.*

GILT. [*Rushing forward*] Oh! Heaven! I am a bankrupt!—Why should I rave? Why does not the blow stun or kill me? I had not the strength to meet my ruin at my post, like a brave man; so, like a coward, I have slunk away, to hide me from the world's contempt. Vain act! My self-contempt pursues me here, and makes this solitude more odious than man's sneer could be. And I, bereft of all, have no bosom, to lay this aching forehead on; no tongue, to sing of hope, amidst the dreadful tempest that bursts around me.—Oh! helpless misery![55] It seems to me, as if all the curses of a bad man's life were gathered in one mass, and hurled from Heaven on my devoted head. [*Enter Shorn, accompanied by Policemen, who remain at the door*]

SHORN. Edward! [*Embracing him*]

GILT. It is all over, James. I am a broken merchant!

SHORN. Heaven grant, that may be the worst!

GILT. If you have any mercy, do not mention the other degrading thing: I will not hear her name.

SHORN. Edward, do you see those officers?

GILT. What then? I have done nothing to offend the law.

SHORN. The law thinks otherwise. Those men are here to arrest you for firing your warehouse.

GILT. What foul injustice! It needs only that a man should be weak, to find oppressors at every corner.

SHORN. Be patient, if you can.

GILT. Talk not of patience to a desperate wretch, without a single hold on life. I have pistols here; and as I am next door to madness, with my sufferings, I will not be taken alive!

SHORN. I pity you sincerely, Edward. I have known men who, in your case, would not have borne this malice of fortune tamely,—brave hearts who would rush on death, rather than wait his tardy coming, and find within his arms a sweet release from all their torments. [*Opens a pistol case upon the table, and gazes at it thoughtfully*] Were I in your state—so abject, so forlorn, so hopeless—I would—[*Pauses*]

GILT. What would you do?

SHORN. I cannot tell but I should be tempted to blow my brains out.

GILT. That would settle all. One pang would cure the aches of many years. Do me a favor,—the last I'll ever ask: Withdraw those villains from the door one moment.

SHORN. I'll try. [*Going*]

GILT. James, a word. I am going where I may not hear of her any more; and, I suppose that, in a situation such as this, it were not unmanly in me to ask of Amy—

SHORN. She has fled, I know not where.

THE BANKRUPT

GILT. Avaunt! Your words sting me like a serpent's fangs! [*Exit Shorn with the Policemen*] Why do I pause? [*Takes up a pistol*] 'Tis but a gentle motion, a mere touch of the finger—and then all is darkness,—unending and untroubled sleep. There's but one thing: Could I only see her and bid her a last farewell, I would not falter in this act.[56] Oh! shame upon me! I love her still! Courage, thou bankrupt wittol!—Courage, thou beggarly incendiary! It asks but resolution. [*Puts the pistol to his head*]

AMY. [*Without, faintly*] Edward!—Edward!

GILT. Was that voice from Heaven? [*Lays down the pistol*]

AMY. [*Without, nearer*] Edward! Edward! [*Enters, followed by Tapeley, Pike, with Shorn in custody, and others*]

GILT. Amy, herself!

AMY. [*Falling upon his bosom*] My husband! Nay, do not put me from you. I am pure; all these will bear witness. You are the only one, in the wide world, who thinks me guilty. Even that bad man is dumb: he dare not, now, deny it.

PIKE. Speak, Captain—if you wish to lie a little more—speak out!

GILT. How is this?

PIKE. Simple enough. Mr. Shelvill Shorton Shorn is the most outrageous scoundrel in the whole human menagerie of such beasts, and you have been his victim. There's a short character, which I am willing to give him in writing.

GILT. James!

SHORN. Pshaw! go bill and coo with your prodigal wife! I am sick of you all.

AMY. Edward, your notes are paid—the *Occident* is safely arrived—the children—Ha! ha! ha! [*Laughing*] Oh! Heaven, spare my reason!

GILT. Amy!—dear Amy!—[*Embracing her*]

AMY. You forgive me, Edward?

GILT. I should ask mercy, on my knees, of you.

AMY. 'Twas not your fault. There is much to be explained.—

SHORN. And something to be done! Think you my plans shall reach this sickly end? that you shall riot in your happiness, while I rot in a dungeon? Think you, Amy Startle, that you shall not suffer a long life through, pining to death by slow degrees, with a most deathly sickness of the heart? Let this be the answer to my question! [*Snatches up the pistol and levels it at Giltwood. As he fires, Amy springs before her husband; and Pike, who, during Shorn's speech, has stolen close to him, strikes up his arm*]

PIKE. Very well intended, Captain! Indeed, I may say that your intentions are always good. But, luckily for the security of Mrs. Giltwood's life, and your own valuable neck, I was just in time to save her from the grave, and you from the gallows. Come along, you murderer at heart! [*Seizes him*] They are, perhaps, twisting hemp for you in the rope-walks;—who knows? At all events, you have done enough for the present. So come along!—Easy, easy, now!

SHORN. The devil palsy your officious arm! Hands off! [*Dashes Pike aside*] I'll walk alone!

PIKE. Isn't he game? [*Exit Shorn slowly, followed by Pike and Policemen*]

AMY. Edward, do you need further proof of this man's villainy?

GILT. No, my dear wife.

AMY. Wife! wife! yes, that is the word I wished to hear again! You hear that, he acknowledged me; and the foul blot cast on my children, by their mistaken father, is wiped away forever! [*Enter Crum, running, followed by Mrs. Startle with Amy's children*]

CRUM. [*Panting*] Oh! mam, am I in time?

AMY. For what, Betsy?

CRUM. To see Shorn hung. I heared all about it. And I thought P'lice Pike 'ud hang 'im up, in the middle of the room, like a chandelier. And, then, we'd all dance around 'im and be so happy! And then—

GILT. [*Interrupting her*] Be quiet, Betsy!

CRUM. Mrs. Giltwood, all I've got to say—

AMY. [*Interrupting her*] Be quiet, Betsy!

CRUM. I vow, Mrs. Startle—

MRS. S. Be quiet, Betsy! be quiet!

CRUM. Mr.—What's your name—

TAP. Silence! woman!

CRUM. Well, I'm a-goin'—I'm a-goin', Mrs. Giltwood! and when you see me agin, you'll be glad to hear me talk.

AMY. Where are you going, Betsy?

CRUM. To the deef and dum asylum, Mrs. Giltwood, where you think I ought'er be.

AMY. Oh! Betsy, Betsy, how foolish you talk!

CRUM. I can't help it, mam. Natur gave me a tongue, and it 'ud be flyin' in the face of Providence not to use it. Well, mam, I suppose, I'm out of place in the drawin'-room, you think? I suppose, the kitchin is Betsy Crum's speer? Very well, mam; I'll go to my speer—I'll go to my speer! I'll go—I'll go—I'll go—[*Exit loftily*]

AMY. Edward, embrace your children. Only long years of kindness can pardon the wrong you did them. Uncle Paul, shake Edward's hand.

Tap. We shall be friends for the future, Edward.

Gilt. Willingly. My hand and heart are both at Amy's command. [*They shake hands*]

Amy. As they have always been. You must be happy, Edward; yet, in your happiness, do not forget the troubles that have passed. The fruits of sorrow are more wholesome and lasting, than the fleeting blossoms of joy. I hope the storm of today may clear your mind for tomorrow; though I would not have you slight, amid your prosperity, the lesson taught to the bankrupt.[57]

THE END

NOTES

THE BANKRUPT

[1] MS II is a typescript bearing the title: *A Commercial Crisis: A Play: by: George H. Boker: Philadelphia*: 1886.

[2] MS I originally gave the remainder of this speech as follows. The later deletions were followed in MS II:

". . . Your unjust tyranny imposed upon me my first degree in crime—branded me with a felon's name—poisoned the purity of my young mind—suspected me until I deserved suspicion—and then howled me forth to destruction. Ten years ago, I left you poor, persecuted, yet innocent; now I return to you rich, powerful, yet guilty. Oh! what a change! The hypocrites, who trod my boyish virtue out under their merciless feet, bow their obsequious foreheads to the Dust before the full-grown criminal. I spit upon your adulation! I will make you sob in your houses, and lament in your streets! I will cram you with new grief, until it equals my old sorrow! Every step, over your pitiless tones, renews the recollection of my sufferings, and recalls the terrible curse with which my soul cursed you when my parched and choking throat refused me utterance. For ten long years I have cherished that curse. For ten long years I have toiled for the golden power to make it deadly; and, at length, I will pour it upon you, not in words, but in deeds that shall seem rained over you by the unsparing hand of fate. Woe! to you who trampled upon my reputation!—Woe! to her who trampled upon my heart! I will glide among you like a serpent; no rustle of the grass, no warning rattle, shall betray my progress, until you feel my fangs at your hearts. There was but one man, among this multitude of men, who raised a voice in my behalf when the world disowned me. Now, Heaven, hear one swear! if need be, over his ruin, over all that he holds dear, over his very corpse, will I stride to my revenge!—stern as justice, calm as religion, inflexible as fate! You, who keep watch above us, know that I love him, that the only prayers I ever breathed were for him—register my vow! If he stands in my path of vengeance, I will crush him—I will crush my own heart—but I will not turn aside. This will I do; and then, unnatural mother, city of my birth and infamy, farewell forever! [*Enter Dreggs*]"

[3] MS II reads "around."

[4] MS I reads "heirs," later changed to "ones."

[5] In MS I the following is deleted. It is omitted in MS II: "You never had a match in your life, and you never aughter have, you lonely, miserable, rickety, bad piece of furnitur! —Ugh."

[6] MS II reads "awake."

[7] MS II reads "on."

[8] MS II omits this sentence.

[9] MS II omits this speech, ending the act with Amy's speech, preceding.

[10] In MS I the following is deleted. It is omitted in MS II: "Some of the richest storehouses in the place have been consumed."

[11] In MS I the following is deleted. It is omitted in MS II: "No! as soon shall the tremendous cataract, that thunders on our northern borders, pause, and leap back across its rocky barrier, or ebb into a dull, inactive pool, as I pause in my onward course."

[12] In MS I the following is deleted. It is omitted in MS II: "And groans of anguish? Oh! ye sterile plains, that stretch your boundless wastes between us and the new found land of gold, have I not filled your desolation with my groans? Have I not made you more horrible with my cries than when the famished wolf, with dripping jaws, howls on the bloody track of the fear-frantic bison? Are not the restless winds of California still doleful with my sighs? Have I

THE BANKRUPT 117

not climbed, for weary hours, through the crumbling snows of the Nevada, stood upon their topmost peaks, and shrieked my anguish into Heaven? Who heard me then?"

13 In MS I the following is deleted. It is omitted in MS II: "Nature lay dumb before me; the great hills shut up their reeky ears, and refused even to echo me. On, then! I will avenge myself on all of you. You, reluctant nature, shall not now deny me your harmful elements. Your fire consumes, at once, my enemies goods, his love for his wife, and her half-broken heart. Ruin hangs over him, like a tottering rock; and my hands shall speed and direct the fall."

14 In MS I the following is deleted. It is omitted in MS II: "Hundreds of his tools, who think themselves his comrades, have passed through my hands; yet I could not wring the slightest sign from them."

15 In MS I the following is deleted. It is omitted in MS II: "He fills up his ranks, as fast as I can thin them."

16 "should" deleted in MS I, omitted in MS II.

17 MS II reads "come to consider."

18 In MS I the following is deleted. It is omitted in MS II: "I have been all astray a thousand times."

19 In MS I the following is deleted. It is omitted in MS II: "The banks have promised me more than enough."

20 In MS I the following is deleted. It is omitted in MS II: "For if I should not hit upon the right ones, or should excite his suspicions, all my plans would be knocked in the head."

21 In MS I the following is deleted. It is omitted in MS II: "His trunks have not come from the hotel yet; so I'll go there, as a porter, and carry them over for him. There is not much use in that though. I have rummaged through his trunks a dozen times, without finding anything but the wardrobe of a gentleman."

22 In MS I the following is deleted. It is omitted in MS II: "The sagacious ancients pictured Love as a blind child, only to show what real power was lodged in his seeming weakness. That same sightless infant could make Jupiter tremble amid his thunderbolts, and brawny Hercules sob beneath his lion's skin."

23 In MS I the following is deleted. It is omitted in MS II: "You spat upon it—made it a joke among his acquaintances;"

24 In MS I the following is deleted. It is omitted in MS II: "while his hot pulses smote against my hand, like the vibrations of a tense-drawn chord."

25 In MS I the following is deleted. It is omitted in MS II: "She struck the arrow through my heart, and I have crawled, far from my home, to perish in strange lands."

26 The speech originally concluded: "Yet bear no hate to her." The phrase is deleted in MS I and omitted in MS II.

27 "twenty" is deleted in MS II.

28 In MS I the following is deleted. It is omitted in MS II: "Go talk to despots of your base designs! Heaven is too near this liberal land of ours, to suffer the stain of public or private tyranny to pollute us."

29 In MS I the following is deleted. It is omitted in MS II: "[*Aside*] what a dull fool is a man in a passion."

30 In MS I the following is deleted. It is omitted in MS II: "If Mr. Shorn wants to take naps in day time, he may make his bed up hisself."

31 In MS I the following is deleted. It is omitted in MS II: "I'll tell you why, Miss Crum, because I know you to be a lady of sense, edecation and discreetion—it's because he tumbles it so, and gives you so much trouble to make it up."

32 Omitted in MS II.

33 Omitted in MS II.

34 In MS I the following is deleted. It is omitted in MS II: "Now, sir, I do not believe you to be the devil, nor my other counsellor Saint Anthony; and I tell you both that, if you felt as I feel, you would each show an agony equal to mine."

35 In MS I the following is deleted. It is omitted in MS II: "The world is sinking into a refined barbarism, to which man's savage state seems noble."

36 In MS I the following is deleted. It is omitted in MS II: "I have thought this matter over, step by step, I may be passionate in my determination, but I am fixed as the star above the pole."

37 In MS I the following is deleted. It is omitted in MS II: "I abjure the common softness of our nature."

38 In MS I the following is deleted. It is omitted in MS II: "and your jaundiced eye makes all things yellow."

39 In MS I the following is deleted. It is omitted in MS II: "Repeat that word, and I cannot answer what use my anger may make of my hands."

40 In MS I the following is deleted. It is omitted in MS II: " . . . Your breath is poisonous, and breeds a pestilence."

41 This speech, in MS I, is written as blank verse, although not all the lines have initial capitals.

42 In MS I the following is deleted. It is omitted in MS II: "Can the soul be foul, and the body pure?"

43 In MS I the following is deleted. It is omitted in MS II: "Then, know that only long use can make it seem so. When, for the first time, it bursts upon a fresh and natural sense, it shows as loathsome as an inclosed tomb, foul with the storage of an hundred years."

44 In MS I the following is deleted. It is omitted in MS II: " . . . with all the rhetoric of my wrongs."

45 In MS I the following is deleted. It is omitted in MS II: " . . . and she did it against mine, her father's, and all her friends' wishes. But, since their union, she seemed so happy, and he has been so kind to her, that I began to be reconciled to the match. Then, she became such a woman of fashion, and dashed out at so grand a rate, that her own mother hardly knew her."

46 In MS I the following is deleted. It is omitted in MS II: " . . . whether you be worthy of it or not. . . ."

47 In MS I Mrs. Startle's speech is broken by the following speech of Amy, later deleted in MS I and omitted in MS II: "If I acted as you do—and there is One above us who knows how hard it is to do our simplest duty thoroughly—he would more than repay me with the content that springs from him alone."

48 In MS I the following is deleted. It is omitted in MS II: "—a king of sorrow, to whom I could be queen?"

49 MS I reads "gentlest mimic arts."

50 In MS I the following is deleted. It is omitted in MS II: "—rich perfumes, drowsy with delicious rest, and more luxurious than Paphian's dreams. There birds, as brilliant as the gems that strew this island's shores flame through the ashy dawn—sing up the rising sun—blow the triumphant clarions of his daily march—and lull his rest, as in his grand repose, he lies along the glowing bosom of the West, calm as a weary god."

51 In MS I the following is deleted. It is omitted in MS II: " . . . for she, distrustful of our tyrant race, has fenced her isle with edged coral—reefs, wall beyond wall, o'er which the angry waves shout high defiance to intruding barks."

52 For "had been" MS II reads "were."

53 This sentence is omitted in MS II.

54 In MS I the following is deleted. It is omitted in MS II: "No foundling hospitals, or almshouses, to fatten the directors, and starve the poor under their care, after I am gone. No, indeed! I have no desire for that kind of selfish glory. If I leave my money in good private hands, I shall do the world more real benefit than if I squander it on any insolent set of thankless speculators, who abuse the name and uses of a corporation. I would rather have my good deeds remembered in Heaven than on my tombstone."

55 This sentence omitted in MS II.

56 MS II reads "Could I only see Amy, even in her guilt—loathsome with sin and laughter—making my misery her jest—could I only see her," etc.

57 MS II reads "taught by a Commercial Crisis."

GLAUCUS

DRAMATIS PERSONAE[1]

GLAUCUS, *a Greek nobleman*

ARBACES, *an Egyptian prince*

CALENUS, *a priest of Isis*

APAECIDES, *a neophyte priest of Isis, brother of Ione*

CLODIUS, *a Roman, friend of Glaucus*

SALLUST, *a Roman gentleman*

PRAETOR, *a governor of Pompeii*

DUDUS, *a Roman fop*

LYDON, *a gladiator*

BURBO, *a retired gladiator*

SAPHAX, *a freedman of Glaucus*

IONE, *a Greek lady*

NYDIA, *a flower girl*

STRATONICE, *wife of Burbo*

GLADIATORS, LICTORS, ATTENDANTS, FREEDMEN, SLAVES, SOLDIERS, ETC.

SCENE: POMPEII. TIME: A.D. 79 AUGUST—FIRST YEAR OF THE REIGN OF TITUS

ACT I.

SCENE: *The part of Pompeii bordering on the Bay of Naples, laid out as a pleasure ground, with seats, etc., surrounded with palaces. The back of the stage crowded with gaily colored booths, etc., and thronged with buyers and sellers. Fishing boats, filled with fishermen, occasionally arrive at side of scene, well back, from which fishermen disembark with nets, fish, etc. Vesuvius, a highly cultivated mountain, covered with villas, gardens, etc., seen in the distance. [R. of C.] Hetairae gaily dressed in transparent costumes, mounted in chariots, conducted by slaves, drive across the stage, accompanied by throngs of young gentlemen who offer the Hetairae flowers, wreaths, presents, etc. The richly curtained litters of ladies of rank, borne and accompanied by slaves, occasionally cross the scene.*[2] *Enter [L.2. and 3.E.] as from the games, Dudus, Burbo, Stratonice and a miscellaneous throng of soldiers, citizens, etc. Clodius and Sallust land from a boat, and advance.*

CLOD. [*To Burbo*] Are the games over?
BUR. For today, my lord.
    And you not there!
CLOD. State business called me hence,
    As far as Baiae. Who was victor?
STRA. Who?—
    Shut up your mouth, you Burbo! The worst use
    You make of it is to be talking thus,
    Unless you are guzzling.
BUR. Stratonice, now!
    His lordship spoke to me—
STRA. He knows you not;
    Or he had better spoken to a parrot.
    Why will you talk and talk, while no one listens?
    Who, your lordship, who won the first prize?
    Why, Lydon, Lydon ever.
SAL. Lydon again:
    Then I win half a talent.
STRA. A mere boy;
    But then he meets but pigmies. In my day,
    When I turned hulking Burbo on his back,

       Like a great tortoise, with my net's first cast;
       And he screamed out for mercy, which for fun,
       For sheer fun all the laughing people gave—
       I wish they had not: he is such a care:[8]
       Then there were women in the bloody ring
       That would have given this Lydon more to do
       Than what you now call men,—call gladiators!
       Fie! gladiators, without strength enough
       To sweep my kitchen out. Take that, and that,
       For all your gladiators! [*Cuffs Burbo*]
Dud. Gracious Venus!
       Is that a matrimonial rite?
Sal. Take warning.
       It is not safe, my Dudus, as you see,
       To wed a gladiator, he or she.
Clod. You were in the arena, Stratonice,
       Some years, I think?
Bur. She was—
Stra. [*Putting her hand over Burbo's mouth*] Five years, my lord.
Dud. Dear, dear!
Stra. And vanquished only twice.
Dud. The men
       Of your day were polite.
Stra. Polite! Young man,
       Feel this right arm.
Bur. [*Interposing jealously*] Nay, nay—
Stra. [*Flinging him aside*] Out, double ass!
       Polite! Feel this. [*Bending and unbending her arm*]
Dud. [*Retreating*] Gods! I would rather not,
       As Burbo feels it.
Sal. But, besides myself,
       Who won on Lydon?
Dud. Glaucus won enough
       To build a temple.
Sal. The sagacious Greek!
Stra. There is a man for you! By Hercules!
       When he was born a gentleman, the games
       Lost a great fighter. Just the other day,
       Out of mere sport, there in the fencing-school,
       He took a foil, and drove this very Lydon

       Around the ring, as if he were a cur.
       Why Lydon panted like a winded horse;
       But Glaucus did not draw one heavy breath
       Through his bright, laughing lips. I'd love to kiss them.
Bur. Nay Stratonice—
Stra. Ass!
Dud. The gods forbid
       Poor Glaucus such a fortune!
Stra. Look you here,
       You gilded toga, you fine heap of clothes,
       With no more man within them, than enough
       To carry them about for show,—feel this! [*Offers her arm*]
Bur. Nay, Stratonice, nay my dearest dove,
       My little pidgy, widdgy! why, oh why
       Are you forever flirting with that youth? [*Pats her cheek*]
Stra. Flirting? you oaf!
Bur. Yes, darling; that's the way
       You flirt with me.
Sal. [*To Clodius*] Was it not strange, that freak
       Of Glaucus, Stratonice told?
Clod. Oh! no;
       He is Achilles in his woman's garb.
       Luxurious indolence has not quite quelled
       The man within him. If he had a cause,
       Great as himself, to which his heart was given,
       There might arise a hero in a day
       Degenerate as is ours.
Sal. Well, Clodius,
       You are the best of friends.
Clod. How so?
Sal. To make
       A hero of that Attic fop.
Clod. Wait, man,
       Till some strong passion moves him—love or hate.
Sal. When will that be?
Clod. Who knows? There is a maid,
       Of Greek descent too, fairest of the fair,
       Rich, graceful, cultured, of a noble stock;
       Heart free, as spotless as Diana's cheek,
       In all ways fit for Glaucus: I would give

        A half year's income, just to bring those two
        Closely in contact; while I stood aloof,
        And watched the issue.
SAL. Grand experiment!
        Who is this paragon, before whose feet
        You'd sacrifice poor Glaucus?
CLOD. Guess you not?
        That damsel of Neapolis, Ione—
        Arbaces' ward. You must have seen the girl,
        Despite the jealous care with which her guardian
        Secludes her from the public, all he can.
        She's now of age, free from his tutelage:
        Has her own household on the street of Fortune;
        Welcomes her guests, and like a princess too,
        And entertains them, as Aspasia might,
        Had the light dame been pure as is this maid.
SAL. Hey, Clodius! you are eloquent today!
        Arbaces' ward? I like not that.
CLOD. Nor I.
SAL. They give him out a sorcerer. And we see
        How he has turned this city upside down
        With his new worship of Egyptian Isis.
        God's, man! her temple elbows Jupiter's,
        And puts our ancient Thunderer to shame,
        With her increasing crowds of devotees,
        While his cold shrine stands empty.[4]
CLOD. In good faith,
        If our old Latin gods gave us no aid—
        In spite of sacrifices and processions—
        During the recent earthquakes; do you blame
        The silly folk for flying to new gods,
        After the old ones fail them? I do not.
        As for Arbaces, he is rich, and lives
        In Oriental splendor; and there is
        A world of mystic beauty in his face,
        Dark as the grave, and as unfathomable,
        That wins the curious gazer at a glance.
SAL. He has the evil eye; to that I'll swear.
        All things are blighted that he looks upon.

CLOD. Pish! I have supped with him; and such a feast
    I shall not see again until the gods
    Transport me to Olympus. Look at me:
    Do I look blighted with the evil eye?
SAL. Not yet; but wait: the bane is slow but sure.
    But when came Glaucus back?
CLOD. A few days since;
    While we were witnessing that wondrous show,
    The Emperor's coronation rites at Rome.
SAL. Was he not there?
CLOD. He! it is said he told
    His old friend Titus, to his very teeth,
    That he would never see an emperor crowned,
    While Greece remains enslaved.
SAL. And Titus?
CLOD. Oh!
    He only laughed: he and the Greek are friends.
    Too close to quarrel.
SAL. And for that, 'tis said,
    Our Praetor scowls on Glaucus; and suspects
    He will be ousted from his office here,
    Since Titus reigns, for certain sentences,
    Against the Greeks, which Glaucus has denounced
    As cruelties. Let Glaucus have a care;
    Or, ere he gain his end, the Praetor's hand
    Will fall upon him.
CLOD. Have no fear for him.
    What are our stupid Romans at intrigue
    Against the subtle Greeks, and, of all men,
    Against a man of Glaucus' influence,
    Wealth, wit, and boundless popularity.
    Fear for the Praetor, Sallust.
SAL. As for him,
    I wish him all the ill the gods may send,
    And to his crony, that Egyptian snake,
    You are so fond of supping with.
CLOD. [*Laughing*] Ha! ha!
    When he invites you, you will change your tune.[5]
NYD. [*Sings without*]
    The land of all lands is the land of my love,

Whose bosom the gods, from their gardens above,
Have buried in flowers, and have watered with dew,
Made grandest of nations, and fairest to view.
O land of the hero, O pride of the earth,
O mother of beauty, and wisdom and mirth,
The glory of battle, the splendor of peace,
The boast of the ages, my beautiful Greece!

In bonds thou art standing, a shame to the host
Of barbarians who smiled when thy freedom was lost;
A shame to thyself, that thou resteth in fear,
While liberty whispers her dream in thy ear.
O Pallas Athenae, awaken our trance!
Make dreadful thy shrine with the buckler and lance!
Lead forward thy children! let war never cease—
Strike, strike from our land, for our beautiful Greece! [*Enter Nydia*]

STRA. Here comes that little termagant again,
  Singing her treason. You blind idiot.
  Ha! would you have me make you sing, you slut,
  Another song? [*Threatens Nydia*]
BUR. Yes, answer that! [*Pushes Nydia rudely*]
STRA. Hands off!
  By Pollux, if you touch my slave!—Come here,
  You Grecian baggage! Sing a song like this. [*Sings grotesquely*]
      Buy flowers—buy flowers—for—for—for—
      Buy flowers—for—for—
DUD. Brava! for what? to fill your purse? Here girl,
  Here is a piece of gold for you. Take care
  Your mistress do not see it. [*Gives her a coin*]
BUR. What, real gold? [*Tries to snatch it*]
STRA. Of course, it is. [*Pushing him aside*] You do not think a youth,
  So sweet-faced and so gay, would give a maid—
  A poor, blind damsel—anything but gold? [*Takes and pockets the coin*]
BUR. I thought so, Chucky; and I wished to see—
STRA. "You wished to see!" You wished to see it melt
  In wine, you tosspot! No, no; this is safe,
  To feed our children, after you have drowned
  Your life in liquor.
BUR. "Children?" We have none.

GLAUCUS

Stra. But who knows what might happen? Go, girl, go!
　　　Your market waits you.—Vixen, hop, and sing!
　Nyd. [*Sings, offering her flowers for sale to all. Some take and others reject her flowers*]

　　Buy my flowers, buy my flowers, at early morn,
　　To garland the front and the gilded horn
　　Of the sacred beast, that bows to the priest,
　　Where the altar burns and the fumes arise
　　To the gods in a holy sacrifice.
　　　Buy my flowers.

　　Buy my flowers, buy my flowers, at golden noon,
　　For armlet and girdle and long festoon,
　　To fetter in one, while the rites are done,
　　Both Cupid and Hymen, as side by side
　　Stand the gallant groom and the blooming bride.
　　　Buy my flowers.

　　Buy my flowers, buy my flowers, at shady eve,
　　And goblet and flask with the roses weave.
　　Let the chaplets shine through the mist of wine,
　　Till the table reel, and each mellow man
　　Lie stretched in the flowers like a drunken Pan.
　　　Buy my flowers.

　　Buy my flowers, buy my flowers, at gloomy night,
　　To crown those features, so solemn and white,
　　Which the Unrevealed hath both signed and sealed,
　　With a name that makes rosy Love grow pale,
　　And his sceptre fall, and his spirit fail.
　　　Buy my flowers.
　　　　　　　　[*Exit, followed at a distance by Burbo and Stratonice, watching her. Shouts, music, etc., without. Enter a procession of Gladiators, bearing Lydon, crowned with a wreath, in a litter upon their shoulders. All singing*]

　　The day is done, and the victory won,
　　And the victor sits his throne upon.
　　And the dusty sand has drunk the blood
　　Of those who our hero's sword withstood.
　　　Sing hi, sing ho! 'twas a jolly show,
　　　As the buckler rang to the falchion's blow,

  And the people shouted, Ho, ho, ho!
  As the vanquished fled to the shades below.
  Sing hi, sing ho! 'twas a jolly show!

 Alone he stands on the bloody sands,
 Mid waving garments and clapping hands,
 Victor o'er all, and lord and king
 Of the laurel crown; so sing, boys, sing,
  Sing hi, sing ho! 'twas a jolly show,
  As the buckler rang to the falchion's blow,
  And the people shouted, Ho, ho, ho!
  As the vanquished fled to the shades below.
  Sing hi, sing ho! 'twas a jolly show!

[*Lydon descends from the litter. The Gladiators disperse about the stage. Music. Enter Soldiers, who force aside the people, then enter the Praetor, attended by Officers, Guards, Slaves, etc.*]

PRAE. Halus, come here! Let not a thing like this
  Happen again. You were remiss today.
  The majesty of Rome is trample on
  By such a scene.
1ST OFF. My lord, we could not pass
  Without a use of weapons.
PRAE. Use them, then,
  On such occasion. Shall a Praetor stop,
  To let a Greek light from his chariot;
  And before all, this demagogue, this Glaucus,
  Who spends his wealth in ostentatious shows
  Of charity, to win the rabble's shouts?
  Go over him, and all his following,
  When next we meet.
1ST OFF. I shall obey, my lord.
  But Glaucus—
PRAE. Glaucus! Fellow, that man's name
  Is wormwood to me. Let him watch his house,
  Or I may tumble it about his ears.
  March on, without a pause; and let the mob
  Care for its toes and heels.
1ST OFF. Attention! March! [*Exeunt the Praetor and train, driving the people aside*]

GLAUCUS

SAL. Pray mark that, Clodius, how his majesty
    Crushes the people underneath his feet!
CLOD. Gods, yes! I wonder when the brute will wipe
    Our senatorial purple with his hoofs?
LYD. Hey, comrades, did we risk our lives all day
    In the arena, to amuse that man,
    To have our bodies prodded with his spears,
    Here, in the peaceful street?
1ST GLAD. By Hercules.
    I'd like to catch him once upon our ground,
    When spears were flying!
LYD. Yes, you mighty man,
    You'd run from him, just as you did from me,
    This very morning. [*All the Gladiators laugh*]
1ST GLAD. Lydon, won't you, now,
    Allow a fellow to agree with you?[8] [*Music. Enter Glaucus, followed by Saphax, Freedmen, Attendants, etc. Two Ethiopians fanning him with large peacock fans*]
SAL. You are most welcome back, my lord.
GLAU. Your slave,
    Good Sallust! Clodius! Dudus!—Do you mind,
    Standing a little off, to let the breeze
    Have passage to me? It is very hot:
    I drove home from the game, and eat a fig,
    And that fatigued me. [*Seats himself, languidly*]
SAL. That fatigued you! Ah!
    You find it hard work living?
GLAU. Very hard.
    If one could only live without the strain
    Of eating, drinking, drawing breath, and, oh!
    Eternal dressing; life to me might be,
    Quite tolerable. Fan me. [*Negroes fan violently*]
    And Eolus, you chill me. Gently now Boreas.
    Give me a zephyr, not a hurricane.
    Clodius, some day these things of ebony
    Will blow me quite away.
SAL. How pitiful!
GLAU. You have a kind heart, Sallust.
SAL. Tell me, Glaucus,
    Where were you for the last six months?

GLAU. Ah me!
   It is a labor to remember that.
   Voyaging about the world, in search of rest.
   I was so bored with Egypt, India,
   And what I saw of rugged Scythia,
   That I came back to find my mansion here
   Split through with earthquakes, all my frescoes cracked,
   And half the people houseless. Why will not
   The earth keep still; and at least until I die?
DUD. He's simply perfect! Shall I ever be
   Just like him?
GLAU. Clodius, have you ever read
   Strabo, our Naturalist?
CLOD. No.
GLAU. Sallust, you?
SAL. We are not scholars.
GLAU. Nor am I. It must
   Be most fatiguing to learn anything;
   So useless too. They say, our Strabo says,
   Yon pigmy mountain—no more than a wart
   On nature's face—yonder Vesuvius—
   Was once volcanic. That was long ago,
   Ere history began. And that same Strabo—
   That quite unpleasant person—further says,
   That at some future day, Vesuvius
   May take it in its silly head once more
   To burst in flame and lava on the world.
DUD. What a sensation that would make!
GLAU. Well said!
   You are the prince of dandies. [*Patting Dudus*]
CLOD. But, my lord,
   The thought is terrible.
SAL. We dwellers here
   Would not be safe.
GLAU. Safe, Sallust! We would be
   Cooked, like so many capons, in our fat.
DUD. How very droll!
CLOD. Now I remember, once,
   I heard Arbaces say the self same thing;
   But as a prophet, not a naturalist.

GLAUCUS

Dud. Then I will bet a talent, more or less,
    It is a lie, and will not come to pass.
Glau. Hey, Dudus, sceptical?
Dud. Of him, my lord.
    I have laid up a fortune, by my bets
    Against the oracles of Isis. Yes:
    I'll give you two to one, no prophecy,
    Made in her temple, ever is fulfilled.
Glau. Speaking of betting; was not Lydon here?
Dud. Yes. Lydon, Lydon! [*Bring Lydon forward*]
Glau. So you won today?
Lyd. My lord, before you, I should blush with shame
    For my poor adversaries. They must be
    Weaklings indeed in your sight.
Glau. Nay; why so?
Lyd. Have you forgot our practice, when you drove me
    Before you like a feather? I would face
    A storm of lightning sooner than your blade.
Glau. But that was play, my Lydon.
Lyd. Not to me;
    I did my best. I was so furious,
    I would have killed you if I could; my lord,
    Had I your arm and skill, I'd go to Rome,
    And face the champions of the world; for that
    Might hasten matters.
Glau. Hasten what?
Lyd. My end,
    Or something better. Do not think, my lord,
    I am a brute from taste, to maim and kill
    My comrades but to hear the arena roar.
Glau. You are an honest fellow. Out with it!
    I'd like to have a reason why a man
    Should be a gladiator.
Lyd. Oh! this world
    Is hard to some of us. I have a father,
    Old and half blind, whose dulness feels the lash
    When he is halting.—In a word, a slave.
    You know what that means, when the taskmaster
    Is pitiless.
Glau. Ye gods! And so you fight—

LYD. But to win gold enough to set him free.
GLAU. Saphax!
SAPH. My lord. [*Advances*]
GLAU. Take Lydon, and go buy
His father's freedom.
SAPH. At what price, my lord?
GLAU. How do I know? His owner will tell that.
By Pallas, one day I shall go insane
With men's eternal questions. Fan me, boys!
LYD. My lord—
GLAU. Oh! yes; I see your eyes. Enough!—
Do not excite me.
LYD. Only this, then, more.
If you should ever need a man to die,
Smiling and happy, for you—
GLAU. Pray, be gone!
You make me warm. [*Exeunt Lydon and Saphax*]
Forgive me this disturbance.
Lydon is dreadful with his gratitude.
But then I won some money on the knave,
And owe him that much for his victory.
SAL. Who lost?
GLAU. The Praetor lost to me. He let
His spite outrun his judgment.
CLOD. That accounts
For why he used the crowd so brutally,
As he passed by.
GLAU. Yes, yes; he is a brute—
Like all Romans.
SAL. Thanks!
GLAU. For what?—the truth?
Do you so seldom hear it? Poor, poor Praetor!
Some people tell me it is very hard
To be a gentleman.
DUD. Delicious!
GLAU. Hum!
I must displace this Praetor, when I have time
To write to Titus. And, meanwhile, one pig,
One Roman pig, is like another.

CLOD. Glaucus,
     You can say anything.
GLAU. Like truth, I hope.
     I am so weary! Would you mind, my friends,
     To talk a little less?
DUD. The gods be thanked
     For such a man among us! [*Enter Ione, borne in a litter, followed by Waiting Women, Attendants, etc.*]
GLAU. [*Regarding her intently*] Who is that?
SAL. A woman.
GLAU. Nay, a goddess, if they grace
     Our wretched planet, as they did of old.
CLOD. Hey! Glaucus! you are waking.
GLAU. Who is she?
CLOD. Ione of Neapolis; a Greek—
     And so far like yourself—rich, cultured, young,
     And as you see her. Is she beautiful,
     According to your fancy?
GLAU. Marvellously!
CLOD. Shall I present you?
GLAU. If she will. [*Clodius approaches Ione*]
CLOD. Hail, fairest!
IONE. Welcome, most courteous Clodius!
CLOD. May your slave
     Present a friend, Glaucus of Athens, to you?
IONE. How now, the sybarite, the woman-scorner?
     What has bewitched him?
CLOD. Ask that of your eyes;
     Or, better still, of him.
IONE. Well, I confess,
     I have a woman's curiosity
     To know why he would meet me.
CLOD. You are gracious. [*Goes to Glaucus, and returns with him to Ione*]
     Permit me lady, to present my friend,
     Glaucus of Athens. As you both are Greek,
     I leave you to your treasonable talk
     Against poor Rome. [*Retires*]
GLAU. The treason of the slave,
     To curse his chains, to love his native land;

          And, above all, to love that liberty
          Which is, or should be, all men's heritage.
IONE. What's that? [*Springing from her litter eagerly*]
GLAU. What Clodius would call treason. Lady,
          I hope it is not treason to your ears. [*They sit*]
IONE. To mine? Oh, no! These are the noblest words
          I ever heard; though startling, as from you.
          My Greece—oh, let me say our Greece—my dream
          Of glory is to see her marble face
          Once more ablaze with that grand liberty
          Which made her forehead beautiful of old.
GLAU. Yes, beautiful as yours, her faithful child;
          Faithful amid the false!
IONE. How men have wronged
          Your nature, Glaucus!
GLAU. Hardly. I was born,
          Save in my blood, a Roman. All my race,
          Since our subjection, held great offices,
          And power and wealth, under almighty Rome,
          Trampling upon their country, as the slave,
          Put in the master's place, will ever do.
          I am ashamed to utter what you hear;
          But, Heaven knows, not ashamed of what I feel,
          In spite of that which made my boyhood base,
          And my youth idle. What is the career
          A Greek may follow, while the heavy heel
          Of Rome is resting on his country's neck
          With hopeless weight? What can the slave do now
          But serve the master?
IONE. He can strike, and die.
GLAU. Yet to no purpose; and cheerless fact
          Has made an idler of me, in a world
          Where action is in vain, and mankind groans
          Under a burden he cannot shake off.
IONE. Is this the trifler, Glaucus?—this strong man,
          Alive with thoughts of empire for his race,
          Albeit desperate?
GLAU. Never would I be
          A trifler in your eyes. You have aroused
          Feelings that slept, and only dreamed, sometimes,

GLAUCUS

        Of possible fulfilment, till your soul
        Looked into mine, and made the dream appear
        Reality, and you the living type
        Of Grecian liberty. Pray, pardon me!
        But we must not be strangers; for my heart
        Was ready as a temple, for the shrine
        And statue of the goddess, ere you came
        To make my life your worship.
IONE. [*Aside*] What is this,
    This fiery current setting to my heart?
    Lie quiet, traitor! It is not the man;
    It is my country wakes you into life. [*Enter Apaecides*]
APAE. Sister!
IONE. My brother, welcome! [*They embrace*] Pray you know
    Glaucus of Athens. [*They bow stifly*]
APAE. Who does not know him,
    Who has an eye for glitter and for pomp?
GLAU. I pray you, do not make me blush, to hear
    How I am known. Perhaps there is a soul,
    Under my garb, more worth the knowing.
IONE. Yes;
    For that I answer.
APAE. You!
GLAU. A neophyte
    Of Isis, by your robe?
IONE. A neophyte,
    No more; not yet a priest.
APAE. Nor e'er to be,
    Perhaps; a scholar merely.
GLAU. Then you read,
    Our Grecian sages, the philosophers?
APAE. Not I.
GLAU. Not Plato even?
APAE. [*Aside*] Ye gods, 'tis strange!
    [*Aloud*] Do you know Plato?
GLAU. Yes, almost by rote.[7]
    Let me commend to you the fountainhead
    Of human wisdom, whose exhaustless flow
    Springs from the earth, and soars into the heavens;
    Links creature to Creator; makes our life

     One with its Source, immortal as the Power
     Which is the central soul of all that is.
Ione. This is pure teaching, Glaucus.
Apae. [*Aside*] I am stunned:
     Such words from him!
 Glau. Are you not curious
     To have a glimpse of Plato's heaven?
Apae. I am.
 Glau. Come to my house then. I have roll on roll
     Of Plato's writings in my library.
Apae. You have a library!
 Glau. In Greek alone.
     'Tis hard to tempt a man so bigoted
     To read the works of the barbarians.
Ione.[8] O Brother, Brother, you should not neglect
     The writers of our country. Where on earth
     Find you such poets and philosophers,
     Such dramatists, and such historians,
     So full of beauty, power and sacred truth,
     As in the writers of our native land?
Apae. I shall accept your hospitality;
     Perhaps to own a teacher in yourself.
     [*Aside*] This is the strangest of strange things; to find
     A scholar hidden in the glittering garb
     Of Glaucus, the Athenian fop! [*Enter Arbaces, Calenus and a brilliant train of Freedmen, Slaves, etc.*]
 Arb. How now!
     Your litter waiting in the public streets!
Ione. Where 'er it is, it waits without your leave,
     Asked or expected.
 Arb. Pardon me. I saw
     The child that used to run with outstretched arms,
     Into my bosom from a stranger's face.
     I still forget the change.
Ione. Remember it.
     You should not wish to make a child of me
     Before the world. Permit me to present
     Glaucus of Athens.
 Arb. Glaucus? We have met
     Before, I think.

GLAU. I cannot recollect.
ARB. Your memory is as bad then as your manners.
GLAU. My lord, I try to make my company
    Better than either.
ARB. You are keen.
GLAU. What, I?
    Only by contrast with a duller wit.
ARB. By Horus!—
IONE. Peace! Do not forget my presence.
ARB. 'Twere better, than to see you sitting thus,
    Like an Aspasia, in a public place.
GLAU. Strange words from an Egyptian. In your land,
    For ages, women held the public place—
    Did the man's duties, as we know them here;
    While he with distaff in his puny hand,
    Or babe on knee, sat with his modesty
    Safely secluded in his wife's abode.
    This thing was so, or else your chronicles
    Lie about that, as well as other things.
ARB. Ha! ha! it moves my mirth, to hear a Greek
    Be so ungrateful, as to cast a slur
    Upon the land to which he owes the birth
    Of all his saucy greatness. Where were art,
    Religion, wisdom, all that makes you proud,
    Had you not stolen from Egypt everything.
GLAU. And bettered all, so that its owner knew,
    But by tradition, that the thing was his.
    Or if, indeed, the mother germ of all
    Slumbered not in the twilight of the race,
    And wakened when the worthiest called.
CAL. [*Aside*] Ha! now,
    Here is a nimble wit, and rich. I wonder
    If service with him might not pay me more
    Than starving with Arbaces. Gold is gold,
    Wherever it be mined.[9] [*Enter Nydia, running, pursued by Stratonice, Burbo and a laughing crowd*]
STRA. Ha! nimble legs,
    You will outrun your mistress then! [*Seizes Nydia*]
IONE. [*To Glaucus*] My lord—
BUR. Take that! [*Offers to strike Nydia*]

GLAU. [*Hurling him aside*] Off wretch! What beast begot you then,
    That you dare lift your impious hand against
    Your mother's sex? [*Nydia shelters herself behind Glaucus*]
1ST CIT. [*To Burbo*] Go at him, man!
BUR. Not I:
    His grip is torture.
GLAU. What is this about?
BUR. Why not ask that before you cripple me?
STRA. Bah! sheep, you crippled! With a club, you sot,
    He could not kill you! Pray, your lordship, hear.
    She is my slave—
GLAU. Your slave! That is name
    To raise up all mankind in her defense.
IONE. 'Tis nobly said.
GLAU. What then?
STRA. She is the most
    Unbidable, cross-grained and crooked thing
    That ever eat my victuals. You bad brat,
    Let me but get these hooks into your skin,
    And you shall know it!
GLAU. What is her offense?
STRA. What—what? This morning, I commanded her
    To wash, and dress, and put her finery on,
    And go to Lord Arbaces' house—
ARB. [*Apart to her*] Hush, hush!
STRA. That's all; she would not go.
GLAU. Why not?
NYD. My lord,
    I am a damsel; and I cannot go
    To that licentious house, where riot raves
    From night till morning—
ARB. [*Apart to her*] Silence!
NYD. [*Shuddering*] He is here!
    I dare not speak. Or if I do, her whip
    Will tear the skin from my shoulders.
STRA. Yes;
    That is a safe prediction. [*Trumpets, etc. Enter the Praetor and train*]

PRAE. What is this?
    Must all our byways be obstructed thus,
    To wait for you, Lord Glaucus?
GLAU. I, my lord?
    I am most innocent of this. Behold,
    A public illustration of the charms
    Of your domestic slavery. That blocks
    The thoroughfare, and makes the heart
    Hard as the stones we tread on.
PRAE. [*Saluting her*] Fair Ione! [*She bows coldly*]
    My noble friend Arbaces. [*They salute cordially*]
    Tell me now,
    Why is the rabble gathered thus? To hear
    A lecture on the naked, sovereign man,
    Or the nobility of poverty,
    From one whose race runs backward to the gods;
    And whose poor fortune, turned to gold, would sink
    Caesar's best galley. [*He, Arbaces and their followers laugh*]
ARB. 'Twas a tumult raised
    With these good people, Burbo and his wife,
    By that Greek gentleman, about a slave,—
    Yon girl beside him. I will finish it.
    Sell me the slave.
NYD. O gods, no! not to him.
    Save me, my lord, if you have ever loved
    Sister or mother! [*To Glaucus*]
GLAU. Burbo, let the girl
    Go to my house. My steward will pay your price.
STRA. Well, but—
ARB. O Praetor, mark this insolence.
    Mine is the prior right. I offered first.
PRAE. What say you, Burbo?
STRA. Say! The slave is mine:
    And he is mine.
PRAE. Well, well, what say you then?
STRA. The girl earns me a living, selling flowers,
    And making music for the gentlemen
    At feasts and suppers. In the temples, too
    She sings at festivals—the bonny bird!

        She is a proper and religious girl:
        'Twould break my heart to part with her.
Bur. [*Weeping*] Ye gods!—
Stra. But if the gentlemen would have her, I
        Will not prevent her bettering herself,
        Poor innocent!—I therefore say, my lord,
        Let him who'll pay the highest price for her,
        Take the poor child from my maternal arms. [*Weeps*]
All Cit. Shame!—shame!
Stra. Oh, go to Pluto with your "shame"!
Prae. Most provident affection! Be it so.
Bur. But this is hard—so hard!—[*Weeping*]
Stra. Stop, ass! we've had
        Enough of that.
Prae. My lord Arbaces, bid.
        Yours is the first chance.
Arb. Let the Greek speak first:
        I waive my right.
Glau. I do protest, my lord,
        Against this thing as most unseemly. What,
        Make a slave market of the pleasure ground
        Of the whole people!
Prae. Oh, "the people"—pah!
        You always have the people in your mouth.
Glau. I am but one of them.
Prae. Come bid, come bid! [*Glaucus looks at Ione, who smiles assent to him*]
Glau. Then I will give a talent more for her
        Than any bid the Egyptian may make.
Cal. Now have a care. If you go very high,
        He'll let you take the girl. Beware Greek tricks! [*Apart to Arbaces*]
Arb. Well thought of. 'Tis a farce. She is not worth
        The tenth part of a talent. I am not
        A fool!
Cal. No, not that way. Who ever said
        Arbaces was a fool in lavishness? [*Aside laughing*]
Prae. Then you abandon bidding?
Arb. I will not
        Stand here, to be a butt, before the mob,
        To his audacious wealth. The infernal gods

Give you the profit of your purchase, Greek!
Add Nydia to your Harem. You must have
A singing girl among your other things.
GLAU. My lord, this foul-tongued fellow, who respects
Neither a lady's presence nor the truth,
Should have a bridle in his liquorish mouth.
ARB. Poh! it is public scandal.
GLAU. Then, as such,
Whisper it darkly to your sister crones
Over your sewing.
PRAE. Peace; no more of this!
The girl is yours.
NYD. The gods be thanked! [*Kisses Glaucus's hand*]
BUR. My lord,
The price you bid—
STRA. A talent—that it was—
An Attic talent, all in pure, bright gold.
GLAU. Yes, yes.
CAL. You two are little less than thieves;
To sell a blind girl at a price like that.
GLAU. Blind! Is she blind?
STRA. Not blinder than the fools
That make their offerings at Isis' shrine.
CAL. Blind as that woman's conscience. You would not
Purchase a goat on such scrutiny.
GLAU. One cannot err in purchasing a slave
Meant for my uses at the seller's price.
The more infirm, afflicted, useless, valueless—
The more in danger of the tyrant's rod—
The more her worth to me.
NYD. I need not eyes
To serve you, master. Take another sense
From my defective body, leave me but
My willing heart, and I could do more work
For you, my lord, than any stalwart slave
Dare venture on.
PRAE. Bold promises sometimes
Forerun a faint performance. I have heard,
It was your boast, you never owned a slave.

    Perhaps it is your policy to talk
    In that way to the people.
Glau. Policy?
    No, when I have the people's ear, I feel
    That I am talking to my brothers. Gods,
    Forget me and my fortunes, when I dare,
    Under your eyes, forget my fellow man!
    I never owned a slave, 'tis true, my lord,
    Longer than time was needed to set free
    The hapless being. Fair Ione, deign
    To give this girl the shelter of your house.
Ione. Most willingly.
Arb.   Ione, I protest
    Against your taking up this gutter filth,
    This tramper of the streets, this sightless toy
    Of every scamp to whom she sells a flower,
    To give her lodging in your spotless home.
Nyd. Send me not from you. Let me stay with you.
    I shall no more disturb your quiet house
    Than a poor mouse. I cannot go, my lord,
    To that great lady's service.
Glau. It were best.
    You are a damsel, and to bide with me
    Would bring you shame, whether deserved or not.
Nyd. True, true, but then—What matter how a slave
    Be thought of?
Ione. Slave! you are a slave no more.
    Hold up your face, alike to gods and men,
    Free citizen of Rome! There are no slaves
    Beneath my roof. No man or woman there
    Serves on compulsion; but for labor done
    Receives that labor's worth.
Nyd. Hear, Mother, hear!
    Bend from your blest abode above the clouds,
    And hear the gentle voice that says your child
    No longer is a slave. Yes, twice a slave,
    If gratitude can hold an honest heart
    Stronger than human bondage. [*Kisses Ione's hand eagerly*]

IONE. Kiss my lips:
    And let the world behold how I esteem
    Your purity, my sister. [*Kisses Nydia*]
NYD. Take my soul!
    My body could not serve you well enough
    To recompense this blessing.
GLAU. [*Aside*] Peerless maid,
    How this new thing discovered in my breast,
    This waking heart, is throbbing at your words!
    Yea, my whole nature, in a storm of light,
    Bursts from its darkness, and votary kneels
    Before your feet,—forever, ever, love!
    The die is cast! No rest can be for me
    Until by deeds, however long and hard,
    I shall have won your virgin lips to own
    A kindred passion. Lo! I am transformed
    Out of my former self, and am become
    Inspired with vigor of the deathless gods.
    What can I not achieve, thus armed, to brave
    Man's puny opposition? [*Ione ascends her litter. Passes along, followed by Nydia, attendants, etc.*]
IONE. Farewell, Glaucus!
GLAU. Will you not change that dreary word, farewell,
    To welcome for me, when we meet again?
    A house so open to the world as yours,
    Should not exclude me. Shall I be received?
    One word, one little word, Ione!—
IONE. Come! [*Glaucus stands looking eagerly after Ione. She, in going, turns her head once, and looks back at him*]

ACT II.

SCENE: *A garden set with statuary, fountains, seats, flowers, etc. overlooking the bay. Vesuvius in the R.C. distance. Maids of Ione are discovered, embroidering, etc. Two or three men pass through the garden, bearing flowers, gifts, etc. and enter the palace of Ione.*

    1ST MAID. More violets!
    2ND MAID. Forever violets!

1st Maid. If we were nearer Greece, I'd say those flowers
   Were gathered on Hymettus.
2nd Maid. Do you know
   The violet is the national flower of Greece?
1st Maid. Oh, yes; on holidays Minerva's fane
   Is loaded with them.
2nd Maid. Cloe, what is the Greek
   For violet?
1st Maid. I know not. Whew!—
2nd Maid. What now?
1st Maid. I stuck my finger. Where is Nydia?
   The darling, how I love her!—she could tell
   The Greek for violet.
2nd Maid. Yes, yes; and what means
   The name of Glaucus. [*They all laugh*]
1st Maid. There is little need
   Of a Thessalian witch to tell us that.
3rd Maid. Mum, girls!
1st Maid. Ask her. [*They all laugh*]
2nd Maid. I dare you to.
3rd Maid. Be still! [*Enter Ione*]
Ione. What are you tittering at?
2nd Maid. At awkward Cloe:
   She stuck her finger.
1st Maid. And it smarted so! Fie,
   Unfeeling girls!
Ione. What are you doing?
1st Maid. [*Shows embroidery*] See.
Ione. There's too much red here, and here too much green.
   Make this all violet.
1st Maid. Violet roses! What,
   And violet leaves! O nature—
Ione. Nature! Why
   Did not this tyrant nature give the rose
   The violet's color and perfume?—Ah, me!
   How much there is in nature, and in fate,
   That might be bettered with a little taste!
   Who has been here?
1st Maid. No one, as yet.

IONE. No one?
   I wonder why my house—pleasant enough—
   Is such a solitude. No one, you said?
1ST MAID. Not even my lord Glaucus.
IONE. Child, I thought
   Nothing of him. For he you know, is not—
   Is not the world. He comes and goes, in faith,
   Just as he chooses. [*Weeps*]
1ST MAID. Ah! my lady!—
IONE. Oh!
   I am so lonely! [*Sits*] Nydia! Nydia! Where
   Is our bird flown?
2ND MAID. Into the streets again.
   She's always homesick for the streets.
IONE. Alas!
   They were her former home.
1ST MAID. A mere pretense.
   I tracked her once. Where do you think she goes?
   Straight to Minerva's temple, where she spends
   Whole hours in prayer and offerings of flowers
   For you, my lady.
IONE. She's a wild bird yet.
   What, Nydia! [*Claps her hands. Enter Nydia rapidly*]
NYD. My lady? [*Sits at Ione's feet*]
IONE. [*Smoothing her head*] You are here,
   At last, you little runaway.
NYD. My heart
   Is always here, dear mistress.
IONE. How, again
   That odious name! I do not like it, child.
   Call me Ione, friend, or sister, please.
NYD. How slavehood shapes the habits of the slave!
   I thank you, lady.
IONE. "Lady"! There again!
   Call me Ione: Try!
NYD. [*Timidly*] Ione.
IONE. Hum!
   Now call my name so all the world may hear,
   Ay, and the listening gods!
NYD. [*Boldly*] Ione!

IONE. Good!
    My Roman citizen!
NYD. But you are sad:
    I hear it in your voice.
IONE. I sad?
NYD. Alas!
IONE. Your ears are better than another's eyes.
    Truly, I am not merry. Sing to me:
    But nothing cheerful. Sing a doleful song;
    Something to make me feel that others are
    As wretched as myself—heigh ho!
NYD. Ah me! [*Sings*]
        What keener woe than for a heart o'erladen
            With love, that flown can never come again—
        Life's venture for a pure and simple maiden—
            A joy to win, to lose a world of pain:
        What if the venture prove in vain, in vain?
        What keener woe!

        What keener woe than to behold above her
            The stormy terrors of a darkening sky;
        No heart to shield her, and no heart to love her,
            The light of hope bedimmed within her eye:
        What can she do but die, but die?
        What keener woe!
IONE. Weeping! Why Nydia, have you known a grief
    So sad as that, and you a very child?
NYD. Child, child! The heart of woman is a flower
    That blossoms early, and the fruits of life
    Follow the bloom apace.
IONE. Too true. What keeps
    That careless man away? Has he no heart
    To tell him that I wait? [*Aside*] What is the hour?
1ST MAID. The tenth.
IONE. And no one here! Surely the world
    Is bathed and trimmed by this.
1ST MAID. [*Apart to other maids*] For world read Glaucus.
3RD MAID. Hush, hush! You reckless thing! [*Enter a servant*]
SERV. Lord Glaucus.

GLAUCUS

IONE. Ha!
    Girls, girls, how do I look? My robes, my hair?
    This girdle sits awry: give it a pull.
    Hand me that bunch of violets. [*Maids busy themselves about her*]
    There, there!
    You may retire. How glorious is the day!
    I thought the morning threatened rain. Go, go!
1ST MAID. Now the whole world is in the house, we must
    "Go, go!" out of the crowd. [*Apart to the others, who retire laughing. Enter Glaucus*]
GLAU. Ione, hail!
IONE. Hail, Glaucus! [*She extends her hand, which he kisses*]
    [*Starting*] Oh! Cannot I give my hand,
    In way of greeting, without having someone
    Kiss it? [*Secretly kisses the hand which he kissed*]
GLAU. It was imprudent to expose
    My weakness to temptation.
IONE. Ah!—my lord,
    Where have you been today? I thought—
GLAU. You thought?
IONE. Nothing.
GLAU. Well thought of! I have been at home,
    Obeying your commands. A loyal slave,
    Even in my sovereign's absence. We have read—
    Apaecides and I—a deal today,
    Plato's Symposium.
IONE. Well, well! And he?
GLAU. Is deeply moved. I left him with his brow
    Knotted in thought; rereading for himself
    Parts of the scroll. I could not wait—
IONE. Not wait?
GLAU. To pay my duty here. [*She extends her hand which he kisses*]
IONE. You are sorely given
    To kissing people's hands.
GLAU. Not all hands.
IONE. Then,
    Apaecides is moved, you say? Perhaps
    'Twill shake his faith in Isis, and the lore,
    The hideous lore of Egypt.

GLAU. So I hope,
    If all that is most beautiful in faith
    Can win a nature, sensitive as his,
    From the degrading ugliness that glares
    From those brute-feathered things, whose history
    Is but a record of repulsive crime.
IONE. Thanks, Pallas! I would have my brother bide
    True to our native gods. Not wander off
    With doubtful strangers. And, besides, I have—
    I know not why—an instinct that should he
    Assume the robe of priesthood, it will end
    In misery to him.
GLAU. It must not be.
NYD. [*Sings*]
    The land of all lands is the land of my love,
    Whose bosom the gods, from the gardens above,
    Have buried in flowers, and have watered with dew,
    Made grandest of nations and fairest to view.
    O land of the hero, O pride of the earth!
    O mother of beauty, and wisdom, and mirth!
    The glory of battle, the splendor of peace,
    The boast of the ages, my beautiful Greece!
IONE. Hark, Glaucus!
GLAU. Yes. Is it the genius
    Of our dear native land that sings, to wake
    Contented slaves to manhood?
IONE. No, alas
    It is the blind girl, Nydia, your gift.
    She is Thessalian, and fiery blood
    Of her wild race is in her daring heart.
    What, Nydia! [*Nydia advances. Glaucus lays his hand upon her head. She starts and cowers with emotion*]
GLAU. My child, where learned you that?
    A song unsuited to the lips of slaves,
    And to their ears.
NYD. Of slaves!
GLAU. Are we not slaves,
    We Grecians, Roman slaves—political,
    If not domestic? Who taught you that song?

NYD. The fierce sun's heat, the arrow of the blast,
   The sounding billows, and the crash and howl
   Of thunder shouted to my echoing heart:
   "Freedom, forever freedom! We are that
   Which Greece should be!" [*Glaucus kisses her forehead*]
GLAU. From her unworthy son,
   Take thus your country's benediction.
NYD. [*Starting with emotion*] Ha!
   The gods have overpaid me!
GLAU. Nydia [*Offering a violet*]
   Know you this flower?
NYD. The violet? Oh yes;
   It is the flower of Greece.
GLAU. Its Grecian name?
NYD. Ion.
GLAU. And hence Ione—fairer flower
   Than ever grew upon our Attic hills;
   More full of sunlight to the darkened heart,
   More full of odor to the weary brain,
   The rest and promise of an aimless soul,
   Nature's supreme consummate flower of flowers—
IONE. My lord, my lord, you are extravagant:
   You drown me with poetic dew. I feel
   Like a poor violet in a deluge. Fie!
   You change the color of your violet
   To burning crimson. Nydia, my lord
   Asked you a question.
NYD. Yes, I know this flower,
   Whence my dear lady takes her gentle name;
   Love-lies-a-bleeding is a flower I know,
   Somewhat too well—the solemn amaranth.
   That never dies itself, but crowns the brows
   Of the pale dead as if in mockery;
   The mortal and immortal side by side.
   Love-lies-a-bleeding: it is often so! [*Exit pensively*]
GLAU. Strange girl!
IONE. What feeling moves her? I so love
   Her gentle nature that my heart would ache
   At any sorrow hidden in her own. [*Enter a servant*]

SERV. The priest Calenus.
IONE. Well, [*Exit Servant. Enter Calenus*]
CAL. Hail! Let me hope
    My presence will not be unwelcome. I
    Come as the herald of my lord. Heaven knows,
    I am tired of blowing on his horn.[10]
    Shorten my skirts, and crop my priestly hair,
    And I would look the slave I really am:
    At a slave's wages too—frowns, growls and sneers,
    And bones to comfort me; but not a glimpse
    Of the dear yellow gold; and he so rich.
    Gods! he must trust me. I could tell—ha! ha! [*Laughing*]
    Were I so minded, what would make this town
    Dance as if shaken with an earthquake. Well,
    The time may come—
GLAU. His trust seems well deserved.
CAL. Mum! He is coming. More anon some day. [*Retires. Enter Arbaces and train*]
ARB. My ward! [*Salutes Ione affectionately. Bows stiffly to Glaucus*]
GLAU. That was.
ARB. [*Fiercely*] You spoke?
GLAU. Sometimes a voice
    Comes from the conscience.
IONE. Nay, nay, gentlemen;
    Why will you bicker—[*A loud rumbling sound. The scenery slightly agitated*]
    What was that?
GLAU. A shock,
    A slight one only, of the earthquake. Earth
    Gives us a hint, to let her children know
    We are resting on her bosom.
IONE. But it made
    My heart leap up, and every pulse stand still.
GLAU. 'Twas but a trifle. Where were you, Ione,
    During the recent earthquake, that so shook
    Our poor Pompeii?
ARB. Ha! he said "Ione";
    And so familiarly!
IONE. I was away,
    Upon the sea, bound to Sorrentum. Yes,

        And fast asleep too. It is terrible,
        To think the earth, in which we firmly trust,
        Can, in a moment, be an enemy
        To all her children—nay, a murderess.
        Are we so little to the gods, that they
        Can sweep us from their sight, as if we were
        A nest of emmets?
ARB. Lo, a mystery,
        That Isis hides behind her triple veil,
        And she alone can answer.
GLAU. Only one,
        Among a thousand, met at every turn.
        Nature is ruthless to the toys she makes:
        One cannot answer whether to create,
        Or to destroy, is more her purpose. Both
        Go on together: the result is—what?
ARB. Is this religion, Greek?
GLAU. No, this is life:
        Faith is above it. Once I stood appalled
        Amid a scene of human sacrifice
        Upon this earthly altar of the gods.
        I was at Smyrna, one bright summer day,
        A day dropped out of Heaven, so fair it was.
        At the seventh hour;—yes, 'twas at very noon—
        A creeping shadow overspread the sky,
        All cloudless heretofore. The dusky sun
        Smouldered above us, like a dying coal,
        Seen through thick smoke. The people held their breath,
        And such a stillness settled on the town
        As made one's life a burden. Then there came
        A sound that drowned all other sounds;—a roar,
        To which the nearest thunder is but tame;
        Pelides' shout, that paralyzed a host,
        Was but a whisper to it. Crash on crash
        Followed the deafening roar, and all the land
        Crept, and vibrated to and fro and swayed,
        Like a dense liquid; as though one might stand
        Upon tempestuous waves, and feel them move
        Under our tottering feet. Great fissures yawned,
        Where once were streets, and their unfathomed mouths

Swallowed a multitude, half stupefied
With wretched sickness and the sulphurous fumes
Exhaling from the earth. House fell on house,
Palace on palace, and the temples reeled
And twisted on their columns, ere they fell
Upon their vainly sacrificing priests.
Amidst the awful din of rending earth,
The rush and crash of falling walls, man's voice
Lifted in terror, moaning in despair,
Was lost; an aimless mob of fugitives,
Howling, unheard of either gods or men;
Mothers with babes hugged to their panting breasts—
I could not hear them, but I saw they shrieked;
Children, uncared for, trampled on, or tossed
Dying above the heads of ruthless men,
Swept back and forth, along the trembling shore:
All thought of sex, or rank, or manly shame
O'erwhelmed in that bewilderment of fear
And omnipresent death. The vision passed;
The dreadful sentence of the frowning gods
Was executed, and the blazing sun
Lighted again our ruined world, and smiled,
In bitter irony, upon the wreck
Of all things human—man and all his works—
In half the time that it has taken me
To dwarf the wonder with my feeble words.
IONE. But you?
GLAU. Nay, think as little of me now,
As then I thought, amidst such dreadful scenes,
Of my poor self.
IONE. But Clodius says your gold
Flowed, like refreshing waters, o'er the town;
Your galleys brought provisions, and thus saved
Those who survived from death.
ARB. Could he do less?
GLAU. Thank you, my lord, for answering for me!
No less, unless I held your ghastly creed
That but the dead are happy.
ARB. Umph! My lord,
Have you no business in the town? for I

GLAUCUS

        Have somewhat with this lady. Have you not
        Another fair to visit with your smiles,
        And your calamities by sea and land,
        That take you longer to narrate than they
        Consumed in happenings?
IONE. [*Apart to him*] Pray you, Glaucus, go:
        Make no reply to him.
GLAU. Is this sweet day
        To be thus clouded with a slanderer's breath?
        I hoped—
IONE. Well, come again; and reunite
        The shattered hours. 'Tis early: come again.
GLAU. O gracious lady, there is in my heart
        That which is burning to discern a way
        Unto your private ear.
IONE. Not now.
GLAU. But when?
IONE. O Glaucus, credit me with shame at least,
        If not with maiden modesty.
GLAU. Dear heart,
        What virtue is there, or in earth or Heaven,
        With which my love has not endowed you?
IONE. Go!
GLAU. I obey; but when shall I return?
IONE. Come when Vesuvius casts her creeping shade
        As far as Pansa's villa.
GLAU. Until then,
        My prayers will be to Phoebus, that he urge
        His fiery horses to the cooling waves.
        Until we meet then, fairest.
IONE. Till we meet. [*Exit Glaucus. Nydia steals in, and seats herself apart, listening*]
ARB. Ione, if a friend may trust his eyes,
        That Grecian dandy has advance apace
        Into your confidence. Perhaps—but that
        I scarce can credit—snake-like, he has squirmed
        Into a vacant corner of your heart.
IONE. If it were so, you are the last whom I
        Should choose for a confessor.

ARB. How is this—
This new distrust of me? Have I not been
A faithful guardian of your infancy,
Your property, your honor;—ay, that now
Comes up for guardianship.

IONE. Of that last care
Henceforth I shall relieve your mind. I am
The proper guardian of my honor.

ARB. Child—
Most inexperienced child—do not mistake
Your innocence for knowledge, or the power
To grapple with a wicked world. Even yet
The last conditions of your father's will
Are not fulfilled. Look here. Read for yourself. [*Hands her a document*]

IONE. [*Reads*] There is a casket in your custody,
Containing among other things, a letter
Of last instructions from my father. This
Is to be opened only at your house,
And in your presence—that is very strange—
When I have reached a marriageable age.
Curious conditions!

ARB. They concern me not.
That is a matter 'twixt your father's will
And your own conscience.

IONE. Very strange!

ARB. Perhaps
'Twill not be so mysterious when you come
To read the letter.

IONE. True. My father's will
Is sacred to me as a voice from Heaven.
Albeit his latter days were clouded o'er
With mental shadows, never was the time
My eyes of love lacked power to penetrate
The meaning of his heart.[11] When shall I come?

ARB. Now, if you will.

IONE. Or later?

ARB. Quite as well.
Ione, of this Glaucus?—

IONE. What of him?
ARB. You know the man, you know the character
    He holds among his fellows, the gay tribe
    That flutters in the sunlight of its days
    Passing the time in revels, shows, or worse,
    Debauches, that draw on the innocent
    To flounder helpless in a mire of guilt,—
    Ruined and ruining.
IONE. My lord, my lord!
    Is Glaucus such as one?
ARB. Why yes; unless
    The world belies him. He does not conceal
    Those vices which he seems to glory in,
    For the weak wonder of the rout he leads
    Into perdition. Ask the first who comes.[12]
    This is not slander; 'tis the common talk
    Of all who know him.
IONE. It is very sad.
    A man of his attainments—
ARB. There it is.[13]
    That makes him more dangerous, more adroit
    In bad inventions, more ingenious
    To hide his wicked ways in treacherous flowers,
    And thus delude the simple eyes that look
    Upon his social acting when he plays
    A virtuous part, as means to a success.
    Ah! there is many a bitter heart that beats
    Here, in Pompeii—of your sex, I mean—
    Which he has rifled, and then cast aside
    In his disdain, to all the world's contempt.
IONE. Alas! alas! Can this be true?
ARB. How else?
    Ask your first friend, ask Sallust, ask that ape,
    Dudus, who strives to imitate, and fails,
    The foppish manners of his model. Yes,
    That grinning idiot said of you, of you—
    Just think of that!—in public at the games—
    That Glaucus holds you now so well in hand,
    That you must follow where a multitude
    Of your fair sisters have already led.

    Yes, and Lord Glaucus smiled to hear the words
    His shallow flatterer uttered. Not a man
    Of those who heard had more grace than to laugh
    In chorus to their master's smile. Ye gods!
    Had I but heard, I'd torn the lying tongue
    Out of his teeth!
 Ione. How pitiful! Are men
    Worse than the innocent can dream? Without! [*Claps her hands.
Nydia advances*]
    Nydia, give orders at my door that none
    Shall enter for the day. I am not well.
 Nyd. Not Glaucus even? [*Apart to Ione*]
 Ione. No one. Pardon me:
    I must retire.
 Arb. Forget not. You will come?
 Ione. Within an hour. [*Exit Nydia*] Oh, heart, poor aching heart,
    How is your dream of happiness, that seemed
    To kiss the earth, and fold me in its arms,
    Shattered by man's unworthiness!
 Arb. Farewell! [*Exit Ione*]
    Triumphant! The first step is safely made:
    The second plain before me. After that
    She will be all my own—must be; for then
    The whole world will reject her, force her back
    To her sole refuge in my loving arms.[14]
    As for this Grecian fop, who crosses me,
    Let him beware a man who never brooked
    A life between him and a settled aim.
    And this of all, the purpose of my life,
    The glory of my future; which to win
    Has made me stoop to falsehood, forgery.
    Degrading guile—I, an Egyptian prince,
    Who should command my fortune from a throne.
    He must be meddling with Apaecides,
    Turning his heart from Isis, to implant
    The shallow creeds of his philosophers
    Within his wavering brain. Goddess supreme,
    Is not that sacrilege? Is not the doom
    For that offense destruction; more than death,—

GLAUCUS

      Annihilation both to flesh and soul? [*Enter Apaecides*]
      My son!
APAE. I seek my sister.
ARB. What of that?
      Have you no word in passing, for the guide
      Who led your youthful steps from height to height
      Of human knowledge, and who stands prepared
      At last to lift old Isis' mystic veil,[15]
      And show you truth—truth absolute and pure—
      Not as man see it, as the gods above?
APAE. Delusion?
ARB. How?
APAE. Delusion was my word.
      Even as the steps, to reach this mystic veil,
      This vestibule of truth, have been through fraud
      Practised upon the people. Say to what
      Can falsehood lead but to the central lie,
      The nothing that sustains it? No my lord,
      Withdraw your hand from Isis' veil for me.
      I have seen enough. I seek to know no more.
      I have seen your oracle, Calenus there,
      Bawling for Isis through a speaking tube
      Unto her wondering worshippers. Alack!
      Our poor Calenus for an oracle![16]
      Here, take your robe of neophyte! I hurl
      The garment at you, buzzing with its lies,
      Like a fallen beehive; and beware the swarm
      Sting not your goddess or yourself! Henceforth
      I walk in freedom; and, for penance, I
      Will blow the secrets of the frauds, wherein
      I was concerned, to the four winds of Heaven.
ARB. Beware!
APAE. I fear you not.
ARB. Recall your oath—
      Its penalty, death, sudden death.
APAE. An oath
      Made in good faith with falsehood, binds me not[17]
      Longer than I can penetrate the lie.
      Death! what is death to this poor mortal frame.
      If lingering or if sudden, while the soul

    Stands ready for its flight in either case?
    But you would so befoul my spirit's wing
    As to unfit it both for life and death.
    Away, imposter! if my soul be pure,
    I may defy your threats!
Arb. Beware, beware!
Apae. Look to your own house, juggler! [*Exit*]
Arb. That I shall.
    Calenus!
Cal. Here, my lord.
Arb. The blow must fall.
Cal. On whom?
Arb. Apaecides. He will betray
    The secrets of the goddess, bring our faith
    Into contempt among the multitude
    By whom we live.
Cal. The villain! As we stand
    Our revenues are small enough; and mine—
    With all my ticklish work at oracles,
    And prodigies, and miracles, and things—
    Scarcely maintains me.
Arb. Miser! You have robbed
    The patient Deity, before her face,
    Of more than I can reckon.
Cal. Ha! ha! ha! [*Laughing*]
Arb. I wonder that you dare, you patent thief,
    Commit such sacrilege, without the fear
    Of Isis' vengeance.
Cal. Oh! come, come, my lord!
    You and I know about her vengeance, since
    We deal it out ourselves. What of the lad?
Arb. Apaecides must die.
Cal. So I suspect:
    That is the fate of all.
Arb. But, suddenly,
    And by your hand.
Cal. Excuse me. That would do
    In Egypt doubtless. Here there is a thing—
    A most impertinent and prying thing—

GLAUCUS

Called Roman law, that sometimes makes the man
Who strikes the blow follow his victim's ghost.

ARB. Amongst your other virtues, you are then
A coward.

CAL. Call me what you please. I'll not
Stand by, and see these precious bones of mine
Fed to a tiger, while you sit at ease,
Among your noble friends, and grin at me,—
Your poor Calenus! I am not a fool:
No; not to that extent.

ARB. I am glad to know
There is a limit to your folly. Well,
Put by your fears. I'll hire some ruffian,
Some gladiator, or some desperate slave,
To do the work. At all events, I'll take
This business on myself. 'Twere surer thus.

CAL. Surer and safer for your humble slave.

ARB. Yes, 'twere absurd to trust you.

CAL. Cunning ape,
You'll get no fiery chestnuts by the paw
Of this poor pussy! [*Aside*] Are you done, my lord?

ARB. Yes, yes; you tire me.

CAL. Then, I'll go and make
The eyes of Isis roll above the worshipers.
I greased her up last night; and now she works
Without a hitch. I have some oracles,
Of double import, for my trumpet too.
Come see, my lord, if you can keep your face,
And not spoil all with your untimely laughter.

ARB. Go, go, you knave!

CAL. Quoth pot to kettle. [*Enter Glaucus followed by Nydia*] Humph!
Here is another customer for you, my lord! [*Salutes Glaucus and exits*]

GLAU. Go, Nydia, to your lady. Take this flower. [*Gives a violet*]
It was a talisman but yesterday,
To make me welcome. There is some mistake.
Deny me, child! Not half an hour ago,
She bade me to return. Say I am here.
According to my promise.

ARB. What is this,
   This mawkish sentiment, so out of place?
   You must have left your manners in the street,
   To force an entrance to a lady's house.
GLAU. If you should find them, do not pick them up:
   They will not fit you.
ARB. Heaven be praised for that!
GLAU. Fly, Nydia. [*Exit Nydia*] My lord, we are alone—
ARB. Not quite so much alone as I would be.
GLAU. I'll not detain you. Go, and have your wish.[18]
   My purpose in addressing you was this:
   You seem to bear me some ill-will—just why
   I neither know nor greatly care. Perhaps
   Your hatred is so deadly, that 'twould suit[19]
   To ease your rancor even with my life.
   Lo! I am at your service. Any day
   During my natural life, however remote,—
   Though we outlast your mummies—I shall be
   Obedient to your call, in any way,
   With any weapons, any time and place,
   Your fancy may determine.
ARB. This indeed
   Is gross self-flattery. Can you think I feel
   So deeply toward so slight a thing as you?
   Ione comes. After she answers you,
   You may feel tamer. [*Enter Ione followed by Nydia*]
IONE. I am here, my lord.
   I understand you will not be denied:
   See me you must. Why is this urgency,
   When I have other cares that need me?
ARB. Good!
   There's frost upon his fire. [*Aside. He retires*]
GLAU. Ione!—What,
   What has changed you? Is it but caprice,—
   Your sex's birthright? Is your memory
   A mere convenience? I beseech you, be
   True to yourself, if not to me.
IONE. My lord,
   Truth to myself compels me to this course.
   I should be false indeed to all I know

GLAUCUS

       Of woman's purity, and the demands
       That custom makes upon a maiden's fame,
       If I consented longer to permit
       Your visits to me.
GLAU. That should be enough
       For pride to hear, without reply. But I—
       Pardon the weakness—have a heart that lies
       Prostrate before your mercy. Not again,
       Though I should tire the ages with my life,
       Can I feel pride towards you; or any passion,
       Save that which overwhelms all else and me,
       The deep humility of sovereign love.
       I do confess, lower than I can kneel,
       A sense of my unworthiness; but you,—
       Goddess in all things, as your form declares,—
       May lift demerit higher than its worth,
       And, with a smile bestow a happiness,
       For which the worthiest victor upon earth
       Would give his laurels.
IONE. You o'erestimate
       A transient feeling. You are of the world,
       A king among the gaudy butterflies
       Of fleeting fashion. Seek your world again
       And there forget me, as you will.
GLAU. Alas!
       Henceforth for me is no forgetfulness.
       Like mortals who have tasted heavenly food—
       The nectar and ambrosia of the gods,
       At an Olympian banquet—I shall thirst
       For that which made my clay almost divine.
IONE. My lord, 'tis needless to prolong our words.
       I am resolved.
GLAU. Resolved! So pitiless!
       What have I done deserving your contempt?
       Grant me no better than my ruder sex,
       Grant I want all that makes you lovable;
       Surely I am no worse than other men,
       Than those you tolerate, to come and go
       Under the roof your presence makes a Heaven.
IONE. Not worse?

GLAU. I know not that I am. If I
         May sit in judgment on myself, I say
         That I am guilty only of such sins
         As thoughtless youth commits. I never wronged
         Man with a lie or woman with a vow.[20]
         I may have had my follies, until you
         Walked, goddess-like, across my path of life,
         And, with a glance, transformed me; made me shake
         The flowers of pleasure from me; made me strive,
         With all resolution of my soul, to be
         Somewhat akin to you in guiltlessness,
         If not in natural purity. Alas!
         Who has maligned me? Who could make your heart
         Do me the wrong of listening with belief
         To false reports? Why do I ask? See, see,
         That dusky shadow which steals back and forth
         Across the scene, an omen of mischance!
         What touch but his could soil the robe of truth
         So darkly and so foully? If I do
         Injustice to the man whom I suspect,
         I ask his pardon. Silent still? O speak!
         Who charges me with aught that should affect
         Your former kindness towards me?
ARB. [*Advancing*] I.
GLAU. Go on.
ARB. I told my ward, and still maintain my words,
        That one of your loose habits, one whose life
        Is given to daily riot, one whose wont
        It is to sneer at woman's purity—
        Pointing your scorn by instance of the girls
        Who gather round your gold with open hands—
        I told this fair and innocent young maid,
        That you are not a proper man to come
        Nearer to her than coldest courtesy
        Sanction if you should come at all.
GLAU. Oh, shame!
         You told her this, yet dare to come yourself,
         Soiled with the orgies of your wicked house?
         You who make lust religion, thinly veil,
         With impious Isis' presence, deeds so foul

GLAUCUS

        That their mere mention makes a wholesome taste
        Sick at their fancy. But go on, go on!
Arb. The goddess will avenge the sacrilege
        Your ignorance has uttered at her rites.
Glau. But was this all?
Arb. Enough I think.
Ione. My lord,
        You told me something personal to me:
        An outrage done to common decency,
        Even though I be so humble that my name
        May be the gossip of abandoned men,
        Reclining idly at the bloody games.
Glau. Ah, ha! I see a light begins to break
        Out through the darkness. What of that?
Arb. Of that?
        Let me remember: I forget. . . . Oh, yes:
        There was a rumor—scandal—what you will:
        Haply not true, but proving, true or false,
        What an unfit associate you are—
        Because of your companionship, my lord—
        For any maiden who regards her fame
        Above her transient pleasure.
Glau. Out with it!
        My heart is standing in my mouth to speak,
        When you are done.
Arb. It was trifling thing—
        I give the rumor as it came to me.
        'Tis said that at the games—some time ago—
        One of your comrades used Ione's name
        Without that reverence which a man should show
        Towards one as unprotected as she is,
        Coupling her name with yours—the merry fool—
        And that you smiled, which made the others laugh.
Glau. Then I deserved to have my carcass thrown,
        Alive and shrieking, to the hungry beasts.
        Do you believe it?
Arb. Nay—
Glau. For if you do,
        Why do you let me live an instant more?
        Methinks her cause would make a coward brave

As angry Herakles. Witness my oath,
Great Power, to whom the secret soul of man
Is as an open volume, if by act or thought
I ever to your fairest creature paid
A less respect than to yourself! Oh, no;
My love is my religion; and its shrine,
Within my heart, is spotless as the maid
To whom 'tis consecrated. Why should I
Stoop to deny a lie so evident?
Or to disclaim what were impossible
To any offspring of my ancient race?
Look you, Egyptian, I am that which you
Cannot conceive of, princely though you are—
I am a gentleman.

ARB. The gods forbid,
I should deny a title of his rank
To one of their descendants. Dearest child,
A madman must be humored, to avoid
Scandal, or worse, even bloodshed in your house.
Get him away. I am not quite a stone,
And he may move me in the end. Be sure,
As I shall tell you in a little while,
That there is more of truth in this report
Than he can meet by anything but rage. [*Apart to Ione*]

GLAU. You are still silent; and in that I read
My fate, even harder than it is unjust.
I have o'erstaid your pleasure it would seem.
If, lady, sometime in the happy life—
Which the gods grant you!—it may ever be
That you shall need a friend—no common friend,
But one who will confront impending death
With solemn pleasure, but to save you pain—
Cry Glaucus, cry it to the listening air,
And, though I be a thousand leagues away,
The sound will reach me; and, with such a speed
As lightning rushes from the hand of Jove,
I shall appear before you. As for you,
Arbaces, traitor to the truth of Heaven,
The world is not so wide, but we shall meet
Before the throne of justice.[21]

ARB. [*Apart to her*] Come, come, child!
    Leave to the vanquished schemer all the good
    Possession of the field may give. For this
    Is not a place where you should linger now;
    As though you doubted that which you have said;
    Thereby inviting him to ask of you
    Another hearing.
IONE. [*Apart to him*] I do doubt indeed.
ARB. Have you not character enough to stand
    Upon your own matured decision, backed
    By the approval of your dearest friend?[22]
    Pshaw! this is weakness, and unworthy her
    Whose reason, from her infancy, I trained,
    Not as a woman's, as a man's, to cope
    With the delusive lures that falsehood spreads
    Before the senses.
IONE. By my brain gives way,
    And from the center of my prophet heart,
    I hear a voice, that cries, in reason's spite:
    Glaucus is true!
ARB. You are bewildered, child.
    Take time to think. I'll answer that this bird
    Will come again whene'er you whistle him.[23]
    Then let tomorrow, if you so decide,
    Heal up the wound that you have given today.
    Come to my house, as you have promised me;—
    I will precede you there a little while;—
    And after you have read your father's letter,
    We may talk over calmly, and without
    This stress of passion, your poor heart affair,
    That, to my colder judgment, now appears
    Both weak and miserable. Pray, be firm.
IONE. Arbaces?
ARB. Dear Ione?
IONE. Fly at once:
    Outstrip the wind, and these delaying thoughts;
    Or I shall stand here, parleying with my heart,
    Until I shame myself!
ARB. [*Aside*] Victorious! [*Exit with Ione, supporting and drawing her off*]

GLAU. Gone! Not a word of parting or regret!
    Gone with that basest, falsest, worst of men;
    Electing him and falsehood for her guides,
    Rather than love and truth—than me. Alas!
    There is the sting, there in my very heart—
    The personal, the selfish, famished cry
    For love bestowed, demanding love's return.[24]
    And yet I thought that, one time, in her eyes
    I saw the dawning light of what might be,
    Full risen, a golden day of love for me.
    Oh, cruel deception! Is it possible,
    The gods should clothe a sorceress, whose guile
    Is to entrap and ruin trusting men,
    In such a winning shape; so outward fair,
    That Solon's self would say the temple's walls
    Must enshrine a goddess radiant with the beams
    Of every heavenly virtue? Oh! shame, shame,
    Upon the doubt! I will not credit it.
    She is both pure and virtuous; or I see
    A prodigy, before unknown on earth,
    Of beauty false unto itself. Poor heart,
    Toil on, toil ever! In this earthly life
    There's but one goal for you. I gird myself,
    Like the Olympian runner, for the race.
    The prize or forfeit, at the course's end,
    I see before me—love or death! [*Enter Nydia*]
NYD. Or death!
    What has the youth and the abounding life
    Of happy Glaucus yet to do with death?
GLAU. Judge your own happiness, my child; but fear
    To answer for another.
NYD. You are wise.
    But what has happened in this house, since I
    Left it so merry, to yourself and her
    Who just fled from it? As I stood beside
    Her litter, as she mounted, I could hear
    Her heart that beat, as an alarm to life,
    While death besieged it.
GLAU. Ask her. It is not
    For me to know why her heart beats.

GLAUCUS

NYD. But why
This bitterness?
GLAU. A moment hence, you'll ask,
Why this strange sweetness? Such is human life.
Where went your mistress?
NYD. To Arbaces' house.
GLAU. Ha!
NYD. You may well exclaim.
GLAU. Why went she there?
NYD. Why goes the dove into the fowler's snare?
I begged her not to go, but all in vain.
I warned her of the danger, vain that too.
She seemed as one who desperately walks
Straight on a peril, full before her set,
Because it is so fated.
GLAU. Why do you
Tarry here safely, while a danger hangs
Over your mistress' head?
NYD. I seek you, Glaucus.
Woman's aid cannot avail her now.
She needs the brain and strong determined hand
That serve your courage.
GLAU. She shall have them.
NYD. Man,
Are you asleep? Will you not take alarm?
Have you not seen, unless you are blinder far
Than I am, that Arbaces, in his way—
His vile, unscrupulous, remorseless way—[25]
Loves her?
GLAU. He loves her!
NYD. Yes, and means this day,
By fair means or by foul, to win her.
GLAU. Gods!
And we stand talking! [*Going*]
NYD. Pause, my lord: one word.
You, singly, cannot rescue her—
GLAU. But I
Can die in the endeavor.—
NYD. That would be
Death and dishonor, at one blow, to both.

Hear me, my lord. I know Arbaces' house
From roof-tree to foundation-stone: I can
Without the knowledge of an inmate there,
So place you that, whene'er she needs your help,
You, in a moment, may be at her side.[26]
Think what depends on this—her life, her love,
Her spotless name, her future and your own.
Success is born of prudence, not of force.

GLAU. Delay no more. But place me face to face
With any wretch that means to do her wrong,
And if I fail to win her, from the mace
Brandished by Herakles, this thing is sure,
That I shall never know it, if by death
We mean oblivion of this world's affairs.

NYD. My signal to you, howso'er you stand,
Victor or vanquished, be my Grecian song:
When you hear that—

GLAU. Away! we waste the time,
While she, perhaps, now stands on peril's brink,
Frozen with horror. Girl, I feel my sword
Creep in its scabbard; my ethereal soul
Loosens its hold upon my grosser clay, and soars,
Like a young eagle, with defying breast,
Fronting the storm of life or calm of death!
We can contrive our plan upon the wing,
As well as here. Delay may mean defeat.

NYD. [*Aside*] Shade of my mother, have I not done well? [*Exeunt rapidly*]

ACT III.

SCENE: *The palace of Arbaces. A great hall, richly furnished, containing strange astrological and alchemical instruments, a library of scrolls, etc. A statue of Isis, with a coffer at the base. A table upon which are papers and a naked sword. In the center of flat a large archway, covered with curtains. As the curtain rises, an orgy of Isis is going on—with music, dancing and drinking, etc. Enter Arbaces hastily.*

ARB. Vanish! I weary of these mummeries. [*Exeunt suddenly all the revellers*]

GLAUCUS

Calenus! sluggard, have you leaden feet? [*Enter Calenus deliberately*]

CAL. The slave reports that she has left her house,
Bound hither.
ARB. Well.
CAL. [*Aside*] For you, mayhap: for her—
ARB. Are the ships ready? All the stores aboard?
CAL. All but the treasure.
ARB. That will be embarked,
Under my eyes.
CAL. [*Aside*] He does not trust me. Well,
I would not trust him were his case my own.
ARB. The captains are instructed, and can cut
Their cables in a trice, and put to sea?
CAL. At any moment.
ARB. And the secret way,
That leads from this room to the shore, has that
Been cleared of rubbish? It has been disused
So long, that it may be encumbered.
CAL. Yes:
And torches are at hand to light the way.
I wonder if I told you—
ARB. Told me what?
CAL. Something about that passage.
ARB. What?
CAL. One day,
About a month ago, when she was here
Singing for you, I met blind Nydia
Feeling her way along the dripping walls
Of that same passage. Why, the gods can tell.
For when I boxed her ears, and questioned her,
She sank into that obstinate, dumb mood,
She is so good at, and made no reply.
I think that little demon knows the house
Better than any rat that ranges it.
ARB. Pshaw! she is harmless.
CAL. Yes; so was the mouse
That gnawed the lion's net.
ARB. You will remain.

Cal. For what?
Arb. To take my property in charge,
And carry on your house of Isis work.
Cal. Oh, Pluto take old Isis and her work!
I am sick of her. Our profits will run down
Almost to nothing if Apaecides
Turn traitor, and go brawling through the streets
About my new machinery, as he threatens.
Ha! ha! the scoffer calls me—think of it—
"The soul of Isis!" Well, as if the goddess
Might not have had a worse soul than myself.
Arb. Apaecides? He must be looked to. You
Think sacrificing him to Isis' wrath
Were dangerous.
Cal. Very: for the worldly law
Might call our good deed by another name—
Murder, for instance.
Arb. Umph! I have a crypt,
Under this very room, of solid rock;
There he might pass the remnant of his days
In penitence to Isis, or relate
His dangerous stories to the listening stones.
Cal. An excellent and pious pastime.
Arb. [Aside] Yes.
Should you become irksome to me, you,
You grasping miser, also may find room
In the same lodging. [Aloud] You must watch the boy:
Track him about the city like a hound;
Know all his doings, from the time he wakes
Until he slumbers.
Cal. How about his dreams?
Arb. His dreams, his dreams! Is not life all a dream—
This chase of phantoms, and this tug with fate—
As we may find when death awakens us?
Are my slaves ready, armed, and at their posts?
The girl shall yield; or must be made to yield:
This day shall end the matter.
Cal. I said, and say
Your orders, to the letter, are obeyed.

ARB. Why do you linger then? It is your charge
 To keep your eye upon my Nubians,
 And bring them when I call.
CAL. I thought, perhaps,
 You might have something else besides a charge
 To give—a credit, say; or, what were better,
 Some solid cash, hey!
ARB. How this avarice
 Grows on you, man! And it is hideous,
 To see a man whose only thought is gold,
 Forever gold! Here, take this bag. [*Gives bag from the table*]
CAL. All gold—
 I think you said, all gold?
ARB. Look for yourself. [*Calenus counts money*]
CAL. But seventeen pieces. Hum! now had it been
 Twenty, to make things even.
ARB. Miscreant!
 Go, ere I brain you.
CAL. Barely seventeen. [*Exit slowly*]
ARB. That knave will quarrel with my patience soon.
 His raging maw would bolt a world of gold,
 And still be hungry. Fellows of his kind
 Cannot be trusted. His fidelity
 Is in his pocket, ready to desert
 To any rival bidder. Well, my man,
 There is a cell, to pocket you alive,
 And all your stealing, if you dare to show
 Treachery to me. [*Re-enter Calenus hastily*]
 How now?
CAL. My lord, the girl
 Is at the door.
ARB. Admit her. Hide yourself:
 Your grin would breed suspicion in a lamb.
CAL. Well for the lamb. [*Exit*]
ARB. Now to assume the sage. [*Seats himself at the table in seeming study*]
 That footfall and the rustle of that robe
 Set my blood bounding. [*Enter Ione, escorted by Arbaces' slaves. Exeunt slaves*]
 Dear Ione, welcome! [*Rises*]

IONE. You show scant hospitality, my lord,
    Not to receive me in your atrium.
ARB. That which you seek is here. [*Pointing to a large coffer*]
    I was absorbed
    In reading o'er your horoscope.
IONE. Ha! ha! [*Laughing*]
    What say the riddling stars about a girl
    As humble as myself?
ARB. Nothing but good,
    If you but heed the stars' interpreter.
IONE. But of the letter.
ARB. [*Hands key*] Open for yourself.
IONE. So then. [*Unlocks coffer*] What's here?—Jewels and gold! Ah! yes;
    Here is a letter. By your leave, my lord. [*Reads*]
ARB. Let me read you, as you peruse the lines.
    Distress?—a frown?—what, anger and disgust?
    No sign of pleasure! Am I come to this?—
    A priest and king of Egypt, of a race
    Older than earth's traditions! Upstart Greek,
    Those looks shall cost you dearly! [*Aside*]
IONE. This is all?
ARB. All that I know of, and that little all
    Seems not to please you.
IONE. Do you know, Arbaces:
    The substance of this letter?
ARB. Certainly:
    Your father read it to me as he wrote.
    It was his darling project; planned, he thought,
    To be your happiness and mine.
IONE. You know
    It is impossible, and always was,
    And always will be. Let me pass. [*Going*]
ARB. [*Preventing her*] Not yet.
    Listen to me. When you were yet a child,
    I but a man, your father solemnly
    Betrothed us two; as far as then he could,
    Joined us as one forever. You have read
    His dying testament, confirming that;
    And then enjoining you, by all the love
    You bear his memory, to obey his will;

    And, at a marriageable age, to give
    Yourself to me in wedlock.
IONE. I cannot:
    The thought is monstrous.
ARB. Why?
IONE. Pray let me go!
    There was no moment in my life or yours,
    When the mere thought of marriage with yourself
    Could have been tolerable to me.
ARB. [*Retaining her*] Alas!
    And I have loved you, ah! so tenderly,
    Not with a parent's or a tutor's love,
    But with the fiery passion of a man
    Who saw before him his one hope in you,
    And bent his life to compass that. For that
    I toiled, I studied, won both wealth and power;
    Made man my subject, and the hands of men
    My willing instruments; became, Ione,
    That which I am, that which you know, I am,
    A giant among pigmies. O, I pray you,
    Pause ere you put this mighty love aside,
    To pick up slighter morsels! You are great;[27]
    Your spirit longs for grandeur and for power;
    See, I can give them. Think you I abide
    In this dull country, rather than the land
    Where I am priest and monarch, for aught else
    Than to crown you my empress? Let us flee
    To the dateless, deathless Egypt; to the realm
    That ruled the world ere history began.
    Come, come, aboard! My ships await us, love,
    Eager to start as I am. Pause, and think:
    Take time for thought.
IONE. I ask for that alone.
    Come to my house tomorrow—
ARB. Ha! ha! ha! [*Laughing*]
    Be sure of this; if you wed me, my own,
    You will not wed a fool.
IONE. How dare you use
    A term like that to me?

Arb. My own you are.
    For when I look about upon these walls,
    Mute, deaf, impenetrable, I almost think
    That you are quite my own. You must decide
    This matter ere we part; for, once at large,
    You might assume your woman's right to change
    Your tender mind. An oath as deep as hell,
    As high as Jove's Olympus, must be bound
    About your soul before you quit my sight.
    What of your father's will?
Ione. O villain, cease!
    Wrong not the dead with falsehood, howsoe'er
    You play the tyrant with his helpless child.
    That letter is a fraud, from first to last,
    As you best know of all men.
Arb. Grant it so;
    Then, of all women, who can better tell
    Than you before what sort of man you stand?
Ione. Arbaces, hear me: would you force my love?—
Arb. Nay, win it, darling.
Ione. Mockery of a man,
    My senses sicken at your loathsome words,
    Call me your slave, your victim; do not dare
    Thus to profane the sanctity of love
    With foul endearments. Have a care! today
    Will not be time's conclusion. I have friends,
    Who will exact a reckoning at your hands
    For all I suffer now.
Arb. Within an hour
    We shall be sailing on the middle sea
    Towards Egypt, my beloved. Once there, where I,
    The son of kings, am master of events,
    Your friends may rage uncared for.
Ione. Gracious gods,
    Are you responsible for such a man,
    Or did the demons form him?
Arb. Come, aboard!
    Go kindly with me, or my slaves shall toss

GLAUCUS

Your haughty beauty, like a bale of goods,
Into my galley. Come, come! [*Seizes her*]
IONE. Pity me!
Pity the child whom once you seemed to love,
Not as a satyr, as a father!
ARB. No!
You have heaped insult on my love; 'tis now
My turn to answer scornful words with deeds. [*She breaks from him and kneels*]
IONE. Pallas Athene, save your helpless child!
Glaucus!—My Glaucus! [*Enter Glaucus from behind the statue of Isis*]
GLAU. [*Drawing*] I am here, beloved!
Call on your gods, Arbaces, for your time
Is dwindled to a span. Have courage, love!
O flower of women, lift your drooping head!
The storm is passed. Behold me at your side.
Now there can be no danger; for the right
Strengthens my arm, and makes my buoyant heart
To dance with joy, that I am here to brave
Nought worse than death in your defense.
ARB. Vile Greek,
Boast when you see the sun again; not now,
While Hell prepares to swallow you! Begone!
Your sight is odious to me! [*Snatches sword from table. They fight; Arbaces is disarmed*]
Murderer!—
Ione, spare me!
IONE. Oh! no blood, no blood!—
Not before me, dear Glaucus!
GLAU. Do I hear?
You said, "dear Glaucus?"
IONE. Now and ever. Hear
The coward's prayer. Henceforward he can have
No portion in our lives.
GLAU. Go, miscreant!
And pass your days in sorrowing o'er yourself.
A voice within me says I am unwise
To spare a broken serpent; but her voice,

    Lifted in supplication, is too sweet
    To be resisted. Trickster, solemn knave,
    Who make an earthly trade of heavenly things,
    Return not to your shallow juggleries
    In Isis' house, or I shall let the world
    Into your frauds. Go wallow in the Nile,
    Whose slime begot you, to make men ashamed
    Of you, their likeness. Come, Ione, come! [*Going with Ione. As they reach the door, Arbaces sounds a sistrum. His guards drive back Glaucus and Ione from the door. Other guards enter from the side, and surround Arbaces. Enter Calenus*]

 ARB. The trap is sprung. Now, insolent, some more
    Of your abounding eloquence! Let me have
    A little more insufferable advice
    About my future life! I wager you,
    You cannot tell as much about your own
    For the next hour or two.
 GLAU. [*Apart to Ione*] Be not dismayed!
    Yet there is hope, if my prevision hold.
    Where, where is Nydia?
 ARB. Seize them! To the ship—
    But tenderly, no rudeness—with the girl.
    The man I shall provide for. There's a cage,
    My Attic linnet, underneath this hall,
    Where you may sing your death-song to yourself,
    Till voice and life both fail you. Seize on them! [*As the guards advance cautiously, dreading Glaucus' sword, Nydia sings without*]
 NYD. [*Sings*] The gods are descending in power from the sky;
    The darkness is broken, and succor is nigh;
    Hell quails at their glance, as their glories increase,
    And light bathes the forehead of beautiful Greece. [*Enter Nydia*]
 GLAU. [*Apart to Ione*] At last! Forget not, darling, that you are
    Almost my wife: be brave!
 NYD. What, Glaucus!
 GLAU. Here:
    Come hither, child! [*She approaches, and whispers Glaucus*]
 ARB. Why do you pause, my men,
    To watch this comedy? Another mouse
    Has fallen into the trap, and that is all.

GLAUCUS

Disarm the Greek! aboard with both the girls!
Athenian fribble, let the latest look
You take of earth, ere you descend forever
Into the darkness of your living tomb,
Be on my triumph! Look! and let that look
Be Hell's affliction to your solitude,
Upon my galleys rocking in the bay;
Ere long to bear me and my lovely bride
Upon our wedding progress. Look your last! [*Flings aside the curtains of the great door, and discovers Clodius, Apaecides, Lydon and an array of Gladiators, heavily armed, standing there in silence. Arbaces' guards, who have been advancing on Glaucus, retreat. Arbaces recoils in confusion*]

GLAU. [*Apart to Arbaces*] Shall it be peace or war? Think, ere you make
    Your house a shambles.
APAE. [*Advancing*] Sister, you are safe.
IONE. Safe evermore. For am I not the prize
    And willing trophy of that brave man's sword?
GLAU. Ione, make me not insane with joy;
    Oh, make me not even grateful to the wretch
    Who brought me such a fortune.
CLOD. [*Advancing*] Glaucus, pray,
    What is the meaning of this summons?
GLAU. [*Apart to him and Apaecides*] Friends,
    I beg your silence. You shall hear anon.
    Arbaces had prepared a spectacle
    Of Isis, to amuse himself and us;
    And so I summoned you for company.
    Somehow, the spectacle has failed to work
    Indeed he seems to be, unwillingly,
    The only spectacle within our view,
    Save that which you present him.
CAL. [*Apart to Arbaces*] So, my lord,
    The game is up.
ARB. [*Apart to him*] Not for another set:
    Not while they leave me life. Be silent, man!
    Today is theirs; tomorrow may be mine.

TABLEAU

ACT IV.

SCENE: *Before the house of Isis. A colossal statue of the goddess seen within. On the right, the entrance to the palace of Arbaces. On the left, the entrance to the theater. Time, before sunset. As the scene darkens, the eyes of the statue of Isis are illumined. The stage is filled with people who have just left, while others are leaving, the theater. Enter from the theater Burbo and Stratonice.*

Bur. Oh, such a lion! Wife, in all your life,
    Did you e'er see a beast like that?
Stra. Yes, dunce,
    A bigger.
Bur. When?
Stra. Why, when I first saw you.
Bur. Ha! ha! you always have your little joke.
1st Cit. What of the lion, Burbo:
Bur. We just saw,
    My wife and I, by favor of a friend,
    Who tends the beasts—
Stra. Well, if my wife and I
    Saw such a sight, let that one tell of it
    Who saw not double. He came in today—
Bur. Brought here by Pansa.—
Stra. Fresh from Africa—
Bur. Wild as a hawk—
Stra. A savage, brave young beast—
Bur. 'Twould make your hair stir but to hear him growl—
Stra. Growl! Will you still be braying, ass? He roars
    Like double thunder.—
Bur. Tears the iron bars—
Stra. Rolls, like a kitten, o'er and o'er again.
    With fury, till his cage rocks.—
Bur. Just to stand
    With no more than those rattling bars between
    Him and yourself.—
Stra. Made Burbo green with fear:
    You shameless coward!—
Bur. Gods! his dreadful tail.
    He thrashed the floor with that same iron tail—

GLAUCUS

STRA. Tail, dummy! Had you seen his ivory teeth,
   As keen lancets—
BUR. And his crooked claws,
   Ripping the boards. What chance would a man stand
   Before the brute?
STRA. And there they'll keep him shut,
   In that vile cage, until he'll grow as weak
   And worthless as my husband.
1ST CIT. What a shame!
   Will not one fight him?
BUR. Were I young again—
STRA. You'd show that lion such a pair of heels,
   That he would take you for an antelope.
   There is no criminal to feed his maw.
BUR. Now, what a godsend were a murderer!
   To let us see the lion do his work
   At crunching bones. By Pollux! there's no man
   Could front him: not a gladiator; no,
   Not Lydon even.
STRA. Lydon; I would like
   To see some nobleman—your Glaucus, hey?—
   That man with thews like Hercules;—if he
   And that young beast together were let loose
   In the arena, you would see some sport—
   Something you would remember. It would be[28]
   Quite even betting too. If Glaucus had
   Sign of weapon, I would lay my purse
   On the Athenian against Africa.
BUR. I tell you what were funny; if young Dudus
   Should have the courage with her slippery hair
   To strangle any girl of his tonight.
   By Jove! to see the lion mouth him!
STRA. Pshaw!
   That beast would take him like a pill. One gulp,
   And all were over. No, I want to see
   A fair, square fight; a long one too. [*A rumbling sound is heard*]
BUR. There, there!
   Do you not feel that?
STRA. What, that little shake?
BUR. It makes me seasick.

STRA. You are given to qualms,
 You bearded woman! 'Twould be well, I think,[20]
 If you and I should interchange our garments,
 To save the family from shame. You flinch
 At every earthquake. Pigeon, use your wings
 When earth has colics.
BUR. If I only had
 The wings to use! I do not like the day:
 This hot dull sun, this smoky air, this smell
 Of burning sulphur. Ever since I rose,
 I have been coughing at that smell.
STRA. Pish! pish!
 How will you do when you must breath those fumes
 Through all eternity? Come home, you sheep! [*Exeunt*]
BUR.[30] Look, look! they come. [*Enter Lydon, bearing a palm branch, and the other Gladiators*]
STRA. Lydon, again! That fellow makes me tired.
 Hail, man of many palms! I heard you said,
 After your daddy gained his liberty
 You'd leave off fighting.
LYD. And so I say still:
 But I am bound to fight this meeting through
 By oath to Pansa.
STRA. If you live so long.
 They say the Praetor rages at the part
 You and your fellows took upon yourselves,
 Last night, at Arbaces' house. Hey, boy,
 What if you all were scourged for that?
LYD. 'Twere better.
 That when my father bore the scourge for nothing.
 From that Lord Glaucus freed him. Let them whip
 This back into a jelly. I shall smile,
 Just as I would upon the bloody cross,
 To know I died for Glaucus.
STRA. Brave old boy!
 Give me your fist; and when you want a hand,
 To help you at your mischief, call on me.
 This arm is not so weakened—Feel my arm:
 Some muscle left yet, hey?—This arm, one time,
 Could wield the trident, cast the fatal net,

GLAUCUS

        And these old legs could hurry round the ring,
        In such a manner as would make them stare
        In these decaying days.
Lyd. No doubt of it:
        For all the giants lived before our time.
Stra. Lydon, see here.
Bur. What, what?
Stra. Does Lydon sound
        Like Burbo? man like monkey? I would speak
        With Lydon, jackass.
Lyd. Well, well.
Stra. Have a care
        Of that Egyptian, for yourself, as well
        As for Lord Glaucus. If I know the man,
        Arbaces' vengeance has a memory
        As long as is Hell's highway. There will be
        A reckoning for last night's affair; and then,
        Let me not find my warning was forgotten.
        Do you see Glaucus ever?
Lyd. But I may.
Stra. Tell him this, and make him credit you:
        Arbaces' man, Calenus, can be bought—
        Bought for a spy, or any dirty use
        That gold e'er purchased. Lydon, by the gods,
        If you neglect my words, let Glaucus' blood
        Be on your head! If you would keep him safe,
        Watch! watch Arbaces.
Lyd. Dear old girl, your words
        Are treasured in my heart. I understand
        Their weight too, trust me.
Stra. Hist, hist! Let's begone. [*Exeunt severally. Enter Arbaces attended*]
Arb. Why am I sighing for almighty power,
        While every sigh but proves me more a man?—
        A human thing, who, to obtain an end,[31]
        Must scheme among the other schemers, weak
        With all their weakness, not a jot more sure
        To rule the future than the savage brute
        That takes his foeman promptly by the throat,
        And sucks the life-blood from his veins. They call
        Me here a wizard; would to Heaven, I were!

That I might spread a glamour o'er the land,
To witch Ione's stubborn heart, and drain
The haughty strength with which that impious Greek
Confronts me, and you, Isis: Will you not
Avenge yourself, O goddess? Dreams, dreams, dreams!
From which I waken, a mere man again,[32]
In conscious impotence—a hypocrite
Who fain would take the desperate chances, born
Of gods in which I have no real belief.
The weak are ever superstitious. I
Call for a power that is not in myself,
And play at self-deception. Isis, speak!
Is what we call religion a trick,
Whereby the cunning rule the imbecile?
And is that deeper faith, our sages hold,
In immortality a product vain
Of human vanity? No answer comes:
The silence seems to mock me. Dreadful Sphinx,
Foreboding future, mother of despair,
Answer your royal priest, if gods have ears—
Yes, if you have a being, and are not,
Like all things earthly, but an empty dream! [*Enter the Praetor and Guards*]

PRAE. Musing, my prince!
ARB. Hail, my unfailing friend!
   This hour is meditation's. As the eye[33]
Watches the sun descending, and the shades
Of evening lengthen, then the heart of man
Seems to go down, and shadows grow about
The central light within our moody breasts:
Life seems most burdensome; and all the sills
That haunt our thoughts, in one stupendous cloud
Settle upon our thoughts. The shackled prisoner
Looks through his walls into the world beyond,
And at the vision groans. The exile's heart
Is tortured with the sweets of home; the lover
Sighs for his absent mistress; once again
The mourner freshly feels the sting of death;
The baffled hopes of youth like spectres rise,
And will not to their ancient graves again;

This heavenly wanderer, which we call the soul,
Yearns in its doleful place of banishment
For its lost birthright, and the broken bond
Aches at its fracture like a cruel wound.
Evening is melancholy's playtime.

PRAE. Yes;
And Prince Arbaces' too. What thing has dashed
Your spirit thus?

ARB. All things.

PRAE. And this report,
Now flying through the town, of something done
Of violence and insult at your house
By that Athenian ruffian;—what of that?—
Backed by a gang of slaves. Do they forget[34]
The lictors' rods? Or does Lord Glaucus know
What it will be to him, should he presume
To outrage Roman law, while I am judge?

ARB. That was drunken riot, nothing more.
Glaucus had supped too well; and in his zeal
Blinded with wine and passion, he mistook
My harmless purpose for I know not what.
Pray pass it over, as I shall; for fear
Lest, should his fault be tossed from tongue to tongue,
It brings a scandal on a lady's name,
Whose fame is dear to me.

PRAE. You show in this
Noble forebearance, like yourself. However,
Remember should he practise pranks like these,
I stand prepared to punish him.

ARB. Thanks, thanks!
Fitter occasion may arise; and then—

PRAE. Not all his wealth, nor all the vulgar howl
Of his dear mob shall save him.

ARB. [*Aside*] Excellent!
Hope smiles again.

PRAE. Farewell!

ARB. Farewell!

PRAE. Observe
That Attic madcap strictly. [*Exit with train*]

ARB. Never fear;
    My eyes were given me for no other use. [*Enter Apaecides*[35] *hastily, Calenus restraining him*]
    Apaecides!
APAE. Dare not pronounce my name.
    Monster of falsehood, do you still pollute
    This city with your presence? Recollect
    Your meditated crime, and hide yourself
    From man and Heaven, till, serpent-like, you crawl
    Back to your native den!
ARB. Misguided youth,
    I pity you, and spare you.
APAE. Spare me, slave!
    It were blaspheming Heaven for me to spare
    You when I find you in the haunts of men,
    Lest the unwary suffer. [*Rushes at Arbaces. Calenus and slaves interpose*]
ARB. There, poor boy,
    You see your weakness. Pray misjudge me not!
    Surely your father's will has some respect
    Of you, although your sister disobey.
APAE. Though you might counterfeit his hand and seal,
    You could not so pervert our faith in him,
    That it did not disown and contradict
    Your written fraud. O sacrilegious wretch,
    To put your lies into a dead man's mouth,
    To bring dishonor on his memory,
    To turn his children's hearts against the man
    To whom they owe all love, and reverence!
    That was the risk you made us undergo,
    Impious imposter; but those twins of Heaven,
    Immortal truth and love, have but one pair
    Of searching eyes, to baffle evil with,
    And they are on you. Go!
ARB. Romantic boy,
    You are too simple for this common world.
    May time call wisdom for you! [*Going. Enter Glaucus, Clodius, Dudus and train, obstructing Arbaces' train*|
    Move!
CAL. My lord—

GLAUCUS

ARB. Who bars the way?
CAL. Lord Glaucus.
ARB. Use your staves!
    Now, by the head of Isis—[*Draws*]
GLAU. Who demands
    The way of me? Arbaces? Men, stand firm!
    I am not used to yield a freeman's right
    To an unpunished criminal. Who stirs [*He and Clodius draw*]
    Walks on the point of my forbidding sword.
    Is it with pomp and impudence like this
    You quit the scene of your misdeeds? Nay, glide,
    Cat-like and stealthy, from our loathing sight,
    Lest justice overtake you, ere you freight
    Your gallies with your guilt.
ARB. I ask no leave
    To go and come, to strike or pitch my tent,[36]
    Of you, Athenian braggart!
APAE. Hold his men
    Back for a moment, till I settle this,
    And all our wrongs together. 'Tis a chance
    I seek and long for.
GLAU. Nay, Apaecides.
    'Twas he began the outrage; let him on,
    And bide the issue of his violence.
ARB. Avoid the fellow, as you would evade
    Unsavory filth. [*To his train*]
GLAU. Yes, follow your wise nose:
    It is a prudent leader for a heart
    As delicate as yours. [*His followers laugh*]
ARB. You act today
    As though Time's hand had dropped his calendar.
    Think of tomorrow; if you will not now,
    Remember, when it comes, what I have said. [*Leads his train around that of Glaucus and exit*]
GLAU. Oh, dear tomorrow, how should I forget,
    Even at a villain's prompting, that the day
    Will usher in my boundless happiness?—
    Will merge in all two lives that yearn to meet,
    Like affluent streams, that henceforth are but one,
    Like kindred hands that join in one salute,

        Like meeting lips that form a single kiss!
        Not in division, but in unity,[37]
        All nature lives. I thank the gracious gods
        That rapt our kindred souls as near to Heaven
        As mortals may aspire, and suffered us
        To join and swell their choral harmony!
CLOD. My Glaucus, O my Glaucus, are you he
        With whom I feasted yesterday, on food
        Cooked in a kitchen, washed with earth-born wine—
        You on whose rapturous lips now overrun
        The nectar and ambrosia of the gods?
APAE. Or are you he, the staid philosopher,
        Who frowned o'er Plato, in a knot of thought;
        While I stood by, to hear your magic tongue
        Make all things clear, as though the puzzling scroll
        Were written with a sunbeam?
DUD.[38] Are you he
        That made this life a burden to yourself,
        That we, your friends, might go the lighter?—You
        Who sighed o'er everything the world contained;
        Grew sick at pain or pleasure, both alike?
        Inveighed against the rose's musky smell,
        The glaring whiteness of the lily's head,
        The noise of music, and the travesty
        Art made of nature—nature, in herself
        Being by no means perfect? You who held
        Of more account a ribbon on your robe
        Than all the foreign policy of Rome?
        Oh, I admired that Glaucus; but I fear
        That you are spoiled forever—
GLAU. Are you done?
        Is this the penance one must undergo
        For showing his true nature? Be it so;
        For I am unconverted. As a proof,
        I bid you to the final sacrifice
        Tomorrow morning. You shall see me go
        As blindly as the dedicated ox
        Goes to the altar and the priestly knife. [*Music without*]
        Hark, hark! the Heavens are bowing down to earth.

GLAUCUS

        I know that strain, and why it makes the wind
        Pause but to hear it.
CLOD. There is wind enough
        To blow us hence. Come, gentlemen, the gods
        Admit no mortals to their councils. Yes;
        We will be there betimes, to see the ox
        Go to the slaughter. [*Exit with Apaecides and Dudus, laughing.*
Enter Ione with attendants and a sacrificial train]
GLAU. Hail, my dearest!
IONE. Glaucus!
GLAU. Be not embarrassed. It is right, my love,
        That you should offer the protecting gods
        Your modest maiden sacrifice. We owe
        More to their grace than human vanity
        Could challenge for itself.
IONE. Yes, yes; but—but—
        Ah, Glaucus, when a woman gives herself
        To any man, as I am given to you,
        Must he be ever in the way? I hoped
        To steal to Heré's temple unobserved,
        At least by you; and, lo, not half way there,
        You start up to confront me, and confuse
        My poor devotions; and—and—
GLAU. You designed
        To pass unnoticed; so your cunning chose
        The Street of Fortune, as a private route;
        Ear-catching music, and a fluttering train
        Of winning girls, begarlanded and decked
        With flying ribbons; all the pomp and stir
        Of coming sacrifice, in which to hide,
        At least from me, your prudish little self!
        You are a very woman.
IONE. Were I not,
        How much would Glaucus love me?
GLAU. Perfect maid,
        I trifle with my happiness. So great
        It seems, and so transfigured is the world
        To something that I never knew before;
        So filled with light and sweetness, that my spirit
        Seems soaring, at a dizzy heavenly height,

On unaccustomed wings. To look below
Awes me, and backward scares the venturous blood
Into its citadel. I dare not think
The mortal thoughts, that ever, prophet-like,
Cry woe, woe, woe! to earthly happiness.
And I, I am too happy for the jealous gods[39]
To tolerate my more than mortal state
Without rebuke. This boding shadow, love,
Cast by the brightness of my dazzling joy,
Will follow me until I clasp you close
Against my heart, and know that fate has made
Our lot secure in making you my wife.

IONE. Glaucus, you dream of good and ill alike,
From the same inspiration. Let my dreams
Be offsets to your own. I only see
Visions of bliss before us. Trust the gods;
For we are in their hands, for joy or grief,
Whether we trust or not. Deserve their grace,
And that may better fortune.

GLAU. Yes, and they
Who spread this glorious nature at their feet,[40]
For their enduring joy, must also show
A new delight in their immortal eyes
When they survey a sight as beautiful,
As pure, as holy as our love. The gods
Be with you, darling, at your sacrifice!
Sound pipe and tabor, fling your streamers out,
Set all your maids to laughing, take the street
Like an imperial triumph, and oncemore
Endeavor thus to steal, all unobserved,
To Heré's temple!

IONE. Glaucus, it is sad
To see how foolish a wise man may be!

GLAU. Oh, look for nothing but the silliest joy
From me, till wedlock make me serious,
Priestess of wisdom!

IONE. Madcap, let me go!
Shall the gods wait to see your folly out?
Well, if you will, here in the public street,

	Insensible to shame!—I am too pressed
	For time, to palter with you.
GLAU.	Nay, my love!
	Here in the privacy of your parade. [*Kisses her*]
IONE.	Then here began my sacrifice; alas!
	And somewhat prematurely. [*Exit with her train*]
GLAU.	O beloved,
	Fairest and best, passion and perfect rest,
	Fire and assuaging dew, consummate marvel
	Of sweetest contraries!—how like a dove,
	That will not quit its mate, my fluttering heart
	Follows your flight with spiritual gaze,
	Broods o'er your tender head with outspread wings.
	By Heaven commissioned! [*Enter Nydia*]
	Nydia!
NYD.	My lord!
GLAU.	You are not with your mistress.
NYD.	Not today.
GLAU.	Why then?
NYD.	I could not—
GLAU.	Could not!
NYD.	Would not—
GLAU.	Would not!
	And at a time so solemn in her life?
NYD.	There may be times as solemn in the lives
	Of others. For my part, I trouble Heaven
	With my thanksgiving at last night's escape:
	That is forever in my mind. My brain
	Refuses to put by the hideous thought
	Of that which might have been to you, had fate
	Given to your foe the upper hand. My lord,
	You do not know how capable of crime—[41]
	Of pitiless, remorseless, deadly crime,
	Is the dark spirit of Arbaces. Now,
	Even now, while all things look so fatal yet.
	Watch, while that demon lives.
GLAU.	Nay, Nydia,
	Whatever be his malice, you o'er-rate
	His power to do me harm.

Nyd. Then I must watch,
   Watch without eyes: my scanty senses must
   Perform the duty that you set at naught.
Glau. I shall not slumber. But bethink you, child,
   With so much happiness before my eyes,
   With Heaven thus beckoning from its open doors,
   How shall I turn my raptured gaze aside,
   To peer into that Hell you shudder at?
Nyd. Happy! are you so happy?
Glau. Can you ask?
Nyd. Ah! then, 'tis not for all, this happiness.
   Thank Heaven that gave it to you: 'Tis so far,[42]
   So very far above the common lot.
   Nor does it always come at love's command:
   Sweet though his gifts be to the fortunate,
   They seem like curses of the angry gods,
   Like the hot arrows of Hyperion's wrath,
   When poured into a heart that cannot share
   Its blessings with another, love for love.
Glau. These are strange thoughts to fill your youthful brain:
   Whence were they gathered?
Nyd. From the tree of life.
   We who pass under, shake its fatal fruit,
   Ripe or rotten, at our startled feet.
   A child may do that. Once I knew a maid,
   Humble as I am, and she loved a king—
   Think of the fool, she loved a very king!—
   Oh, not a king with sceptre, crown and throne,
   The common frippery of sham royalty;
   But a real king, by nature bred and crowned,
   And so acknowledged by a subject world.
Glau. She flew too high.
Nyd. But why has love his wings,
   Unless to soar with? Ah! my lord, you talk
   Like all the world; but not like Glaucus.
Glau. True.
   But of the maiden?
Nyd. I forgot the girl,
   Lost in the splendor of the man she loved.
   Her passion was the secret of her breast:

She dared not tell it to an earthly thing,
Lest gossip echo, from her hollow cave,
Should spread her story to the jeering land.
Oh, no, she whispered to the mystic skies,
Distant and voiceless—to her mother's soul,
Silent as death, that stood between their lives—
The bitter story which she knew too well.
Nothing was pitiful. The raging clouds,
With thunder upon thunder, shouted, fool!
Her mother's voice, as fine and thin as songs
Sung to an ailing infant, murmured, fool!
And her own heart—there was the hopeless pang—
Muttered forever, fool, and fool, and fool!

GLAU. What was her fate?
NYD. What is the fate of all,
Happy or wretched, who begin to die
As soon as they begin to live? the grave
But hiding up the tragedy of life,
Whose course is only dying. Let her nurse
The death within her as a blessed thing,
The only product of her barren love,
And thank the gods for that one mercy!

GLAU. Child,
Can I do aught to soothe her sorrow?
NYD. You!
You least of all men. Hurry to the one
You'll make your bride tomorrow. That way lies
Your duty. Let the maiden bide the fate
You cannot alter. Since I knew, and tried,
Vainly, to rock her history to sleep
Within the cradle of my heart, all love—
Save such as cursed her with its wretchedness—
Seems make-believe and pastime; merry sport
Of triflers, fooling with a deadly thing.
Oh! and its noise of selfish happiness
Drives through me like a weapon.

GLAU. Nydia!
You think too much, and feel too bitterly,
For one so youthful. There's a joy of youth

          In mere existence. Nourish that delight:
          It comes but once.
Nyd. To me it never came.
          What can I do in darkness, in this house
          All windowless, but think, till gracious death
          May give me back my vision? Go, my lord,
          Go to the pageant. It is glorious,
          The people tell me, to behold the things
          I hear and touch. 'Tis all a mystery
          To me. I would that I could understand
          What sight is like.
Glau. Hereafter you may know,
          If the gods love the pure and beautiful. [*Exit*]
Nyd. O Heaven, O Mother, did you hear? He called
          Me pure and beautiful! O abject shame!
          Called me, whose heart is eaten through and through
          With guilty love, with sin, almost with crime;
          Whose wicked soul is tempted, hour by hour,
          To do the things, I should not dare to dream.
          Pure, beautiful! Avenging Nemesis,[48]
          Count not his error as my sin! Alas!
          How little do we know each others' hearts,
          Though we were twinned together! Hark, I hear
          Calenus' step, that shuffling, stealthy tread.
          The kind old miser; often has he saved
          Poor me from insult, when the riot raged,
          High as the vault of hell, in yonder house.
          Well, I must rest. The spirit has o'erworn
          Its dusty covering. One day it will fall
          A crumbling ruin: then the long, long rest. [*Seats herself. Enter Calenus*]
Cal. A dismal place. What demon brought me here?
          Hello, dame Isis! blinking with your eyes:
          But somewhat dimly. I must trim your lamps,
          And freshen up your eyesight. No one here?
          Yes; who is that? But Nydia. Could she see,
          She'd seek a place more cheerful for repose.
          Master Calenus, just a word with you.
          Come here, a moment. Now, in confidence,
          I have a word or two to say to you.

GLAUCUS

You wretched pauper, do you know, I fear
That you will run your gullet in a noose,
If you keep backing up Arbaces' luck.
And then that dream, that nasty dream, thrice dreamt,
Of drowning in a flood of liquid gold,
While fierce Arbaces, scowling o'er the tide,
Pelted my head with coins and ingots. Sure
That dream meant something. Yes, it meant just this—[44]
For, Isis, as you know, I am skilled in dreams—
It meant you'd better shun the company
And dangerous business of your present lord.
His star is waning. Let me see, by Jove,[45]
And Glaucus' is ascending. It was so
At their last bout. If I could hitch myself
Close to this Glaucus and his wealth, perhaps
Things would look brighter for me; much more safe,
Without a question. Ah! but how, but how?
No one will trust you, my Calenus, now,
Since your long service with Arbaces. Right!
By Jove, I would not trust you. Isis, there!
Old lady, give me but a happy thought,
And I will work you and your oracles,
So that you'll take this wondering town by storm.

NYD. [*Sings*] What keener woe than to behold above her
        The stormy terrors of a darkening sky!
    No heart to shield her, and no heart to love her,
        The light of hope bedimmed within her eye:
        What can she do but die, but die?
        What keener woe!

CAL. Nydia, what are singing in the dark? [*She advances*]
Gods! child you make me creep. "What can she do
But die, but die?" A thousand other things.
Dying's the last thing she should think about:
Tell your friend that. Hey, now, my singing bird,
Is her nest soft in rich Ione's house?
I always thought some good would come to you.

NYD. How wise you are for others; not for yourself!

CAL. How so?

Nyd. In hanging to Arbaces' skirts.
    While he walks down to Hades.
Cal. Right, quite right!
    You echo warnings stirring in my brain.
    Does it e'er happen to you pretty one,
    To talk with Glaucus?
Nyd. Rarely.
Cal. But sometimes?
Nyd. Yes; when I will. He is all courtesy.
    A heart so gentle that he would alight,[46]
    As quick as Hermes, from his chariot,
    To ease the sorrows of a dying dog.
    Who may not speak with Glaucus, who has need
    Of any service he can do to man?
Cal. Tut, tut! you talk heroics. He's a Greek:
    Shrewd therefore—not a fool, by any means!
Nyd. Not unless Pallas is.
Cal. High! there you go!
    Stick to this world; talk business; that's my aim.
    Is Glaucus rich?
Nyd. As Midas: at his touch
    Earth turns to gold.—
Cal. Oh! fiddle, faddle, girl!
    Give up your raptures. What you said just now,
    About Arbaces, lingers in my head.
Nyd. Well, what of him?
Cal. That man is dangerous.
Nyd. That I well know.
Cal. Yes, and his purposes
    Make him as dangerous to friends as foes.—
    A little more so, if a man may judge
    By recent happenings. He is rich, 'tis true;
    But what of that? He's meaner than—than—than—
    Hey, now, bring in your gods and goddesses!
Nyd. I would not wrong them by the likeness.
Cal. Good,
    You pious child! Can you keep secrets, girl?
Nyd. I carry one that burns me, like a coal
    Heated in hell, and I shall carry it
    Until the cold grave quench it.

CAL. Promise me,
  If nothing come of what I say to you,
  If we make no agreement, ere we part,
  Or if you cannot win your perfect lord
  To share our compact, you will lay my words
  Beside that coal which worries you so much.
  Hey, will you swear it?
NYD. [Aside] If I catch his drift,
  The man is ripe to play Arbaces false;
  And that, well covered, may assure my lord
  Freedom from peril. [Aloud] Yes, I swear.
CAL. By what?
  Your gods and goddesses the poets made.
  As for my lady Isis—pshaw! I know
  Too much about her, to confide an oath
  To her loose keeping. Ah! I have it now: [Shows a coin]
  Swear on this aureas, on this trusty gold—
  O you true goddess, let me kiss your face!—[Kisses it]
  That you will keep my counsel.
NYD. So I swear.
CAL. Will you not kiss the image? No? Well, there,
  Go back into your temple. [Pockets the coin]
NYD. Now speak out.
CAL. You know what was Arbaces' plan, that failed
  Last night, perhaps?
NYD. I guess it.
CAL. 'Twas to take
  Lady Ione hence by force, and wed
  Her and her fortune when his galleys reached
  His land of Egypt. That design is yet
  Hot in his mind. He watches for the chance
  To make that project a success.
NYD. Ye gods,
  Must this poor frailty throbbing in my breast
  Be thus forever tempted? Fool, O fool!⁴⁷
  Would her destruction bring poor humble me
  Nearer to him? No; further would I fall.
  His frantic wrath would be a wall of stone
  Between him and all other things. Or grief,
  A grief like mine, would kill him inch by inch.

Could I see that and live? Gods, give me strength,
Me, his bought slave, to serve him to the end;
And see within my mother's shining face
My hard reward at last. [*Aside*]

CAL. Well, little sphinx,
What are you mumbling to yourself?

NYD. Go on.
A blast from hell kindled my coal again:
I shall be patient now.

CAL. But can you be
Trusted with more?

NYD. You know me. Did I break
The oath Arbaces forced from me?

CAL. Not yet;—
I am breaking mine all into little bits;—
And who can tell—Well, I am in for it.[48]
There's peril for me either way; and this
Seems least, most hopeful.

NYD. For yourself?

CAL. Ay, girl.
Do you suppose I waste my precious time,
In taking care of other people? No;
All I can do—and that seems hard enough—
Is but to wriggle one Calenus through
This knotted snare. But others hold a place
Of safety or of danger with myself.
For instance: from the pious love he bears
To yonder lady with the beaming eyes—
Gods, she is winking like a sleepy owl![49]
Shame on you, Isis! keep yourself awake,
And help the fortunes of your faithful priest!
Well, for the love Arbaces bears to her,
He has passed the sentence on Apaecides;
Doomed him to death for treachery to her,
And seeks occasion now to murder him.

NYD. Ha!

CAL. There is something, is it not? By Jove,
'Tis useful information.—Wink, wink, wink!
What, are you going blind, you jade?

NYD. You know,
  I am quite blind.
CAL. I did not speak of you.
  That blinking Isis makes me nervous. Well,
  If he would murder young Apaecides,
  To satisfy his hot religious zeal—
  Ho! ho! religion and Arbaces mix[50]
  Like oil and water. [*Laughing*] If he'd take that life,
  But for his conscience-sake, what will he do
  To Glaucus? Tell me that. He hates your lord—
  Just as I hate those sleepy, ribald priests[51]
  That are neglecting my poor Isis' eyes.
  I'll swing you for it, when I get to you!
  What do you say to that, my Nydia?
NYD. It is most grave. But what do you propose?
CAL. This, if the service can be made to pay,
  I propose to attach myself at once
  To Glaucus; and to do the ticklish work
  He cannot do without me, if he would,
  In keeping him advised of every plan[52]
  Arbaces forms; helping to thwart his plots.
  To save two lives, prevent your lady's theft,
  Et cetera; and, in the end, to deal
  The monster out full justice. Do you see?
  Your poor Calenus will have work enough,
  Meriting handsome wages.
NYD. If you do
  But half you promise, you may swim in gold.
CAL. "May swim in gold!" there is my dream again!
  I cannot fail you; for my treachery[53]
  Would catch me in the outcome. Then, reflect,
  I cannot harm you, if I do no good.
  Keep your own councils, tell me nought; but use
  My information as you please. Besides,
  Nothing for nothing is a golden rule.
NYD. Calenus, I accept you.
CAL. Yes, my child,
  That's very well; but what do you suppose—
  Oh! not to haggle, not for a mere coin—
  What do you think, in gross, the pay will be?

Nyd. More than you dream of.
Cal. Nay, my dreams, sometimes,
　　　Go very far into the fattest purse.
Nyd. Trust me for that.
Cal. I do, as you trust me.
　　　Now Nydia, little mouse, you know that house
　　　Better than I do; or as well, at least.
　　　You know the danger of this work of mine;
　　　You know Arbaces: Well, if, some bright day,
　　　Your poor Calenus suddenly should seem
　　　To quit the world, no warning given to you—
　　　Where would you seek him? what would you suppose?
Nyd. Nay, I know not.
Cal. Dear innocent, I do.
　　　You must suppose Arbaces has found out
　　　Clumsy Calenus, and has stuffed your friend
　　　Into that solid cell, beneath the hall,
　　　With nothing to console his leisure time,
　　　While he is slowly starving, but the thought
　　　Of what a mighty fool he made himself
　　　In reckoning without his host—the man
　　　Who gives him lodging, free of any charge:
　　　Remember that.
Nyd. Grim jesting.
Cal. Jesting, girl!
　　　It may be truth tomorrow. Look you, now:
　　　Should this thing happen, you must get me out,
　　　By hook or crook, by sleight or force; so I
　　　May tell my story in a court of law.
　　　You know the cell?
Nyd. By your description, yes.
Cal. The door to it is hidden in the base
　　　Of Isis' image, in the gallery.
　　　That you must force. Take men enough with you[54]
　　　To overpower resistance: such a gang
　　　As followed you last night. Oh, mighty gold!
　　　What else, by chink and twinkle, could have called
　　　That little army up so suddenly?
Nyd. Calenus, he is coming.
Cal. Who?

GLAUCUS

Nyd. Arbaces:
I know his step.
Cal. Mole-ears, your hearing shames
The eyes of Argus. Fly! [*Exit Nydia swiftly*] So that is done,
And I feel easier, less inclined to muse
Or how it feels to decorate a cross,
Or to be pinched between a lion's jaws,
To please admiring friends. [*Enter Arbaces*]
Arb. It must be done
Tonight, this very night. The boy must die;
And ere the morning, ere she hear of it,
Ione must be safe aboard with me,
With leagues of water 'twixt this town and us.
As for the Greek, why, let him live to feel
My thorough vengeance in his misery.—
Who's there?
Cal. Calenus.
Arb. It grows dark apace.
I did not know you in the shadow there.
Cal. [*Aside*] I wonder if he knows me in the light?
Arb. What do you here?
Cal. I must be somewhere—here,
Or somewhere else. I cannot make myself
Invisible, to please you.
Arb. [*Aside*] So, my man!
There is something new within that brain of yours:
A tone of falsehood in your very voice.
The slave grows insubordinate perhaps.
You must be looked to.
Cal. [*Aside*] Now what brought him out
Tonight, and unattended? I shall watch
Your goings and your comings for a while.
Arb. You are moody.
Cal. I? but quiet. When I'm still,
Be sure that I have nothing much to say.
Arb. What is the matter?
Cal. Curse this thankless world!
Here, I've been working like a gang of slaves,
Year in year out, for other people's good—
And I have done a turn of work for Heaven, [55]

For Isis too; and what is my reward?—
More work, and harder, and more perilous.
And, by and by, you'll leave me in the lurch,
In the law's grip, while you are sailing off,
Secure and happy, with your pretty bride.
That's fine for you; but as for me—My lord,
What shall I do, after the bubble bursts,
And Isis is a by-word? She will be,
As surely as Apaecides reveal
The temple's secrets.

ARB. He will say no more
After tonight, and that will seem to be
The judgment of the goddess to the world.
Go, get you in.

CAL. Look at that statue's eyes:
I swear, they are disgraceful. We are out
Of naphtha for the lamps; and, meanwhile, she
Blinks in that owlish manner, poor old girl!

ARB. Pooh! here is money for your lamps. [*Gives money*]

CAL. Not much:
Enough, mayhap, to serve a month or two. [*Goes into the temple and watches Arbaces from behind a column*]

ARB. That fellow is past service, and begins
To be untrustworthy. It matters not:
I shall not need him shortly. Till we part,
Let him hold closely to his shaking faith!
Or woe betide his treachery! [*Enter Apaecides. Arbaces, observing him, walks up*]

APAE. How dark
The night grows suddenly! A sympathy
With gloom has struck my spirit; for I feel
As though the hand of an impending doom
Hangs o'er my head, and only hesitates
How soon to fall. Where tarries Glaucus? He[56]
Promised to meet me on the way, as soon
As he had seen the sacrificial rites
Duly performed. Come, Glaucus; for I need
Your sunny smile, to light my moody heart.
I will walk further on. Ha! who goes there?

ARB. Apaecides.
APAE. Bold villain! must it be
    That every turn I take still leads to you?
    Away! avoid me! if you hold your life
    Worth the precaution that will save it.
ARB. Ah!
    How kindlier times escape a memory
    As blind with rage as yours! Look back, my son,
    Upon the guardian of your youth, the man
    Who loved you as a father,[57] and displayed
    That love in every action.
APAE. Whining hound,
    What, will you cower, because you have been cuffed?
    Out of my way! My fingers clench and burn
    To do you justice here, before that block
    You call a goddess.
ARB. Isis, hear him not!
    Spare him for me, your faithful worshiper!
APAE. Prodigious hypocrite, embodied lie,
    Base counterfeiter of the coin of Heaven.
    Who are so false that one can neither trust[58]
    Your seeming virtues nor your vices. Faugh!
    My stomach sickens at the sight of you:
    And at your prayers, to any power above[59]
    That holds mankind responsible, my skin
    Creeps with sheer horror. Bide another day
    Here, in Pompeii, with your impious frauds—
    Your Isis and your oracles, with your own[60]
    Sham piety, you shameless mountebank—
    And I will make your gods, your rites and you
    The jeer and by-word of the market place!
ARB. Demented atheist! [*Stabs him suddenly*] Take that, and that!
    O Isis, to your earthly sovereignty—
    You know with what regret—I offer up
    My erring son; and may his death atone
    For his transgressions!
APAE. Vile assassin, hark!
    When the stone falls, between the blow and death,
    Think of this deed, and may its memory
    Be your first pang of hell! Oh!—Oh! [*Dies*]

Arb. I struck
Too rashly; but the torrent of my rage
Swept of my judgment. [*Calenus advances slowly*]
Back! [*Draws*] Another step
Is death to one of us.
Cal. Um!
Arb. Only you?
Calenus, quick; we must be rid of this.
Cal. Ay, if you could. This act will last awhile,
And draw its consequences after it.
Arb. You moralizing fool! the act is done!
We must bestow the body somewhere.
Cal. Where?
Arb. You empty echo! are your wits astray?
Lend me a hand, to bear this lump of clay
Into the temple. You can throw the corpse
Into the pit, among the bones and dregs
Of other sacrifices. Come, at once!
Cal. Oh, mercy, how he bleeds!
Arb. Come, fellow, come!
Cal. I am no fellow for a murderer.
I saw it all.
Arb. Ha!
Cal. Yes; I will not put
My little finger into this affair.
Fate sees the end. I cannot.
Arb. Are you mad?
You shall have gold enough to satisfy
Even your avarice.
Cal. Gold, without my life,
Might be a comfort to my heirs. To me—
Arb. Treacherous villain! what, will you betray
Your master?
Cal. Um! I know not what I'll do—
Arb. I know as well. Within there! [*Seizes Calenus. Enter slaves from Arbaces' house*] In with him! [*Slaves seize Calenus*]
Cal. Help!—
Arb. Silence him. [*Slaves throttle Calenus*] Look at this bloody deed,
Done by his hand—the murder of my boy,
My poor, poor boy! O execrable wretch!

GLAUCUS

      Drag him away, and prison him, fast bound,
      And gagged to silence, in my study. I
      Will deal with him hereafter. On your lives,
      Hold him secure; or I will scourge to death
      The whole gang of you! [*Exeunt slaves with Calenus*]
      Light begins to break!
      The toils are falling from me. I can make
      One traitor answer for the other's death.
      But, at the trial, what the rogue might say
      Would cast suspicion on me. Isis, help!
      My mind is in confusion. Curse the boy!
      He is more trouble to me dead than he
      Was while he lived.
GLAU. [*Without*]   Apaecides! what, ho!
ARB.   Oh, golden fortune! Isis heard my prayer.
      'Tis the Greek's voice. Now let me guide events
      To my own ends. The pit is dug: [*Retires back*]
      One careless step is all I need. [*Enter Glaucus, looking about him*]
GLAU.   'Tis strange.
      Apaecides, where stray you in the dark?
      He promised he would meet me on the way;
      And I am almost home, without a glimpse
      Or sound of him. Can it have been we passed
      Each other in the darkness? [*Arbaces, so placed that the body lies between him and Glaucus*]
ARB.   Oh!—[*Groans*]
GLAU.   A groan!
      Some drunken reveller perchance has fallen
      Here by the wayside. Let me give him aid.
      Heaven knows, if mortals ever need our aid,[61]
      It is when he who stands may help the fallen
      To lift the weary burden of his sins.
ARB.   Oh!—Oh!—[*Groans*]
GLAU.   Again! What's here? A prostrate man! [*Discovers Apaecides' body*]
      Apaecides! My brother, why is this?
      What is this sticky stuff that covers you?
      Blood, blood!—warm blood! Why lie you here? Arouse!
      How still he is! Cheer up! There's succor nigh.
      Apaecides! oh answer! Help! help! help!

ARB. Who is it cracks the silent ear of night
    With such shrill cry?
GLAU. Look you here!—Oh, look
    Upon this piteous sight!—A wounded man—
    Murdered perhaps, if murder have the heart
    To slay the innocent. Who are you?
ARB. Arbaces I of Egypt.
GLAU. Of all men,
    Even now, the most unwelcome. But, my lord,
    Forget our enmity before the claim
    Of such a woe. He is not dead, I know.
    I heard him groan a moment since. Have you
    Skill in such matters?
ARB. Some. But who is he?
GLAU. Apaecides, your ward.
ARB. What?
GLAU. Look at him. [*Arbaces examines the body*]
    Oh, see, he bleeds afresh! It cannot be
    That he is dead. How shall I bear this news
    To poor Ione? Pray what think you?
ARB. Dead;
    But very lately. Ah! incautious boy,
    How did you bring this fate upon your head?
GLAU. How does the lamb die by the butcher's hand?
    He was the most harmless of all living things.[62]
ARB. Help! help!—here's murder—help me, citizens! [*Calling without. Burbo and Stratonice enter with a crowd of citizens, gladiators, soldiers, etc. from different directions, some with torches*]
BUR. This way the cry was.
STRA. What is this?
ARB. A man
    Slain in the streets. [*Enter Clodius, Sallust, Lydon and Nydia*]
LYD. Who is he?
ARB. A young priest
    Of Isis' house, Apaecides.
NYD. Oh, woe!
    Calenus' prophecy is half fulfilled.
    I heard the demon's voice a moment since.
    Oh! my poor lady! [*Exit hastily*]
BUR. But who did this?

ARB. Who?
   Why do you ask? [*Retires*]
BUR. That is not far to seek:
   Look at his hands and toga, running blood—
LYD. You are a liar, scoundrel! [*Strikes him*]
CLOD. Peace!
1ST CIT. Stand back!
   Here is a Senator.
CLOD. Glaucus, my friend,
   What means this sight? Why are you here,
   Thus stained with blood?
BUR. Red-handed.
LYD.[63] Have a care:
   My next blow will be earnest.
GLAU. Clodius,
   O tell me it is but a dreadful dream.
   My brain is whirling. All that I can see
   Is blood, blood, blood; and all that I can hear
   Is the shrill shriek from those wan, frozen lips,
   That felt so warm a little hour ago. [*Enter Ione, Nydia, and a train of maids, servants, etc.*]
   O gods, she comes! Where shall I hide myself?
IONE. [*Falls on his bosom*] Glaucus!
GLAU. Divine forgiveness! Half the fault
   Is mine, beloved. I should have guarded him,
   Foreseeing danger.
IONE. Do not blame yourself.
   Apaecides?—
GLAU. Is dead! and I should be
   The happier with him. Dear, I swore to you
   To watch our brother's safety as your own:
   And see, look here! here is my broken oath
   Bleeding from every wound of his.
IONE. Alas!
   We have but human faculties to serve
   Our promises. We are not gods, beloved.
1ST CIT. O lady, quit that man.
IONE. And wherefore, friend?
1ST CIT. Look at his hands.

IONE. But that is guiltless blood.
    Come, let me kiss them: they are pure as mine. [*Kisses his hands*]
    Rather suspect me of this bloody deed
    Than noble Glaucus.
NYD. [*Aside*] Hear, ye listening gods!
    This is a love like mine. [*Cries without of, "Way, way!" Then enter the Praetor with lictors bearing torches and guards. Arbaces approaches the Praetor*]
PRAE. What mean these cries,
    That break the quiet of our sleeping town,
    And bare the blade of armed authority? [*Approaches the body*]
    A murdered man! Who is he? [*To Arbaces*] Speak, my lord,
    If you know aught concerning the affair.
ARB. I speak reluctantly, because 'tis known
    Glaucus and I have been at enmity:
    So people say, and so perhaps it is.—[*Pauses*]
GLAU. Forget all that. I have a vow in Heaven,
    Recorded there among its sacred things,
    To hunt the murderer of Apaecides
    Through land, through flood, through earth or howling sea—
    By night and day, wherever he may bide—
    Yea, though the gods of darkness shelter him—
    And drag him to the cross, the hungry beast,
    Or wheresoever the hand of Justice point!
ARB. Remember this, when you stand face to face
    Before the truth.
PRAE. What know you? Let there be
    No further interruptions. Speak, my lord!
ARB. Pray you, excuse me;—I am ill at ease;—
    I know not what to say. Indeed, the facts
    Are so suspicious, from my point of view,
    As I was forced to see them—[*Pauses*]
PRAE. By the gods,
    It seems to me you seek to shield the wretch
    Who did this crime. If that be your design,
    Look to yourself, ere you be self-condemned
    As an accomplice!
GLAU. O my lord, speak out!
    You one time called this murdered youth your son,
    Your ward he was; if any trace of love

GLAUCUS

        Rest in your heart toward his memory,
        Give it full way. Do you know anything
        That may have happened, ere you heard me call,
        And found him lying dead within my arms?
ARB. Indeed, indeed, I loved him as a son.
        Poor orphan, during twenty patient years,
        To him and to his sister, I supplied
        A father's place—
PRAE. By Jupiter, my blood
        Boils at your girlish sentiment! If you,
        By these fond maunderings, seek but to obstruct
        The course of justice, I shall hold you both,
        You two discoverers of the crime—you Greek,
        And you Egyptian—guilty both alike.
        Advance, my lictors! [*The lictors advance*]
ARB. 'Tis not fear, my lord,
        Of the law's prying eye, or vengeful hand,
        That urged me to speak. Oh, no; the ghost
        Of young Apaecides is hovering nigh—
        That tender, beautiful, most harmless youth,[64]
        Differing in sex, but not in loveliness,
        From his dear sister; and I hear the cry
        That, as the delegate of Heaven, he breathes
        Into my ears, demanding blood for blood.
        And, thus adjured, I must tell all I know;
        However much it may add grief to grief,
        And crush the hearts now overweighted.
PRAE. On!
ARB. While on my housetop, studying the stars—
        That seem to threaten some calamity
        Near to this quarter of the world—I heard
        Voices high pitched in quarrel, then a blow;
        Then the dull gurgling sound a wounded man,
        Choking with blood, ejects; and then I heard
        A cry for help.
PRAE. Whose voice?
ARB. I could not tell:
        It might have been Apaecides'.
PRAE. What more?

ARB. I rushed into the street, and when my eyes
  Grew more familiar to the darkness, saw
  Glaucus unholding in his arms the corpse
  Of dear Apaecides—a woeful sight!—
  He seemed half frantic, with remorse or fear;
  Begged me for aid, in wild and rambling terms;
  But, to my sorrow, the unlucky youth
  Was past all aid.
PRAE. What was the weapon used?
ARB. I stumbled on this stylus. [*Shows it*]
PRAE. Let me see. [*Takes it*]
  A common stylus, such as all men bear.
  How were the wounds made?
OFF. As I judge, my lord,
  With some long, slender weapon.
PRAE. Might it be
  With such a thing as this?
OFF. Beyond all doubt.
PRAE. Arrest the Greek. [*Lictors surround Glaucus*]
GLAU. Arrest me! for what cause?
PRAE. The murder of Apaecides.
GLAU. My lord,
  If in Pompeii there is only one
  Who could not have performed that act, 'tis I.
  He was my brother, by the ties of love
  That stronger are than nature's. In a day,
  His sister would have been—nay, will be—I
  Cannot forego that hope as yet—my wife—
IONE. O Glaucus, do you dare to doubt me? Yes,
  Though wicked men accuse you, though the law
  Convict you, and its brutal myrmidons
  Drag you to death—there, at the cross's foot,
  Or where the arena trembles with the roar
  Of the on-bounding lion—if my lord
  Will honor so his handmaid—I will wed
  You and you only; for a voice from Heaven
  Cries in my soul, Glaucus is innocent!
NYD. [*Aside*] She must have heard my mother's voice, that says
  The same thing in my soul. Oh, thank the gods,
  That made me true to her through all temptations!

GLAUCUS

GLAU. Perjured informer, now I see the snare
       Your coward cunning set before my feet.
       I fell therein, because I could not deem
       A man so base as you have shown yourself.
       My lord, this villain, with the spider's craft,
       Has woven a web of most deceptive lies
       Out of a hundred facts, that are not truth
       As he presents them. Let me question him.
PRAE. That you may do, before the judges, when
       He gives his testimony. Officer,
       Take bonds that Lord Arbaces may appear
       Upon the trial. He would shield this man;
       That is too patent.
IONE. You are blind, stone blind.
       Oh, let me speak, dear Glaucus; let me tell
       The story of last night. No maid, nor man,
       Should fear the truth, though every syllable
       Must needs be dyed in blushes.
GLAU. Nay, not now.
       'Twere useless to expose that scandal here,
       To the world's wonder. Maiden character
       Is like the new fallen snow; more easily stained
       From its abounding whiteness. Patience, love!
       There is a power in Heaven that guides the ways
       Of even the wicked to its gracious ends.
       All things, both good and evil, are as one,
       To serve the purpose of the hand that moulds
       Our mortal destinies.
IONE. You are my guide.
       The hand that ruling Heaven extends to me,
       Henceforth forever, on my earthly path.
       Your will I follow meekly, with a faith
       That love alone inspires.
GLAU. Trust me no more
       Than reason justifies. The fire of truth
       Was kindled by the gods, ere man began:
       They watch above it, as a sacred care,
       Lest any spark be lost; and, when they will,
       Like sudden sunrise, they flood Heaven and earth
       With its eternal beams.

PRAE. Delay no more.
   Conduct your prisoner to his cell. Strip off
   His gilded plumage. Let him see and feel
   What 'tis to be like one of that dear mob
   He so admires!
ARB. [*Laughing aside*] Ha! ha!
NYD. Brute, brute! you thing,
   You accident of ill, that, by mischance,
   Have crawled into a place which you disgrace—
   Off with your purple robe, to cover him,
   A natural king of men; and hide your shame
   Under the slavish garb you dare to place
   Upon his royal limbs!
PRAE. Peace, sightless scold!
LYD. Peace, cry you, while yourself made war—
CLOD. [*Restraining Lydon*] Forbear!
   Your crazy love will prejudice his cause.
   Has he not enemies enough, without
   His friends evoking more to ruin him?
PRAE. Present your pikes, men! Does rebellion dare
   Show front before me? [*The people show signs of resistance*]
GLAU. Patience, gentle friends!
   Force cannot clear me of this deadly snare.
   Though blows may rescue, for a little space,
   My outraged body, my imprisoned soul
   Would still be bound in shackles by this charge.
   I have no fear of what bad men can do
   Upon this stage and halting place of life,
   This cradle of eternity, though they
   By fraud, or violence, or death itself,
   Slam to the doors of being in my face,
   And set my spirit free. Move on!—Ione!—[*Exit guarded*]
IONE. Glaucus!—my Glaucus!—[*Faints*]
ARB. [*Aside*] Victory!
NYD. Mark, gods!
   He must be of your kindred.
BUR. Hum! I think
   The lion will have food tomorrow.
LYD. [*Strikes him down*] Beast!

ACT V.

SCENE: *The Forum. At the back of the scene on the right, the doorway of the Basilica, or Court of Justice, a vast building of the Ionic order. Farther to the left, the temple of Jupiter, of the Corinthian order. A mixed crowd of Citizens, Soldiers, Freedmen, Slaves, etc., discovered, waiting to hear the result of the trial of Glaucus. Enter Dudus. Burbo appears at the door of the Basilica.*

BUR. Sentence is passed.
ALL. What sentence?
BUR. Instant death.
ALL. Huzza! [*Enter Stratonice from the Basilica, and advances*]
STRA. What are you howling at? I'll bet
    In aurea, one to ten on Glaucus.
1ST. CIT. How?
    What is the sentence?
STRA. That he be exposed,
    In the arena, to the lion.
1ST CIT. What,
    Bound hand and foot?
STRA. Gods, no!
1ST CIT. Armed then?
STRA. Somewhat;
    With the same stylus that the liars say
    He did the murder with. Oh, we shall have
    A royal fight. I'll make it one to seven
    On Glaucus.
DUD. That he kill the beast?
STRA. No, no;
    But that the beast do not kill him.
1ST CIT. I take it.
DUD. I'll give you that ten times.
1ST CIT. Agreed.
BUR. [*Advances*] Hey, now,
    How is the betting?
DUD. One to seven on Glaucus.
BUR. I'll back the lion—
STRA. [*Taking him by the ear*] No, you'll back yourself.
    I'll teach you, you born ass, to bet against
    My luck!—I'll teach you! [*Shakes him*]

Bur. I am taught. I'll bet
     Ten aurea on the Greek.
1st Cit. How?
Bur. Even money.
All Cit. Taken.
Stra. You wretched idiot, be still!
     You have swept the odds from under me. Ye gods,
     Was ever a woman cursed so in a husband?
     Go to your pots; get drunk; do anything,
     But throw our money in these sharpers' teeth. [*Retires with Burbo.*
Enter from the Basilica, Clodius and Sallust]
All. Room for the Senators!
Sal. [*Advancing with Clodius and Dudus*] This was sharp work.
Clod. A mockery of Roman justice. I
     Am too indignant at the Praetor's course,
     At his indecent haste, and obvious bias
     Against poor Glaucus, that I needs must be
     A passionate counsellor.
Sal. Justice, you say!
     There was no law, no decent form of law,
     Observed or thought of. By the huckster's god,
     Winged Mercury, it made me sick to know
     Such antics could be played in Italy.
Clod. Yes, and ere Glaucus' orator could well
     Get seated, ere his chair was warm, by Jove,
     Out came the sentence—death, immediate death
     In the arena, by the lion's jaws.
     Sallust, we noblemen must look to this.[65]
     'Tis an attack upon our class. The rank
     Of Glaucus gave him right, I think,
     Of trial by the Senate.
Sal. How that dark demon, the Egyptian, grinned
     When all was over; how his evil eyes
     Sparkled and kindled, as though hell had struck
     A recent fire within them. There was more
     Than a mere triumph in that glance. By Jove,
     I should not wonder, if the truth were known,
     That this Arbaces struck the blow himself.
Dud.[66] I will bet one to two that you are right.
     Fie! our dear Glaucus an assassin! No;

GLAUCUS

No man of his refinement could be that.
No man that wore the toga as he did,
With such a presence, such a royal air,
Could be a vulgar murderer. Alas!
Who'll set the fashions in Pompeii now?
It is a public loss.

SAL. Poor Dudus! Each
Has his own spring of tears at Glaucus' fate.

DUD. Did you observe him in his prison garb—
That dirty woollen skirt, unshaved, unkempt?
Among the gold and purple throng, he seemed
The only king.

CLOD. Sallust, that thought of yours,
Which lays the murder on Arbaces' hands,
Should be considered carefully.

DUD. The mob,
Those knaves behind us, have already got
That fancy in their brains. I heard a rogue
Just out of prison—one who ought to know
Crime by inspection—swear he'd go to death,
If yon Arbaces had not killed a man
Within a week; he saw it in his eye.

CLOD. Even Glaucus did not hint at that.

DUD. Not he:
He is too noble to accuse a foe
On mere suspicion.

SAL. Think of this: the priests
Of Isis and they only, had a motive
To kill Apaecides; if it be true
That he adjured their faith, and had declared
Their mysteries, mummeries, and their oracles
And miracles but specious tricks. Then he
Had a wild story of the filthy things
Done in Arbaces' house, on the pretext
Of worship to his goddess. Who but he,
This foreign quack, had motive for the deed?

CLOD. Oh, for an hour with Titus!

SAL. He, alas!
Is on the sea, half way to Syria
Ere this; and Glaucus' doom will be enforced[67]

    This very day, this very hour, unless
    The Praetor, suddenly should show himself
    Less of a brute than the half-famished beast
    That waits our poor friend's coming.
Dud. Look you, now!
    You are so solemn over Glaucus' fate,
    Forget not that long stylus in a hand
    As strong as Hercules! What if he kill
    The lion, as he may do?
Clod. Then the cross
    Awaits him, that was in the sentence too.
Sal.[68] By Jove, it shall not! If he slay the lion
    The people will be with him to a man;
    And I will organize the mutiny.
    And head it too, with voice, and arm, and sword,
    But he shall be set free.
Dud. I'll second you.
Clod. O Senator!—
Sal. "O Senator!" I was
    A man before I was a senator.
    Heaven grant, I be that till I make an end
    Worthy my manhood!
Clod. Come, come; let us talk
    Among the people; set this matter up,
    And see what taste they have for your exploit.
    Hell help the Praetor, if we get the mob
    Once on his heels!
Sal. O Senator!
Clod. Bah, man!
    You set my blood on fire. Look to yourself,
    If it consume your house. I love our Glaucus,
    As dearly as I love my eldest boy,
    His namesake.
Dud. Look, look there! Oh, shame!
Cits. Huzza! [*Enter, from the Basilica, Glaucus guarded by Lictors, the edges of their axes turned toward him, followed by the Praetor, leaning on Arbaces' shoulder. Officers, Guards, etc. Some people hiss and groan*]
 Prae. I have been told there is, among the mob,
    A rumor, prince, that you have saved your life
    By testifying against a guiltless man.

I'll show the beggars what I think of them
And their opinions.
ARB. My gracious lord!
PRAE. Shackle the prisoner. Will you let the wretch
Walk free, and thus invite him to escape? [*Lictors place heavy chains on Glaucus*]
So let him drag his prison to the ring,
And face the justice of the lion's jaws.
CLOD. Sorrow on sorrow! [*Enter Ione in disorder, followed by Attendants, etc. She bursts through the Lictors. Throws herself on his breast*]
IONE. Glaucus!
GLAU. My beloved,
Have you come here, to make life dear again?
Ah, this I hoped that you would spare yourself;
Sweet as it is to me, to turn my eyes,
For the last time, upon my guiding star,
That made my life so beautiful, and tuned
The smallest pulse that beats within my frame
To that eternal harmony which holds
Heaven stable, and secures the blessed gods
Their own unbroken calm.
IONE. O, love, to die
Thus sheltered in your arms! to lapse away,
As if from dream to dream, without a shock,
And leave this misery, with my dust, behind,
Buried with it among earth's other ills!
I have no fear. You men, when you esteem
Death nobler than intolerable life,
Pause not to lay your fate-defying hands
Upon the source of being. Why should we,
Poor women, weaker and less resolute
To cope with fate, not follow where you lead?
GLAU. Life is a trust from Heaven; 'tis not for us
Rashly to squander that which is not ours,
But a confided treasure of the gods.
Let them resume their bounty when they will;
We must not dare forestall them, nor decide
Whether their gift we value less or not.
Ione, live to vindicate my fame;
To see at last the light of truth break through

    The darkness which surrounds me; to see time
    Set his broad seal upon my innocence.
    And mourn somewhat regretfully, I trust,
    Above my outraged memory.
IONE. O Glaucus,
    This is the very tyranny of grief.
    My heart rebels against it, like a slave
    O'ertasked, that must perform some desperate act,
    Or break, or break! What shall I do?
GLAU. Endure,
    Endure like me.
IONE. Oh! if you loved yourself
    With half the love I bear you, it would seem
    Folly to meet the torrent of my heart
    With temperate counsel. But a gleam of hope
    Still lights the future.
GLAU. All we hope or fear
    Is locked in that mysterious future.
IONE. Nay;
    Until your trial, Glaucus—
GLAU. That is past.
IONE. What?
GLAU. Yes; and you must nerve yourself to bear
    Ruthless necessity.
IONE. Oh, speak! The court
    Has not passed sentence on you yet?
GLAU. Even so.
IONE. That was the meaning of your pity then
    Towards me, poor me, forgetful of yourself.
    Fool that I am: I might have known as much.
    Tell me, before I go quite mad, or die
    Here at your feet. The sentence?—
GLAU. Death.
IONE. Death, death!—
    Surely you try my fortitude—not death!
GLAU. What else could justice measure out to guilt,
    For such a crime?
IONE. But you are innocent.
    To know you merely, is to know that well.

GLAUCUS

Glau. Noblest of womankind, your faith in me,
    Condemned of others for your brother's death,
    Lightens the burden of this earthly life,
    Which I must bear a little further on;
    And, with its prophet hand, unfolds the gates
    Of Heaven before me—
Ione. Glaucus, tell me all.
    I waver on the verge of madness. Speak!
Cits. On to the lion with him!
Ione. What was that?
Glau. The people whom I loved, and helped at need,
    Have grown impatient. By the Praetor's doom,
    I am condemned to be exposed today.
    In the arena, to a lion.
Ione. No!
    It cannot be that all the gods are dead:
    There is some justice yet in Heaven. Man, man—
    Or monster rather—[*To the Praetor*]
Glau. Peace, Ione, peace!
    Do not degrade yourself and me with words
    Of prayer or imprecation to that man—
    That puppet of Arbaces' brutish will.
    Speak rather to the lion I must meet,
    As to a noble creature.
Ione. Gracious gods,
    I am so dazed with horror, that my brain
    Seems to refuse to see things as they are;
    And, like the moth about a deadly light,
    Its coming ruin, chases round and round
    Wild fancies in insane bewilderment.
    Is this you, Glaucus? and am I Ione?
    It cannot be that we, of yesterday,
    Were what we are today. Awaken me
    From the dark trance, that, like benumbing death,
    Is settling on my soul.
Glau. Benignant Heaven,
    Spread a kind torpor, like an opiate,
    Over her tortured senses! There will be
    Time in the bitter future for her heart

    To feel its chastening, and to understand
    Your now secreted purpose.
Prae. End the farce
    Between the felon and this blinded girl.
    We have been too indulgent.
Arb. [*Apart to Praetor*] Nay, my lord;
    The desperation of her present state,
    Will work for me hereafter. Fair Ione [*advancing*],
    My ward, my child, if ever you had need
    Of a protector it is now. My heart
    Bleeds for your painful posture. Turn to me,
    With your old confidence, I pray—
Glau. Begone,
    You triple murderer, you incarnate hell,
    Or I will brain you with my shackles!
Ione. Off!
    Your touch would be pollution. Hire yourself
    As headsman or assassin, for the pay
    Your deeds may bring you! Never, while yon Heaven
    Looks on the world, with meaning in its face,
    Shall you see aught of me. [*Arbaces returns to the Praetor*]
Arb. My lord, I pray
    That you will save this damsel from herself.
    She is unfit, as you have seen, to care
    For her own interests. Give her to my charge.
Glau. O Heaven, the misery of any death
    Were bliss to this!
Prae. Arbaces, take the maid
    Back to your wardship.
Clod. [*From among the crowd*] I protest against
    This tyranny.
Prae. How, insolent! Who dares
    Question my will?
Clod. [*Advancing*] A senator from Rome.
Sal. Backed by another. Praetor though you be,
    If you dare venture to impose restraint
    Upon a free-born citizen, whose years
    Place her beyond all tutelage, we'll make
    The wondering capital ring long and loud
    With fury at your act. [*The crowd cheers*]

Prae. O, well, my lords,
    If you will answer for the maiden's weal—
Clod. To Caesar, not to you.
Prae. Then take the girl.
    I could not give her into better hands.
    But mark you, lords, you are responsible.
Clod. Yes, with our heads, that she shall come and go
    As suits her fancy, and the liberty
    The state accords her.
Prae. [*To Ione*] And are you content
    That these two honorable and gracious lords
    Shall care for you?
Ione. Consign me where you will.
    I am the slave of sorrow; how I drudge
    Through the brief remnant of my doleful life
    Concerns me not.
Arb. Destruction be your lot
    You meddling marplots! [*Aside*]
Glau. But a while ago,
    I thought that friendship had abandoned me,
    And, like the Alpine climber, I was hemmed
    On every side in hard and icy hearts.
    Now Clodius, and now Sallust, you shall see
    Your old companion front the lion's glare
    With smiles upon his lips; and in his soul
    Such bounteous thanksgiving to you both
    As the worn mother stammers to the gods,
    When her new-born lies sobbing at her side.
    I have but this to say, to tell you all:—
    I thank you more, a thousandfold, brave men,
    Than if your courage had redeemed my life.
    Take my Ione from my grateful hands,
    My chiefest treasure, and the world's alike.
    But show to her the scrupulous regard
    Due to the widow of a friend, and I
    Will tire the gods for blessings on your heads.
    Farewell!
Clod. O Glaucus, must I be a child
    A second time?
Glau. Dear Sallust!

SAL. If my life
　　　Could ransom yours?
GLAU. Ione, come to me.
　　　Darling, I do believe, as I believe
　　　In nothing else, man's spirit cannot die.
　　　Death is no ill: a universal lot
　　　Cannot be evil. Do you mark me, love?
　　　Heaven knows with what a sorrow I renounce—
　　　As something sweeter than my life deserved—
　　　The golden prospect which our union
　　　Opened before us. Join your hand with mine.
　　　Here, on the verge of earth, before the gods,
　　　I take you for eternity to be
　　　My wedded wife. Earth scants us of our rights;
　　　But to the long endurance of the soul,
　　　And its deep capabilities of bliss,
　　　Time and this life are but little drops
　　　That fall into a boundless sea. You hear?
IONE. Perhaps—I think I do—O Glaucus—
GLAU. Nay,
　　　These words are for your memory. When the world
　　　Looks dark about you, and the Heaven above
　　　Seems but reflecting back its hopeless ills,
　　　Oh, murmur not at what is hidden from you!
　　　Remember, too, that through the darkest cloud,
　　　The spirit's eyes can penetrate; that love
　　　Is the supreme and only law of all—
　　　Of every thing, whether in Heaven or earth—
　　　The Power above has fashioned in accord
　　　With his own being. I shall watch o'er you,
　　　Follow you, guard you, whisper to your heart
　　　That I await you, though your days on earth
　　　Outnumber Nestor's. Oh, remember!
IONE. Glaucus!
　　　I cannot part from you. They will not dare
　　　Tear you away from my entwining arms.
　　　Gods of my fathers, hear me! You are just:
　　　You will not look upon this awful deed,
　　　That drags to unjust death a guiltless man,

GLAUCUS

While the blood-guilty flourish, and defy
You to your faces! [*Cries without of "Glaucus! Glaucus!" Enter hastily, and in disorder, Nydia, followed by Lydon, and other Gladiators, supporting Calenus, ill-clad, suffering, and scarcely recognizable*]

NYD. Glaucus—Glaucus! Heart,
    Stand still, until he answer me!
GLAU. My child!
NYD. Now break, my heart, my mad tumultuous heart,
    Break when you will, and tell the whole world why;
    For I have saved him! This is you indeed,
    My lord, my king! This is your hand, your—gods!
    These are a felon's chains! Off, off with them!
    And pile them, mountain high, upon that wretch—
    That cursed wizard, murderer, perjurer—
    That all that's evil in a single word—
    Arbaces!
PRAE. Girl, you have forgot yourself.
    This fierce, indecent noise is out of place,
    Here, in this presence.
NYD. "In this presence," ha!
    For once I thank you for my blindness, Heaven!
    It is a blessing that I cannot see
    "This presence," as you call it. Lydon, men,
    Bring forth the witness! [*Calenus supported by Lydon and others, advances*]
ARB. Hound of hell, he lives!
    His death, and not his torture, was my need—
    Shortsighted vengeance! [*Aside*]
PRAE. Witness? and of what?
NYD. The murder of Apaecides.
PRAE. That case
    Is settled, and the murderer is judged,
    Sentenced, and now awaits his doom.
CLOD. And you
    Refuse to hear a witness, by whose word
    The guiltless may be saved! Is this your law
    And you its lawyer? Then, by all the gods,
    A curse upon the law and all its tribe!
SAL. You dare not for a quibble, for a form,
    Deny us justice? In a cause like this,

        It is not Glaucus only, but the world
        That claims a right.
PRAE. It is too late, my lord.
CLOD. It cannot ever be too late for man
        To do man justice. Hear, I pray, this man,
        Who totters on the sharp and downward edge
        Of his own grave. From him we may expect,
        So solemn is his station, truth at least.
ALL CITS. Hear him! By Jove, he shall be heard!
PRAE. Then speak.
ARB. My lord, the law has no safe path to tread,[69]
        Save by those forms which the united will
        Of ages of man's wisdom have imposed
        Upon her careful steps. But set that by.
        That wretch before you, asking to be heard,
        Is a mere thief, who robbed my treasury;
        And by myself was prisoned in my house,
        Awaiting the convenience of the law
        To be arraigned. Besides, my followers,
        Some of whom stand behind me, at the first
        Held him to be the murderer of my ward,
        And so to me denounced him. Call my slaves,
        And put them to the torture. They will tell
        Nothing but what I say.
ALL CITS. Oh, silence him!
        Let us hear old Calenus! Speak out, man!
PRAE.[70] [*Apart to Arbaces*] I cannot stem this torrent.
ARB. [*Apart to him*] Then I drown.
PRAE. [*Apart to him*] Not yet: another struggle. [*To Calenus*] Who are you?
CAL. Calenus is my name.
PRAE. A priest of Isis?
CAL. Once; but not so henceforth.
PRAE. Arbaces, then,
        Is your high priest, and to the sacred law
        You are responsible, but not to me.
        I have no jurisdiction in this case,
        My lords. [*To Clodius and Sallust*]
CLOD. The law of Rome doth recognize
        No such high priest nor worship; interdicts

GLAUCUS

      The consecration of a temple, built
      To Isis, throughout Italy; and hence
      Her worshipers must style her den a house,
      But not a temple. All of which you know;
      Or solemn edicts, by the Senate passed,
      Are passed to little purpose.
PRAE. [*To Arbaces*] Foiled again!
      Well, if it be resolved that I shall hear
      The testimony of a common thief,
      And weigh it with the clear, impartial words
      Pronounced by Prince Arbaces; as we know,
      A reputable man, of royal birth—
CITS. That's to be seen.
BUR. Yes, and the lion waits
      For somebody—and to decide my bets.
PRAE. It is a violation of all law,
      After a sentence passed, and—
CITS. Curse your law!
      Let us have justice!
PRAE. [*To Calenus*] Tell your story, man!
CAL. Oh! I am very weak, I have not had
      A bit of bread—since when?—It seems an age:
      And I am old besides. He meant to starve
      My life out; that is plain enough—
PRAE. Go on!
      Your maunderings tire us. Swear to what you say.
CAL. About the gods my mind is somewhat mixed: [*Raises his hand*]
      I know so much about them. To be safe,
      I swear by all the gods of all the lands,
      On which the sun shines, that what I may say
      Shall be the simple truth. Will that oath do?
      If not, propose another. I will swear
      As fast as you propose.
PRAE. Old ribald cease!
      Your oaths were empty howsoe'er you swear.
CITS. Tell us about the murder!
CAL. That I saw.
      I saw the blow; I heard the angry words
      That went before, and all that followed it.
CLOD. Who struck the blow?

CAL. Arbaces.
PRAE. Monstrous!
    This knave endeavors to avoid the guilt
    And penalty of theft by perjury;
    Swearing away the character and life
    Of a most honorable man. For shame!
CITS. Arbaces to the lion!
ARB. Filthy brutes,
    Blind with the blackness of your ignorance,
    Arbaces flings defiance at your heads! [*Praetor waves his hand. Trumpets sound. Enter a body of soldiers whose presence overawes the people*]
PRAE. The story is incredible to us—
    A bald, crude statement, unsustained by facts;
    A mere denunciation, without show
    Of circumstances to back it.
CITS. Hear him out.
PRAE. I have heard enough. On with the prisoner—
    The true and law-convicted criminal—
    To the arena with him!
CITS. No, no, no!
    Arbaces to the lion!
PRAE. March!
GLAU. One word.
    A few brief words is all the grace I ask.
PRAE. No!
GLAU. Not to you shall I address myself,
    Not to the pitying people, whom I thank
    For the wild justice they would execute.
    I reverence the law, and if the law
    Rightly condemns me, I have nought to say.
    That point your lordship must hereafter clear
    With Titus Caesar, my imperial friend.
CLOD.[71] [*To the Citizens*] See how the villain pales!
SAL. Thank Heaven, there is,
    Even in this world, a punishment for crime!
CITS. Let Glaucus speak!
PRAE. I would not lose your love,
    Good people, by opposing your desires:

So, if you will, the criminal may speak
For the last time.
CLOD. [*To Sallust*] The wretched demagogue!
GLAU. It gives me pleasure, at the last, to find
Reason to thank your lordship.
SAL. Clodius,
That hit and stung.
GLAU. Not for myself, I speak.
This life of mine, this fickle, transient breath,
Was given, and may be taken by the gods,
At their good pleasure. For my fellow man,
On the broad ground of justice, and for her,
This tender creature, clinging to my life
In desperate silence, who was almost mine
By the fair rights of marriage.—
IONE. Glaucus!—
NYD. Woe,
Woe to the land that lets this crime be done
Before insulted Heaven!
GLAU. It is to you,
Romans, to you, Ione, whose hard fate
It is to be a widow ere my hand
Unloose your maiden fillet, that I owe
The duty of preserving you a life,
Whose taking would be shameful guilt to you,
Ye Roman citizens, and to my bride
A lifelong loss, a lifelong misery.
'Tis said, perhaps 'tis fabled, that I am
Descended from the ancient gods of Greece:
If it be so, my fathers, in your sight
I lift my guiltless hands, thus manacled,
And call on you, great Glaucus of the seas,
Seated in power upon Olympian heights,
For heavenly justice, here to counterpoise
This manifest injustice of mankind!
NYD. Woe to the land! I hear the gods descend!
Earth trembles at their footsteps!
GLAU. Prophetess!
Look, where my fathers light the dreadful fires
Of their forgotten altar! Bow, and die! [*Flames and dense smoke*

bursts from Vesuvius. Loud rumbling sounds are heard. The columns of the temples reel and fall. The arch and cornice of the Basilica fall upon Arbaces and the Praetor. The people flee in every direction. A tremendous din, and crash of falling buildings goes on, while Glaucus, supporting Ione, Clodius, Sallust, Lydon supporting Calenus, and others, group together. As the darkness descends upon the scene, amidst tumult, Nydia is seen in advance of the group—leading them off. The darkness becomes total; and as it clears away, a large trireme is discovered putting to sea, containing Glaucus, Ione and their friends. Nydia is seated at the bow, a harp in her hands, singing]

NYD. Row mariners, row to the land of my love!
    Spread forth your white sails, like the wings of the dove!
    Bend, bend to the oar! for the god of the sea
    Would know that his son is as spotless and free
    As the fame of the goddess, now reigning in peace
    O'er the land of her love, over beautiful Greece!

CURTAIN

NOTES

Glaucus

PUBLISHERS' NOTE. *Through a mistake in following the editor's typescript, which was not detected in time to make possible the necessary changes, the blank verse in this play* Glaucus *was not set so as to show adequately the author's conception of the organic rhythm of the lines. As it appears here, the five-stress verse is not clearly indicated, especially where the lines are broken by a change of speakers. The publishers wish, by means of this footnote, to explain to those readers who may well be confused by the setting of the verse as here given. It need hardly be said that this mistake is in no way attributable to the editor of this volume, whose typescript was in the proper form.*

[1] MS I bears the typed notation "Begun Oct. 18, 1885 and finished January 9, 1886—83 days."
[2] This sentence is deleted in MS II.
[3] This, and the two lines preceding are deleted in MS II.
[4] MS II reads "shrine deserted stands."
[5] MS II omits from Sallust's speech, beginning "They give him out a sorcerer" to this point.
[6] The last four speeches are deleted in MS I and omitted in MS II.
[7] From this point this speech and the next five are deleted in both MSS.
[8] This speech is deleted in both MSS.
[9] The five preceding speeches are deleted in both MSS.
[10] The remainder of this speech is deleted in both MSS.
[11] From Ione's speech "Very strange," above, to this point is deleted in both MSS.
[12] This and the preceding line are deleted in both MSS.
[13] The following lines, to "means to a success" are deleted in both MSS.
[14] The remainder of the speech is deleted in both MSS.
[15] From here to Apaecides' phrase "no, my lord," below, is deleted in both MSS.
[16] The remainder of the speech is deleted in both MSS.
[17] The next six lines are deleted in both MSS.
[18] MS II reads "Go, and be alone."
[19] MS I read "Your courage to have time and place and chance."
[20] The next seven lines are deleted in both MSS.
[21] At this point begins the new material which was added as an Appendix to the copy designated as MS II. It consisted of a new ending for Act II and a completely new Act III. It would somewhat shorten the acting time of the play, but does not alter the narrative. It has been omitted in this edition.
[22] From here to Ione's phrase, "My prophet heart," below, is deleted in both MSS.
[23] The next two lines are deleted in both MSS.
[24] The next eleven lines are deleted in both MSS.
[25] This line is added in MS II.
[26] The next three lines are cut in MS I, but restored in MS II.
[27] This phrase, and the following passage to the word "Empress" is deleted in both MSS.
[28] This phrase, and the next three lines are deleted in both MSS.
[29] This half-line, and all to Burbo's "wings to use," below, is deleted in both MSS.
[30] This and the following fifteen speeches are cut in both MSS.
[31] This line and the following to the word "veins" are deleted in both MSS.
[32] This line and the remainder of the speech are deleted in both MSS.
[33] This phrase, the remainder of this speech, and the next two speeches are deleted in MS II.

34 This line and the following three lines are deleted in both MSS.
35 From "enter Apaecides" to "enter Glaucus," below, deleted in both MSS.
36 This line was omitted in MS II.
37 This line, and the remainder of the speech deleted in both MSS.
38 This speech is deleted in both MSS.
39 This line, and the remainder of this speech, are deleted in both MSS.
40 This line and the four following are deleted in both MSS.
41 This line and the following three lines are deleted in both MSS.
42 This line and the next are deleted in both MSS.
43 This line and the remainder of the speech are deleted in both MSS.
44 This line and the next are deleted in MS II.
45 This line and the remainder of the speech are deleted in both MSS.
46 This line and the next two are deleted in both MSS.
47 This phrase and the remainder of the speech are deleted in both MSS.
48 This line and the preceding occur in this order in MS II. In MS I they were reversed.
49 This line and the next three are deleted in both MSS.
50 This and the next line are deleted in both MSS.
51 This and the next two lines are deleted in both MSS.
52 This and the next four lines are deleted in both MSS.
53 This and the next two lines are deleted in both MSS.
54 This and the next four lines are deleted in both MSS.
55 This and the next two lines are deleted in both MSS.
56 The present text follows MS II. In MS I this line was expanded into five lines, as follows:

>"How, and how soon to fall. Oh fie! if one
>Felt a presentiment of every ill,
>Man would abide in terror all his days,
>So thickly sorrows and calamities
>Beset our lives. Where tarries Glaucus? He"

57 In MS II the speech ends here.
58 This and the next line are deleted in both MSS.
59 This phrase and the remainder of the sentence are deleted in both MSS.
60 This and the next line are deleted in both MSS.
61 This and the next two lines are deleted in both MSS.
62 This line is deleted in both MSS.
63 This speech is deleted in both MSS.
64 This line and the next four lines are deleted in both MSS.
65 This line and the remainder of the speech are deleted in both MSS.
66 This speech and the next seven speeches are deleted in both MSS.
67 This line and the next four lines are deleted in both MSS.
68 From this point to "*Enter from the Basilica,*" below, is deleted in both MSS.
69 This line and the next three lines are deleted in both MSS.
70 The next eighteen speeches are deleted in both MSS.
71 This and the next speech are deleted in both MSS.

www.ingramcontent.com/pod-product-compliance
Lightning Source LLC
Chambersburg PA
CBHW032107090426
42743CB00007B/266